tear here

Common Sound Blaster Problems and Solutions

PROBLEM	SOLUTION
System crashes.	Resolve IRQ, DMA channel, or base I/O address conflict. (Chapters 6, 12, and 13)
CD-ROM doesn't play.	Re-install CD-ROM software. (Chapter 13)
MIDI doesn't play in Windows.	Re-install Sound Blaster software; turn volume up with Creative Mixer or SB16SET. (Chapter 14)
WAV files don't play in Windows.	Re-install Sound Blaster software; turn volume up with Creative Mixer or SB16SET. (Chapter 14)
No sound from CD-ROM drive.	Connect audio cable from drive to Sound Blaster. (Chapter 13)
Crackly sound.	Plug speakers firmly into Sound Blaster. (Chapter 9 and 13)
No sound or music in DOS games.	Use game setup software to select sound card type. (Chapter 13)
AWE32 MIDI sounds bad in Windows 95.	Reset MIDI driver in Control Panel. (Chapter 11)

For more information about troubleshooting Sound Blaster, read Chapters 13 and 14.

Common Definitions

digital audio A form of audio that your computer can read and play. Most often, digital audio files have the WAV file name extension.

frequency modulation synthesis (FM synthesis) An older method for sound cards used to create MIDI music. An on-board chip synthetically creates the sound of an instrument. This often is called "synthesizer music."

MIDI (Musical Instrument Digital Interface) A standard for connecting digital musical instruments, including your Sound Blaster, together. It also standardizes music creation with these instruments. Most often, MIDI files have the MID file extension name.

sequencer software A type of software for putting together and editing MIDI compositions. The Cakewalk Apprentice sequencer comes with some versions of Sound Blaster and the MusicMagic sequencer is on the CD-ROM that accompanies this book.

wave-table synthesis A newer method of creating MIDI music. This method plays back digital samples of actual instruments, which creates a more realistic sound than FM synthesis.

Common Sound and Music Tasks

Following is a list of tasks you can do with Sound Blaster and the software you would use. Note, however, that not all versions of Sound Blaster come with the appropriate software. To learn more about what software comes with which package, read Chapter 5.

TO	USE
Change playback volume	SB16SET; Creative Mixer (Chapter 15)
Change recording levels	SB16SET; Ensemble Mixer (Chapter 15)
Control all music and sound players	Ensemble Remote (Chapter 16)
Convert text to voice	TextAssist (Chapter 18)
Convert voice to Windows commands	Voice Assist (Chapter 18)
Edit a WAV file	Creative WaveStudio (Chapter 22)
Embed sound in a document	Soundo'LE (Chapter 19)
Play an Audio CD	Play; EnsembleCD (Chapter 16)
Play a MIDI file	Play; EnsembleMIDI (Chapter 16)
Play a WAV file	Play; EnsembleWAVE (Chapter 16)
Record a WAV file	Record; Soundo'LE; Creative WaveStudio (Chapters 19, 21, 22)
Create a MIDI song	Cakewalk Apprentice; Midisoft Studio (Chapters 23, 24)

The COMPLETE IDIOT'S GUIDE TO Sound Blaster

by David Haskin

A Division of Macmillan Computer Publishing
A Prentice Hall Macmillan Company
201 West 103rd Street, Indianapolis, IN 46290 USA

To my favorite Schmit inlaws and outlaws: Tom, Tom, Cathy, Kathy, Elizabeth, Bob, and Joan.

©1995 by Que®

International Standard Book Number: 1-56761-651-8
Library of Congress Catalog Card Number: 95-079785

98 97 96 95   8 7 6 5 4 3 2 1

Interpretation of the printing code: the rightmost double-digit number is the year of the book's first printing; the rightmost single-digit number is the number of the book's printing. For example, a printing code of 95-1 shows that this copy of the book was printed during the first printing of the book in 1995.

Screen reproductions in this book were created by means of the program Collage Plus from Inner Media, Inc., Hollis, NH.

Printed in the United States of America

Publisher
Roland Elgey

Vice President and Publisher
Marie Butler-Knight

Editorial Services Director
Elizabeth Keaffaber

Publishing Manager
Barry Pruett

Managing Editor
Michael Cunningham

Product Development Specialists
Lisa Bucki and Heather Stith

Technical Editing
Discovery Computing

Production Editor
Kelly Oliver

Manuscript Editor
San Dee Phillips

Illustrator
Judd Winick

Book Designer
Barbara Kordesh

Cover Designer
Karen Ruggles

Indexer
Kathy Venable

Production Team
Anne Dickerson
Chad Dressler
DiMonique Ford
John Hulse
Daryl Kessler
Scott Tullis

Contents at a Glance

Contents

ix

Introduction

Idiots and sound cards *should* go together about like fish and bicycles. But I remember what an idiot I felt like when I was installing my first sound card.

I started out being very excited about purchasing my sound card. I bought it about the time of the first big explosion of computer games with cool sound effects and music. Before that, most games either had no sound or music or they depended on the pathetic speakers that come with PCs. I was going to get this sound card installed and be the envy of all my friends.

But a day later, not only was the &@$#! card not installed, but my system was crashing regularly. I got frustrated and—yes—I felt like a total idiot.

Two days later, after running up a humongous telephone bill to the sound card vendor's technical support department, I finally got the job done. And I vowed never again to feel like an idiot when it came to installing sound cards—or any other cards or software, for that matter.

Well, as I came to learn, I wasn't the only person who felt frustrated when trying to install a sound card. All these years later, sound cards—and especially Sound Blaster cards from Creative Labs—sound much better than that prehistoric 8-bit number I installed back then. But installing PC sound cards still can induce feelings of idiocy.

What's wrong with this picture? What's wrong is that sound cards should be fun. This book will help you get to the fun part of your Sound Blaster fast without straining your self-esteem.

Then, once you're up and running, this book's aim is to help you understand how to get the absolute most out of your Sound Blaster card. The features Sound Blaster offers are, as the name implies, a blast, and after spending your hard-earned money, you deserve to have fun, fun, fun.

To that end, I put together a CD-ROM, tucked into the back cover, that is full of cool sounds, music and programs. You'll have fun—guaranteed. And you'll never feel like an idiot—guaranteed.

Sound Blasters are great sound cards. So read on and learn how to get the most out of yours.

Who Should Read This Book?

This book assumes that you have things to do with your life—such as riding your bicycle or eating fresh fish—other than learning how to deal with your Sound Blaster.

Basically, I assume that you already know how to start your PC and how to start and navigate Windows. Beyond that, you don't have to know anything else about computers to read this book.

How Do I Use This Book?

While undoubtedly a great work of literature, this book is more along the lines of great *reference* literature. That means that it doesn't have much of a plot. Or, put differently, you don't have to read it from beginning to end.

Instead, this book is designed so you can quickly find what you need, and then get on with your life. If you have a question about something, look it up in the table of contents or the index, and then go to the referenced pages. Learn what you need to know and go back to having fun with your Sound Blaster. Or with whatever floats your boat.

I'll make the descriptions and instructions clear. I'll also provide special types of information that you can find by looking for visual clues. Those special types of information are in special shaded boxes like the ones shown here.

> **By the Way** These sidebars can offer a variety of helpful info. For example, they give simple definitions of computer jargon so, if you want, you can show off at parties; tips that streamline how to do specific tasks; and warnings about what can go wrong; and help getting yourself out of it when it does go wrong.

Techno Nerd Teaches

Provides more detailed descriptions of technical issues, should you want to learn them.

The Least You Need To Know section at the end of each chapter sums up all its main points. If you read only this section at the end of each chapter, you will know enough to convince others you're a computer geek.

Acknowledgments

No book is an island; neither are the people who write them. This book wouldn't have been created without the help of many people.

I'd like to start with my family. Thanks to Sam, who came home from college to guide me through some of the fine points of Cakewalk Apprentice (and, of course, to use the washing machine). Thanks, also, to Liz and Mary for their patience and love and for not giving me *too* hard a time when I was making such a racket with Sound Blaster.

As always, my profound appreciation to the gang at Que, particularly Barry Pruett, Heather Stith, Kelly Oliver, San Dee Phillips, and Martha O'Sullivan. Lots of thanks to a great editor, Lisa Bucki, for making sense of it all. Also, thanks to Cari Skaggs for assembling the CD-ROM.

Finally, big thanks to the folks at Creative Labs, particularly to Theresa Pulido and Scott Taylor, who saved my bacon any number of times during the writing of this book.

Trademarks

All terms mentioned in this book that are known to be or are suspected of being trademarks or service marks have been appropriately capitalized. Que Corporation cannot attest to the accuracy of this information. Use of a term in this book should not be regarded as affecting the validity of any trademark or service mark.

Part 1
Sound Blaster Basics

Maybe it's a guy thing, or maybe it's just me. But I have a tendency to, shall we say, dive in deep before I know all the specifics. I needn't go into details here, but my family and friends could give you some highly embarrassing particulars.

In this part, you'll learn some of the basics about sound, Sound Blaster, and the other pieces that work together with Sound Blaster. The goal of this part is to help you avoid the embarrassment that can occur if you have the same malady I have.

The Least You Need to Know

Several years ago after I finished installing my first sound card, I suddenly remembered the ending of one of my all-time favorite movies, *The Candidate*. A young Robert Redford plays a charismatic candidate for the U.S. Senate. After endless political shenanigans by his manipulative handlers, the naive Redford character actually wins the election; his shocked response is, "Now what?"

I had just installed this wonderful new bit of hardware in my wonderful new computer, and I wasn't quite sure what to do with it. This, frankly, is a common feeling for me and, as I have since learned, for many other computer users.

In this chapter, you'll learn what you can do with your Sound Blaster. You'll also learn about some of Sound Blaster's virtues. Hopefully, this will make you glad—and excited—that you bought it and tackled the process of installing it.

Now, a Word About Sound Cards

In the beginning, PCs couldn't sing like Macintosh computers. Macintoshes have a built-in capability to create and play back sounds and music. But PCs... they were, relatively speaking, deaf and mute.

Then, a number of years ago came Sound Blaster. These are so-called *add-in cards* (also known as adapters or expansion cards). As I'll explain later in this part, you insert Sound Blaster into your computer and, after some setup procedures, it plays sounds and music.

Sound Card
This is a circuit board you insert into your PC. It's dedicated to the task of helping your PC play sounds and music.

Alas, nothing in this world is free. On the one hand, Sound Blasters started a PC sound revolution. Previously silent PCs began to sound like an orchestra or a sound effects factory. On the other hand, installing them, making sure they run right, and getting the most out of them was a bear.

Well, Sound Blasters sound better than ever these days, but installing and tweaking them still can be trying. Hence, this book. The information in it will help you install, troubleshoot, and wring the best sounds and music out of your Sound Blaster sound card.

The Top Few Things You Should Know About Sound Blaster

I'm a fan of Top 10 lists, but when I have to create them, I suffer from performance anxiety—I worry about whether I'll come up with the requisite number of items.

So I avoided the pressure by deciding to create a "Top Few" list of things you should know about Sound Blaster. That way, *you'll* learn what's important about Sound Blaster, and *I* won't have to worry about how many items are on the list. (As it turns out, when I was finished with this list of important things about Sound Blaster, the number came out to ten! Today's my lucky day!) So, without further ado, here's the list:

10. **Sound Blaster gives you lots of giggles.** Giggles and grins—if you like those two items, you'll love Sound Blaster. Parts 3 and 4 of the book discuss getting the most of everything out of your Sound Blaster card.

9. **These babies work.** The folks at Creative Labs know how to build sound cards to work well and to work under a wide variety of conditions. Frankly, many competing sound cards are good, but some don't measure up to Sound Blaster. When you install a Sound Blaster sound card, you know it will work as advertised.

8. **If you've never had a sound card before, you'll never want to live without one again.** I remember asking in 1983, "What would I do with a color monitor?" What once seemed like luxury soon became necessity. That's certainly true with sound cards. Once you become accustomed to a PC with sound, living without sound is strange indeed. Sure, your PC comes with a little speaker, but that speaker can't play music, and its capability to create sound effects is pathetic. Part 3 of this book discusses how to get the most sound and music out of your Sound Blaster card.

7. **You'll appreciate Sound Blaster's compatibility.** When you buy other sound cards, you have to worry about how compatible they are with your software. That's never a concern with Sound Blaster because it's the standard for PC sound cards. Practically speaking, this means that when software vendors create software, they make sure it works with Sound Blaster cards. As a result, other sound card vendors must make their sound cards "Sound Blaster-compatible." In theory, a Sound Blaster-compatible sound card will work with all software. In my experience, however, the phrase "Sound Blaster-compatible" doesn't count for much. I've owned sound cards that claimed to be Sound Blaster-compatible that didn't work with some software. When you use a Sound Blaster card, you are, by definition, assured that it will work with virtually all software.

6. **Creative Labs makes installation simple—relatively.** I want to be perfectly clear—when talking about sound cards (and other add-in cards for your PC), the words "simple" and "installation" don't work in the same sentence. Sound Blaster is no exception. Installation *can* be confusing and frustrating.

   While Creative Labs did a very good job of simplifying installation, there are still some things you need to know before you install. That's why Chapter 6 describes some of the ins and outs of installing hardware, Chapters 7 and 8 describe the installation process for different types of Sound Blaster cards, and Chapter 13 provides installation troubleshooting.

5. **The Sound Blaster family is large and sometimes confusing.** There are four basic types of Sound Blaster cards: plain old Sound Blaster, Sound Blaster Pro, Sound Blaster 16, and AWE32. As I will discuss in Chapter 5, Sound Blaster and Sound Blaster Pro are based on older, inexpensive (and nearly obsolete) 8-bit technology. As a result, I won't discuss those older cards much in this book. Creative Labs offers the Sound Blaster 16 in a mind-boggling array of packages that come with different options. The card is essentially the same in all these packages, but the optional hardware and software that come with it change. If you haven't already bought your Sound Blaster, or if you're not sure you got the right one, read Chapter 5 for details about all the different Sound Blaster 16 options.

4. **You can play all day with Sound Blaster.** Sound Blaster comes with a startlingly large amount of software. Depending on the specific package you bought, it comes with software that enables you to create and edit sounds, record and edit music, and

even create fancy multimedia presentations. Part 3 tells you about all that software. The CD-ROM accompanying this book also provides some interesting ways to have fun with your Sound Blaster.

3. **There's a lot more you can do with Sound Blaster than simply *listen* to sounds.** If you're like me, you probably bought your Sound Blaster mostly to hear sounds and music, such as those you would find, say, in your favorite game. But there are many "more advanced topics" pertaining to music that you can dive into if you're so inclined. This is a book for Sound Blaster beginners, and creating music is most definitely an advanced topic. Still, I'll touch on the subject many times during the course of this book, particularly in Parts 3 and 4.

2. **Sound Blaster is a trade name, not a generic name.** Many people use the generic term *sound blaster* to describe any sound card. This is a problem that the folks at Creative Labs share with the companies that bring you products such as Kleenex and Coke. *Sound Blaster* is a trade name referring to a specific line of products sold by Creative Labs. Often, airline cabin attendants will remind you of the destination of the flight before take-off and suggest that you leave the plane if you're not going to that destination. Similarly, I feel obligated to tell you that this book is about Sound Blaster sound cards from Creative Labs. If you bought another type of sound card, this book probably won't help you much.

1. **If you bought your Sound Blaster a la carte, keep your credit card warm.** Many people buy Sound Blaster as part of a "multimedia upgrade kit," which includes all the pieces you need to use multimedia on your PC. This kit probably also includes all the pieces you need to make Sound Blaster work, most notably speakers. But if you simply went to the store and bought a Sound Blaster card and nothing else, you may need to buy more stuff. For example, you'll most assuredly need speakers designed to work with your computer. You may also want other hardware such as a CD-ROM drive. Read Chapter 4 to learn more about other hardware that will enhance your Sound Blaster experience.

The Sound Blaster To-Do List

Now you know some of the most important things about Sound Blaster, but I still haven't told you what you can *do* with it. That's what the rest of the chapter is about.

Havin' Fun

Remember "giggles and grins?" I listed that as one of the top 10 things you should know about Sound Blaster sound cards. That's certainly the main reason that people buy a Sound Blaster—for fun.

The most obvious way to have fun with a Sound Blaster is to play games. Sure, you can play most games without a sound card, but a PC's internal speaker only creates the most pathetic of sounds. If you play a game (such as those that come with *The Complete Idiot's Guide to PC Games*) without a sound card, here's what you'll hear: *beep... bink... boop...*

But when you add a Sound Blaster to your computer, your games come to life. A laser blast sounds like a laser blast. A monster dying an agonizing death sounds like... well, you get the idea.

But games aren't the only way to have fun with sound. Multimedia applications, such as CD-ROM "edutainment" titles, use sound extensively. For example, I just saw a CD-ROM about air warfare during World War II. For each different type of plane described on the disc, there was a recording of the sound the plane made. The sound of the Stukka dive bomber, particularly, sent chills down my spine.

On an even lighter note, you can add sounds to particular Windows events. For example, without buying separate software, you can attach a special sound effect (such as the one from the CD-ROM that accompanies this book) to play whenever you exit Windows. This is fun, and it breaks up the monotony.

Makin' Music

Music soothes the savage beast, I'm told. As a PC game player, I tend to think that music also accompanies the on-screen appearance of the savage beast.

However it works, music is a universal language; with a Sound Blaster card, you not only can listen to music, you can create it, too. As you'll learn in Chapters 20 and 21, you can record sound and music.

For me, though, the greatest musical pleasure afforded by the Sound Blaster is music appreciation. There are several CD-ROMs that not only play music but also teach you how to appreciate it. One of my favorite discs, for example, is Microsoft's Multimedia Beethoven. Whatever kind of music you like or want to create, there's software that works with your Sound Blaster.

Doin' Business

Sure, most people buy Sound Blaster for giggles and grins, but an increasing number of business applications use sound, as well. Here are some examples:

➤ **You can record an explanation of a specific cell in a spreadsheet.** Then, when you give the spreadsheet to a work colleague, that person can double-click the cell and hear your explanation. The same concept works with virtually any other type of business application, such as databases or word processing documents. (Of course, the other person must have a sound card, too.)

➤ **Voice-enabled electronic mail.** This means you can send music or sound effects via electronic mail to other people with sound cards. A marketing person, for example, can send a recording of a proposed new advertising jingle to his or her colleagues for comments and approval.

➤ **Multimedia presentations.** Computer-generated presentations have become a staple of sales personnel and virtually everybody else who must make a point in front of an audience. Adding multimedia elements such as sound to these presentations is becoming increasingly common. With Sound Blaster, you can add a musical background to an on-screen presentation and then show a video of your company president discussing an important merger or acquisition.

➤ **Turn your PC into a phone center.** These days, some modems can handle incoming voice calls and save those calls on your hard disk. Similarly, you can use this software and a microphone to turn your PC into a speakerphone—if you have a sound card such as Sound Blaster.

The Least You Need to Know

In this chapter, you learned some important things about Sound Blaster and what you can do with a Sound Blaster card. You learned that:

➤ Sound Blaster is the standard in sound cards. This means that software vendors create software to work with it. This, in turn, means that you shouldn't encounter compatibility problems.

➤ Sound cards such as Sound Blaster make games seem much more realistic.

➤ If you use a sound card like Sound Blaster, you can actually create music.

➤ There are an increasing number of business uses for sound cards, including multimedia presentations and voice explanations for documents.

Giving Your Computer a Voice

In grade school, I learned that sound moves through the air in waves, and I wondered: If all these waves are hitting me, why don't they knock me over? It wasn't until my teenage years that I learned, much to my parents' chagrin, that if you play music loud enough, sound waves *will* knock you over.

You can't see sound waves, but they're all around us. However, left to their own devices, computers can't hear and play sound waves. Nope, computers only understand computer language. That's why you need a Sound Blaster—to translate between sound waves and computer language.

This chapter is a brief refresher course about the nature of sound, both the type that zips through the air to your ears and the type that your computer can create and play.

I find this an interesting topic. But it's also a useful topic. That's because if you understand the basics of sound, you'll better understand how your Sound Blaster works.

And if you understand how Sound Blaster works, you'll better be able to fix problems and enhance your listening pleasure.

Riding the (Sound) Wave

Let's do the technical thing for just a moment. Most people know that sound travels through the air in waves. But sound waves are hardly generic; depending on how long they are and how quickly they vibrate, they produce different tones.

Sound is created by waves, or vibrations, moving through the air. Our ears collect these waves and send them to the brain for processing. We don't "hear" until our brain processes the sound waves. This reminds me of the old riddle about whether a tree makes noise if it falls in the forest and nobody is around to hear it.

The Windup... and the Pitch

Frequency Frequency is measured in *hertz* (abbreviated *Hz*), which refers to the number of times in a second that a sound wave vibrates. Experts say that the sounds humans normally can hear range from 20 hertz (20 vibrations per second or 20Hz) to 20 kilohertz (20,000 vibrations per second or 20KHz).

Hertz Named after Heinrich Hertz who made a study of such things, hertz (Hz) refers to the number of times per second something occurs. Kilohertz (KHz) refers to how many *thousands* of times per second something occurs.

Sound waves with random characteristics make random, disorganized sounds. You know, like the sound of someone's nails running across a chalkboard.

However, consistently repeated sound waves with specific characteristics, such as a consistent speed at which the wave vibrates, create sounds with a specific pitch. If you were Superperson and could see sound waves, you'd notice that sound waves for a high pitch are different from sound waves for a low pitch. The wave from the lower pitch vibrates less frequently.

These factors make *frequency* an important concept. Sound waves for high tones vibrate much more frequently during a specific period of time than sound waves for low tones.

All this hoopla about sound waves and vibrations is easy to test with a rubber band. Stretch the band between your fingers until it's taut, and then pluck it. You'll get a relatively high note. If you loosen your grip (on the rubber band, that is) and pluck it again, you'll get a lower note. If you look closely at the band, you'll see that it vibrates more slowly for the lower rubber band note than for the higher rubber band note.

Besides rubber bands, all musical instruments operate on this principal in one form or another, and so do our voices and everything else that makes sounds. By hitting a taught wire (such as on a piano or guitar), by blowing on something that vibrates (such as with woodwind instruments), or by vibrating our larynxes, we can create a variety of tones.

Put together carefully, these vibrations can create songs, speech, and various recognizable sounds. If you don't put them together carefully, the result is noise.

Turn Up the Volume

Pitch is one thing, but how about volume? Volume arises out of another characteristic of sound waves called *amplitude*. I already knew about sound waves and pitch as a youngster; it was amplitude that I discovered in my teenage years.

Let me put this in simple terms that are easy to visualize. While *wavelength* refers to the length of the wave, *amplitude* refers to the height. The higher the amplitude, the louder the sound.

Amplitude This is a measure of the intensity, or loudness, of a sound wave. The higher the amplitude, the louder the sound. It makes sense, then, that when you *amplify* sound, you increase its amplitude.

How Computers Make Sounds

The theory of sound is swell, you're probably saying, but what does it have to do with me? Truthfully, if you just want to listen to sounds and don't care about the technical stuff, skip the rest of this chapter and the next. But if you have a healthy interest in how things work (and also how to fix them when they go wrong), read on.

The rest of the chapter discusses how the basic principles of sound apply to computers and specifically to sound cards. I'll discuss some important concepts that pertain to how well your sound card reproduces sound.

I find this stuff interesting and useful. An extra benefit is that it makes for great defensive party talk. When I get cornered at a party by a techno-nerd wannabe, I dazzle him or her with this stuff, and the pseudo-geek is gone in a matter of minutes.

You Say Analog... I Say Digital

Let's go back to sound waves. The sound waves we've been talking about are *analog*. That is to say, they occur in the physical world and, when they occur, you can hear the result.

Analog Analog means that something occurs in the physical world; when it occurs, you hear, see, feel, smell, or touch it. I have a computer geek friend who refers to a handshake as an *analog interpersonal interface.* He's spent way too much time in front of his monitor, but I like him anyway.

Analog sounds are easy to produce by using mechanical means such as with musical instruments, with your voice, or by dragging your nails across a blackboard. The sound characteristics change constantly as the nature of the wave—and the instrument creating the wave—changes.

Here, however, is the rub: computers don't do analog. The best way to make your computer vibrate is to wait for an earthquake, which is a blessedly rare event where I'm from. And even then, it's hard to control the earthquake so the computer vibrates at just the right frequency and creates the pitch you want.

Nope, computers are *digital.* That is, they only recognize digital code, which is a series of 1s and 0s that, when put together in a specific pattern, creates a specific result. If 1 and 0 doesn't make sense, think of it as on and off. This literally refers to the voltage that flows through your computer's chips. In simple terms, the instructions are transmitted by whether the flow of electricity is momentarily on or momentarily off. As you can tell, this is a very different approach than analog sounds, in which vibrations are constantly changing. The result might be an episode of DOOM, or one of those spreadsheet thingies that people sometimes use computers for, or, as we'll discuss further, digital sounds.

Analog Control Chip This chip, which resides on your sound card, is as adept as any translator for the United Nations. In this case, the analog control chip converts analog sounds to digital and vice versa.

Because the world is analog and computers are digital, one of a sound card's primary tasks is to translate between the two. The sound card, working with various software, takes digital computer code that represents sound, translates it, and sends the translation out through the speakers. Speakers create analog sounds you can hear.

Conversely, your sound card also can collect analog sounds, such as when you speak into a microphone, and convert it into digital files your computer can process. That means that an important part of your sound card is the *audio control chip*, which is the chip that converts the analog sounds to digital files.

There Are Sounds... and There Are Sounds

Okay, so we must convert between the analog sounds that occur in the natural world around us and digital sounds that computers can handle. But there are sounds... and

12

there are *sounds*. Your sound card and computer can handle different types of digital sounds.

There are two types of sounds that are most common in the world of PCs. You've undoubtedly heard both types of sounds many times, and each plays an important role. They are the most common types of sound and music, but certainly not the only kind. They do work with Sound Blaster and virtually all other sound cards. The next several sections describe these two different types of sounds, which are called *waveform* and *MIDI*.

Waveform Files

You're stalking through a dark cavern on another planet, when all of a sudden laser fire erupts. Now, I don't expect you to stop playing your game to think about the sound—you've got enough on your hands with those menacing bad guys shooting lethal futuristic weapons at you. But if you did stop to think about those sounds, you'd notice this about them:

➤ They are relatively short in duration—far shorter than, say, the average song.

➤ They mimic some real (or, in the case of lasers, an imagined) sound that occurs in the real world. It might be laser fire, but it also might be a bird chirping or your company president introducing a new product.

Digital files containing sounds from the real world are called *waveform* files. That's because they are recordings, saved in a digital format, of sounds that have sound waves—a.k.a. analog sounds. Waveform files also are called WAV files because that is the file name extension conventionally used when you save these files in this format.

Waveform (WAV) Files
Birds chirping, bigwigs speaking, cars roaring—if you've heard sounds like these on your computer, chances are they were stored as WAV files. WAV files are essentially digital recordings of sounds.

Often, WAV files are obtained simply by recording sounds via equipment and software that converts the sounds directly into digital format. Sound Blaster includes the tools for doing that. Read Chapter 21 to learn how to create waveform files.

The advantage of WAV files is that because they essentially are recordings, they sound realistic. Another advantage is that you can easily edit them so you can add special effects like the reverb or echo. You also can mix together two or more WAV files to make humorous or strange sounds. Again, as you'll learn in Chapter 21, Sound Blaster comes with programs to let you do this.

A significant disadvantage of WAV files is that they require a lot of hard disk storage space. That explains why the sounds contained in WAV files are relatively short ones, like sound effects.

A WAV file containing the *William Tell Overture,* for example, would require more hard disk storage space than most PC owners can even dream about. This isn't a problem with the other type of sound most frequently played by sound cards: *MIDI* sound. I'll discuss MIDI a bit later in this chapter in the "Maxi, Mini... MIDI" section.

How Many Bits Are Enough?

When your Sound Blaster plays a WAV file, it actually is playing, in rapid succession, a series of short sounds called *samples*. If you play enough samples quickly enough, it sounds like the recorded sound.

Samples This is what Willy Loman carried in *Death of a Salesman*. It also refers to a sample of a real sound. Played at a rapid rate, samples combine to re-create a sound.

Sampling Rate This *could* refer to how fast I eat my way through the dessert section of a buffet. In this case, though, it refers to how many sound samples per second a sound card plays.

Here's an analogy. A drop of water is a drop of water, right? But it takes many drops of water all flowing together to make a shower. It's like that with sound samples. A sound sample is a sound, but it's not a *recognizable* sound until it's played together with a lot of other sound samples.

How many samples do you need to get good quality sound? A lot. Even low-end sound cards have a *sampling rate* of at least 22 kilohertz (or 22KHz).

Remember, hertz refers to the number of times per second something occurs, and kilohertz refers to the number of times something occurs per second *measured in thousands*. In other words, 22KHz means that a sound card usually plays 22,000 samples per second or more.

The higher the sampling rate, the better the sound. 22KHz might sound like a high sampling rate, but it isn't. Cards with a maximum sampling rate of only 22KHz are called *8-bit sound cards*, like the original Sound Blaster and the Sound Blaster Pro. Creative Labs still sells these cards, but since they are quickly becoming obsolete, we won't cover them in this book.

Nope, this book focuses on 16-bit cards that, as the name implies, have a maximum sampling rate that's twice as high as 8-bit cards—44KHz. Put differently, a high-quality two-second WAV clip of a dog barking requires your 44KHz sound card to play more than 80,000 samples.

14

Maxi, Mini... MIDI

Waveform files most often are used for sound effects or short vocal narrations. But what about music?

MIDI, which stands for *Musical Instrument Digital Interface*, is a computer-assisted method of creating music. While a WAV file is a digitized recording of actual sounds, a MIDI file (which has the .MID filename extension) is a set of instructions telling your sound card what tones to play, with a particular duration and volume.

MIDI

MIDI is a method by which your computer and sound card creates synthesized music. MIDI first became popular in the early '80s before PCs as we now know them became popular. In fact, some of the early MIDI synthesizers now are highly prized for the "retro" sounds they create.

MIDI became popular with the introduction of early synthesizers like the Moog synthesizer. In fact, creating MIDI music doesn't require that you use a computer. But if you have a computer with a sound card like a Sound Blaster, you can easily create and modify MIDI music. MIDI music is also extremely common in all kinds of computer applications, like games.

MIDI music files contain multiple tracks, each of which plays a different synthesized instrument. As a result, you can create complex songs and have fine control over each instrument's volume, pitch, and tempo.

You can edit and alter MIDI music with a *sequencer*, which lets you set the instrument and characteristics for each track. Not surprisingly, Sound Blaster cards come with a sequencer. Read how to use a sequencer in Chapter 23.

MIDI actually is a standard. The fact that it is a standard is useful for a number of reasons:

➤ It provides specific numbers and types of synthesized instruments. Specifically, the MIDI standard allows 128 general sounds and 64 percussion sounds.

Sequencer
Software that you use to edit MIDI music. A good sequencer will let you assign a specific synthesized instrument to each track and also assign specific characteristics, such as pitch and volume, to each track.

➤ It provides a standard way for connecting MIDI devices, like keyboards, to your sound card.

We'll discuss this topic more in the next chapter, but you should know that your Sound Blaster—and every other sound card—includes a *synthesis chip*. This is the chip that actually creates the synthesized sounds based on the instructions in the MIDI file.

In Chapter 3, I'll discuss the specific ways the Sound Blaster cards—and particularly the Sound Blaster 16 and the AWE32—create sounds.

The Least You Need to Know

This chapter described the basics of how sound is created and how computers and sound cards, like Sound Blaster, re-create music. You learned that:

➤ In the natural world, sound consists of waves. The wave's characteristics determine the pitch and the volume of the wave. For example, sound waves that vibrate faster are higher pitched.

➤ The sound you hear is analog sound; that is, it is continually changing sound created in the real world. Computers, however, are digital and operate discrete instructions. Sound cards translate between analog and digital.

➤ WAV files are digital recordings of analog sounds.

➤ MIDI files contain instructions that tell your sound card how to synthesize musical instruments.

Chapter 3

Putting It Together with Sound Blaster

In This Chapter

➤ Making synthesizer music

➤ Hearing realistic wave-tables

➤ How sound works in a PC system

In the last chapter, I sounded off about the basics of sound. Now, class, things get a bit more specific. So listen up.

In this chapter, you'll dive into more detail about how Sound Blaster works. You'll also learn about the special characteristics of your Sound Blaster card. This chapter isn't meant to help you earn an advanced degree. Rather, it should help you enjoy your Sound Blaster more and enable you to correct problems should they occur.

Listening to Sound Blaster's FM Synthesis

We covered the basics of WAV playback in Chapter 2, but there's still much to say about how sound cards play MIDI music. There are fundamental differences between sound cards in this regard—including the difference between the Sound Blaster 16 and the AWE32.

The synthesis chip on a sound card uses instructions from the MIDI file to synthesize the sounds of instruments playing. It then intertwines the synthesized instruments, each with their own pitches and other characteristics. The result is a song.

Until recently, the most common way that sound cards and synthesis chips created these sounds was *frequency modulation synthesis*, or *FM synthesis* for short. This created what sometimes is thought of as *synthesized music*.

Frequency Modulation (FM Synthesis) A common method used by sound cards for creating MIDI music. While effective and even beloved by some people, it creates synthetic-sounding instruments. That's why music created this way often is called *synthesizer music*.

FM synthesis still is widely used in sound cards. In fact, it is the method used by the Sound Blaster 16 for creating MIDI music. It's a tried and true technology and it's also inexpensive. However, there's one undeniable fact about FM synthesis: it sounds, by definition, synthesized. It creates MIDI violins that sound like, well, synthesized violins. The same is true for virtually all instruments.

This failing sent engineers, including those at Creative Labs, in search of a better method of creating music. That better method is the subject of the next section.

Putting Your Cards on the Wave-Table

I can just envision some scientist in a white lab coat mulling over the problem of synthetic-sounding music when, suddenly, a light bulb went on over his head. "Aha!" the scientist must have exclaimed. "Why not use waveform sounds to create MIDI?"

Okay—so this breakthrough moment doesn't exactly send shivers down your spine, but this magic moment, or some moment like it, led to a more realistic-sounding method of creating MIDI music called *wave-table synthesis*. This, in turn, led to the current generation of wave-table synthesis cards, such as the AWE32. By the way, AWE stands for Advanced WavEffects, which is a Creative Labs trade name.

Wave-table Synthesis This is a method of creating MIDI music that uses waveform sound samples of actual instruments rather than synthesized versions of those instruments. The result is MIDI music that is much more realistic than FM synthesis.

In simple terms, wave-table synthesis cards store sound samples of the various MIDI instruments in special memory chips on the sound card. When the sound card reads the instructions in the MIDI file, it plays back those samples instead of synthesizing the sounds.

It's not difficult to understand why wave-table synthesis sounds much more realistic than FM synthesis, but not all wave-table synthesis cards are created equally. Specifically, the differences include:

➤ The quality of the sound samples. I've listened to a number of different wave-table sound cards, and some play back specific instruments better than others. This often is the result of differences in the quality of the sound samples. The Sound Blaster AWE32, I believe, has strong sound quality for all instruments.

➤ The quantity of sound samples. Much of the sound quantity issue relates to the amount of memory on the sound card devoted to holding the sound samples. The AWE32 has 1M of on-board storage for sound samples, which is pretty standard. But you can upgrade the AWE32's on-board random-access memory (RAM) to as much as 28M to contain more sounds. Whenever you start your computer, these extra sounds load into AEW32's on-board RAM. Read Chapter 20 about adding RAM and more sounds.

If realistic music is important to you and you still haven't bought your sound card, wave-table is the way to go. As with all new and good things, however, you'll pay a premium. While the marketplace for wave-table cards has become quite competitive, you'll still pay at least $100 more than you would for an FM synthesis card.

But, of course, as always in the computer biz, prices are coming down quickly. Today, if you shop carefully, you can find 16-bit cards for $100 or less. The price you pay for an AWE32 is about the same as you would have paid for a 16-bit card less than three years ago.

Other Noteworthy Sound Blaster Parts

There are more doohickeys on your Sound Blaster card than simply the synthesis chip, wave-table memory, and audio control chip that you've already read about. (You have been paying attention, haven't you?) In fact, there are doohickeys galore on that Sound Blaster card of yours. This section briefly describes them and their benefits.

Many sound cards, including several versions of Sound Blaster, include:

➤ **Digital signal processors (DSPs)**   Ordinarily, when your sound card creates sound, it works in conjunction with your computer's central processing unit (CPU), which is the "main brain" of your computer. However, this slows down your computer's capability to do other chores. A DSP on your sound card does some of that computing grunt work that would otherwise distract and slow down your computer.

➤ **CD-ROM interfaces**   Sound Blaster cards include built-in interfaces to make your CD-ROM drive run. Depending on which model of Sound Blaster you buy, you can buy a connector for CD-ROM drives from Sony, Mitsumi, and Creative Labs. This

Digital Signal Processor (DSP) Handy little chips that come on Sound Blaster cards. Because they assume some of the duties that creating sounds normally imposes on your computer, they prevent your computer from bogging down.

Joystick Computer joysticks are a favorite of hard-core game players. They are modeled after the joysticks in airplanes, which explains their popularity for games involving simulated flight. However, they're also popular for many other types of games, particularly action games.

means if you use one of those drives, you won't have to add a CD-ROM interface.

In addition, the Sound Blaster 16 SCSI-2 comes with an adapter, called a SCSI adapter, for connecting virtually any other CD-ROM drive. Read Chapter 9 to learn how to install the SCSI-2 adapter and how to connect your CD-ROM drive.

➤ **A CD-ROM/audio connector** This is for playing sound generated from internal CD-ROM drives. An internal CD-ROM drive resides within your computer, as opposed to an external unit that resides outside your computer.

➤ **Joystick/MIDI port** This is a plug-in in the back of your Sound Blaster. Joysticks are a popular method of controlling games. You use the same port for plugging MIDI devices, such as keyboards or drum kits, into Sound Blaster. You then use software to record and edit the music you create with those devices.

➤ **Various and sundry connectors** You'll learn more about these connectors in Chapters 7 and 8. For now, suffice it to say these are the places into which you plug things such as your speakers, headphones, microphones, and even audio CD players.

Of course, you also need software for doing things such as listening to sounds and music. Sound Blaster comes with a lot of software and the CD-ROM that comes with this book has even more. Much of the second half of this book is devoted to that software. Chapter 24 tells you about the CD-ROM.

Sound Blaster: A Cog in the (PC) Machine

Just one more thing and I'll be off this how-does-it-work kick. I usually find it useful, after learning some specific information, to see how things work in the big picture.

So far, we've only talked about how sound cards work, but the sound card is only one part of the big picture. There also are the other components that work with your sound card. Those components include:

➤ Data storage devices, such as a CD-ROM drive and your hard drive.

➤ Random-access memory (RAM), which temporarily stores data and instructions from your software.

➤ Your PC's motherboard, which is the central circuit board for your PC. It's kind of like a big junction through which information and program instructions must pass on their way to other parts of your computer.

➤ Your computer's central processing unit, or CPU. As I mentioned before, this is the chip that does most of the "thinking" for your computer. It's located on the motherboard.

➤ A video system, which includes a video adapter and a monitor.

➤ So-called input devices such as your keyboard or mouse.

➤ So-called output devices such as a printer.

Some of these items, such as RAM and the CPU, are built into the motherboard. Others, such as Sound Blaster and your video adapter, plug into your computer's motherboard. Other items connect to the items that plug into the motherboard. For example, you plug your sound card into a slot in the motherboard, and then you plug your speakers into the sound card.

Binding Arbitration: Making All the Pieces Work

Making all these items work together is a miracle of arbitration. By that, I mean that your computer system must sort out the needs of these various components. Then it must make everything work in such a way that it feels normal to you when you use your computer.

For example, say you are playing a game and when a character dies, there's a horrific sound effect and blood gushing from the unfortunate digital character. You sure wouldn't want to see the gushing blood and the falling-over dead part, and then wait three seconds for the horrific sound effect. Nope, that would definitely detract from the experience.

Making all this happen the way it should is *system software*. There are two types of system software: your operating system, such as DOS, and system software that is built into your motherboard.

System Software

System software is, in many ways, the master arbitrator. Among its many chores, system software routes data and instructions to the proper component in a PC so that, to the user, everything occurs in the precise sequence that it should. There are two types of system software: BIOS, which is like a traffic cop for input and output, and operating systems, which control how you manage files and programs.

Without going into much detail (after all, computer scientists earn doctorates on this subject), the system software helps route data and information to where it belongs. To demonstrate how all these components work with your system software, say you are playing a game like the ubiquitous DOOM that you control with a joystick. Say you unexpectedly confront an evil hellspawn. Behind the scenes, here's what happens:

1. To avoid danger, you move the joystick to the side. What really happens is that the signal moves from the joystick to the joystick port in your Sound Blaster. Sound Blaster sends the signal through the motherboard, which routes it to the video adapter, which shows your change in direction on-screen.

2. You press a joystick button to fire a weapon at the evil hellspawn. Again, the signal goes from your joystick to... eventually the monitor. But one more thing occurs: another signal, generated by the game, goes to your Sound Blaster. The Sound Blaster converts this digital signal to the analog sound of your weapon and sends that signal out through your speakers.

3. After you kill the demon, you save your game. This time, you press keys in your keyboard. The signal goes from your keyboard to the motherboard and from there to the device that controls your hard drive. That device instructs your hard drive to save your game.

The remarkable thing is that all this occurs almost simultaneously and in the order in which it is supposed to occur. For that, thank the geniuses who created your system software. Sure, it's not always fun to bump into these techies at parties, but I'm sure grateful that they exist.

The Least You Need to Know

In the last chapter, you learned some basics about sound. In this chapter, you learned some basics about your Sound Blaster and about how it works with the rest of your PC. Specifically, you learned:

➤ There are two ways that sound cards create MIDI music: with FM synthesis and wave-table synthesis.

➤ FM synthesis often sounds synthetic, which is why it often is called *synthesizer music*. Wave-table synthesis creates far more realistic music.

➤ Sound Blaster is just one piece out of many in your PC that must work in synch with the other hardware and software in your system. Much of the responsibility for making this happen falls to system software that includes your operating system, such as DOS.

Chapter 4

Other Gotta-Have-It Hardware

In This Chapter

➤ Listening to speakers (and what you're listening for)

➤ The CD-ROM connection

➤ What about mike(rophone)?

Once, on a hurried business trip to New York, I forgot to pack socks. As I was paying for new socks in a clothing store, the salesperson asked with a straight face, "Can I show you a suit to go along with the socks?"

Just because you own a sound card doesn't mean you don't need to buy a complete outfit. Heavens, no. But there are many other things that you'll need or want to go along with your sound card. This chapter briefly outlines those items and describes what to look for when you buy them.

Speaking About Speakers

When it comes to PC speakers, it's easy to act like the birdies and be cheap. Most of us have no problem justifying large and relatively expensive speakers for our stereos. Some of us would even consider spending a chunk of the kids' college tuition for these speakers.

But speakers for a PC... there's something about the idea that shouts, "CHEAP!" Here's one bit of advice I've learned the hard way: get good PC speakers. If you don't, you're wasting much of your Sound Blaster's capabilities.

Here are some things to look for when buying speakers for your PC. Specifically, speakers should:

➤ **Be magnetically shielded.** Magnets wreak havoc with computers. They can corrupt data on your hard drive and distort the image of your monitor. And guess what? Speakers have magnets in them. That's why you should use speakers specifically designed for PCs; don't try to use your old bookshelf speakers. PC speakers are magnetically shielded.

Speakers Need Power

And that means they require an AC adapter. But caveat emptor: some speakers don't include the adapter, so you'll have to buy one separately. This isn't expensive, but it is a pain. So check to see whether the adapter comes with the speakers before you fork over the dough.

➤ **Be self-amplified.** That's because, like all other sound cards, Sound Blaster cards provide some amplification power but not as much as you'll sometimes want. As a result, most PC speakers are self-powered by batteries, an AC adapter, or both.

➤ **Sound clear in all sound ranges.** Poor-quality speakers typically sound muddy. Even speakers for which you spend a fair amount of money may sound good in the middle ranges but muddy in the lows and highs. Listen to the speakers before you buy and make sure their tone is pleasing to you.

Many people buy their sound cards as part of a "multimedia upgrade kit," which contains all the pieces necessary to make your PC play multimedia. These kits typically include a sound card, a reputable CD-ROM drive, and a good selection of software.

Usually, the speakers in multimedia upgrade kits are not highly regarded by audiophiles. If you want really good speakers, be ready to shell out at least $100. In my experience, $200 can get you absolutely top-notch speakers.

A final word about speakers: increasingly, vendors are combining speakers with other elements of their computers. I've seen speakers built into monitors and I've even seen a couple of keyboards with built-in speakers.

I'll say one thing about these combinations: they're convenient. You needn't futz with setting up the monitor or keyboard and then setting up the speakers. And they save space since you don't have to find a place on your desk for the speakers.

Big, Bad Bass I'm a bass hound. I love a deep, rumbly bass sound. As a result, my newest set of PC speakers has a subwoofer. This is a freestanding unit that only plays the lowest part of the bass range and, to my ear, it makes a significant improvement to sound quality.

If you have reasonably relaxed standards for sound, these combinations sometimes might work for you. I've seen and heard enough of them, however, to know that you won't get great sound. If you really care about sound quality, buy your speakers separately.

Read Chapter 9 to learn how to attach your speakers to your Sound Blaster card.

Don't Forget Mike(rophone)

This section will be short since your Sound Blaster probably came with a microphone and you won't need to buy another one.

Microphones often are handy for use with your sound card. Specifically, you will need a microphone for:

➤ **Speech recognition.** This enables you to run your computing environment with your voice. Sound Blaster comes with speech recognition software—Chapter 18 teaches you about that software.

➤ **Recording voice and sounds.** This is useful for spicing up multimedia presentations and for annotating your business applications. You could, for example, record an explanation of a particular record in a database that plays whenever somebody accesses that record.

Read Chapter 9 to learn how to attach your microphone to your Sound Blaster card.

It's CD-ROMania Time

In the last few years, the sales of CD-ROM (compact disc read-only memory) drives and discs have grown at a phenomenal rate. Sound cards are one of the few items that have grown as quickly.

CD-ROMs often are thought to be synonymous with multimedia. True, most decent multimedia applications come on CD-ROM. For the record, though, CD-ROM refers to a method of storing data. That data can be text only; many text-based databases of interest to specific professionals such as doctors, lawyers, and chemists come on CD-ROMs.

These database discs are extremely useful, but they aren't multimedia and they appeal only to a narrow range of people. For most of us, CD-ROM means games or "edutainment" titles such as encyclopedias that mix sound with video, animation, still images, and text.

In many ways, CD-ROM drives and audio CD players are similar. Both take digital data and convert it to analog information, such as sound. In fact, you can play audio CDs on most CD-ROM drives. However, CD-ROM drives also can play digital versions of videos, animations, and still images.

The way the data is stored on a CD-ROM is similar, but not identical, to the way data is stored on audio CDs. You can play audio CDs on most CD-ROM drives, but since audio CD players only handle one type of data—music—they can't handle CD-ROMs, which contain many types of data.

When buying a CD-ROM drive, speed is the key ingredient. In the beginning, CD-ROM drives were slooooow. Then, about three years ago, a new generation of CD-ROM drives appeared that operated twice as fast as the original CD-ROM drives. These were called *double-spin drives* because the mechanism that spins the disc operated twice as fast as the original drives.

Double Your Pleasure... and Your Spin

Double-spin drives quickly became the standard. Even though at this writing, you can still find some single-spin drives for a song, many newer multimedia titles won't work with them. As a result, resist the temptation to save money by purchasing a single-spin drive. Buy, at the very minimum, a double-spin drive. Even better, if you can, buy a quad-spin drive.

Quad-spin drives are becoming increasingly common. Formerly about twice as expensive as double-spin drives, prices are now plummeting on these units. Increasingly, multimedia upgrade kits use quad-spin drives.

And, in the "relentless march of progress" department, the newest generation of CD-ROM drives is starting to appear, even though, at this writing, nobody knows what to call them. These drives spin six times as fast as the original CD-ROM drives. Do we call them *sextuple-spin* drives? I don't know, but I'll sure welcome the increased speed.

In Your CD-ROM Interface

CD-ROM drives don't operate by themselves. You also need a *CD-ROM interface*. These are adapters that plug into your computer's motherboard and control what your CD-ROM drive does.

In simple terms, the CD-ROM interface exchanges information between the CD-ROM and drive and the rest of your computer system. For example, if you are playing a CD-ROM-based game and it is the appropriate time for music to play, the software on the disc passes the information about the music to the CD-ROM interface. The CD-ROM interface, in turn, sends that instruction on to your Sound Blaster, which then plays the music. Chapter 9 provides more details about how all this stuff works.

Chances are, you already own a CD-ROM interface. Most versions of Sound Blaster have at least one CD-ROM interface built in. Some versions have CD-ROM interfaces that can handle any drive, and some support only CD-ROM drives from Sony, Mitsumi, Panasonic, and Creative Labs.

CD-ROM Interface This little baby usually plugs into your computer's motherboard. Then, you plug your CD-ROM drive into the CD-ROM interface. Many sound cards, including most versions of Sound Blaster, come with built-in CD-ROM interfaces.

I'll cover CD-ROM interfaces in more depth in Chapter 9; my purpose isn't to confuse you with technical minutiae. Rather, my purpose is to make you a wiser shopper and to take some of the mystery out of this sometimes mysterious area of computer hardware. Adding a generic CD-ROM interface can be a frustrating process and your Sound Blaster, with its built-in capabilities, simplifies the process greatly.

The Joy of Joysticks

Game Controllers Joysticks and game pads that connect to your Sound Blaster are, by far, the most popular way of controlling games. However, there also are controller-like yokes that resemble the yokes used by pilots for controlling aircraft. Another interesting twist is wireless controllers that don't clutter your desk with wires.

Game controllers are, as the name implies, devices you use to control your games. The best known type of game controller is a *joystick*; a *game pad* is another type. Game pads are similar to the controllers used with game machines such as those created by Nintendo and Sega.

Joysticks and other devices for controlling your games connect to sound cards in the most literal way. Sound Blasters include an adapter to which you connect game controllers. Unless you buy a sound card with a joystick port, you'll have to go through the hassle of installing the port separately.

Chapter 9 tells you how to plug your game controller into your Sound Blaster card.

Other Multimedia Bits and Pieces

Some multimedia upgrade kits come with tons of stuff. This often is stuff that you wouldn't think of buying yourself but will use if you already have it.

The following is a short list of multimedia bits and pieces you may or may not need, or even care about. I offer it just so you know about them.

➤ **Headphones** Just like a stereo, headphones are useful for listening to music and other sounds without disturbing others. Most CD-ROM drives come with a jack in their front panel for headphones. You also can plug the headphones into your Sound Blaster card, as described in Chapter 9. Depending on your CD-ROM drive, you may need headphones for listening to audio CDs.

➤ **Disc caddies** Some CD-ROM drives work like this: you insert your CD-ROM or audio CD into a caddie. Then you insert the caddie into the drive. It's a bit of a pain, but it keeps the disc clean and prevents distorted sounds.

➤ **Good speaker wire** Audiophiles will tell you that you can lose sound quality because of mediocre speaker wires. With cheap speakers, you can't easily change the speaker wire. But with most high-quality speakers, you can.

The Least You Need to Know

Simply installing a Sound Blaster by itself doesn't assure you of listening pleasure. There are other pieces you must add, too.

➤ It's easy to skimp on speakers for your PC, but this is penny-wise and pound-foolish. Good speakers maximize your listening pleasure.

➤ A CD-ROM drive and CD-ROM interface are necessary for enjoying some of the best multimedia available.

➤ While not related to sounds or music, game controllers plug into your Sound Blaster card.

Chapter 5

The Sound Blaster Family Tree

In This Chapter

➤ Take a look at 8- and 16-bit sound cards

➤ Introducing the AWEsome AWE32

➤ Options for Sound Blaster 16

I'll end this part of the book focusing on basics with what, to me, is one of the most confusing things about Sound Blaster: the Sound Blaster family tree. Creative Labs has several different types of sound cards and places those cards in a large number of different packages.

Each package offers different capabilities. Some packages come with a lot of software; some come with less software. Some packages include special hardware such as a CD-ROM interface; some don't.

This chapter describes the various Sound Blaster packages. The intent isn't to provide free advertising for Creative Labs. Rather, the intent is to help you make heads or tails out of the packages that they sell. In this way, if you haven't already bought your Sound Blaster, you will be better informed about which package to buy.

Basic Cards: Sound Blaster and Sound Blaster Pro

Before describing the plethora of Sound Blaster options, let's first review the differences between the various cards.

As you learned in Chapter 3, 8-bit cards have a limited capability to play back sound samples. As a result, 8-bit cards provide lower sound quality than other sound cards. However, there are mono and stereo 8-bit cards; obviously, stereo cards will provide better sound quality than mono cards because they have two channels of sound playing at the same time. Mono cards only have one channel of sound.

Sound Blaster is the 8-bit mono Sound Blaster card; *Sound Blaster Pro* is the 8-bit stereo Sound Blaster card. We will not cover either of those cards in this book, because 8-bit sound card technology is quickly becoming obsolete. At this writing, these cards still are available, but their appeal is waning as better-sounding 16-bit cards are becoming almost as cheap. Because you can buy basic 16-bit cards for under $100, it's likely you can afford a 16-bit card.

16-Bit Cards: The Next Generation

You can subdivide the 16-bit Sound Blaster cards based on their capability to play back MIDI music files. *FM synthesis* cards rely on older technology to synthesize the instruments. The **Sound Blaster 16** Creative Labs product produces 16-bit.

Wave-table synthesis is a more advanced—and more real-sounding—method of playing back MIDI music. **AWE32** is the Creative Labs sound board that produces 16-bit wave-table synthesis.

32 Notes, Not 32 Bits

Note that, despite its name, the AWE32 is *not* a 32-bit sound card; however, it can play back 32 notes at a time.

The Sound Blaster 16 and the AWE32 are the two cards that we will cover in this book. These two cards come in a dizzying array of packages, each of which costs a different amount and offers different capabilities and software. The rest of this chapter describes the leading packages that include the Sound Blaster 16 and the AWE32.

Here's one important caveat. Like any company, Creative Labs (the makers of Sound Blaster) has both a research and development department and a marketing department. At the drop of a hat, the former can create new products and the latter can create new combinations of packages to put on your retailer's shelves. As a result, the information in this chapter, while up to date as of this writing, is subject to change.

One area that I know will change is that Creative Labs will offer different types of CD-ROM interfaces with their sound cards. The new type of interface is an IDE interface. If you see a Sound Blaster package in the store with the phrase IDE on the box, this will be one of the new packages. Specifically, the IDE is a general controller; you can use it to connect most quad-spin drives.

As a result, Creative Labs is eliminating the connections for Sony and Mitsumi drives from its cards, although it will maintain connections for its own drives and Panasonic drives, which are identical. Note, however, that the sound card itself won't change—just the way it can handle CD-ROM drives.

Getting More for Your Buck: The Value Editions

Say you want a Sound Blaster—nothing else will do—but you're on a tight budget. That's where so-called "Value Editions" come in. Creative Labs includes a Sound Blaster AWE32 Value Edition; also new is the budget-priced Sound Blaster 32 and the Sound Blaster 16 Value Edition.

Both of these packages include the basic sound cards—either the Sound Blaster 16 or the AWE32. However, Value Edition packages scale back the selection of accompanying software and the capabilities on the sound cards.

The basic sound cards are the same and produce the same sound. But the less expensive versions (Value Edition and Sound Blaster 32) are far less expandable in terms of memory. This makes them less attractive for those who want to create music, although they are the equal of the standard edition for playing games.

In the next section, I'll tell you about the confusing array of packages based on the Sound Blaster 16, including the Sound Blaster 16 Value Edition. The AWE32 lineup, however, is much simpler to understand.

Listen Up!

My advice: if your primary interest is merely spicing up your multimedia and games with sound, the Value Editions should suffice. But if you want more out of life—and more out of your Sound Blaster—buy the more advanced packages.

Awesome AWE32 Choices

The three basic packages that include the AWE32 are the Value Edition, the standard edition, and Sound Blaster 32. The card included in the standard AWE32 package enables you to increase the on-card memory used to store sound. Also, the standard package comes with a microphone; the Value Edition and Sound Blaster 32 don't.

You'll also get more software with the standard product. Most notably, the standard AWE32 package comes with a wonderful and powerful product called HSC InterActive Special Edition. This software lets you create advanced, professional-looking multimedia presentations.

You also get a product called Cakewalk Apprentice, which lets you create and modify MIDI music. This is a scaled down version of a very powerful MIDI product that many serious MIDI musicians use.

Advanced Sound Blaster 16

While the options for the AWE32 are relatively simple, things become complicated with the different varieties of Sound Blaster 16. Here are the five most common packages, in order of price (from cheapest to most expensive):

➤ **Sound Blaster 16 Value Edition**   As mentioned in the last section, this is the basic card that comes with basic software. For example, the included software would enable you to record WAV files. Also, you can only connect two types of CD-ROM drives to the card in the Value Edition: the Panasonic and Creative Labs CD-ROM drives.

➤ **Sound Blaster 16 MultiCD**   "MultiCD" refers to the fact that you connect Panasonic, Creative Labs, Sony, and Mitsumi CD-ROM drives to this card. Otherwise, the card itself is substantially similar to that in the Value Edition, although you'll get more software such as HSC InterActive. Note, though, that as Creative Labs phases in its cards with IDE connections for your CD-ROM drive, it will only offer cards with that connection and a connection for Creative Labs and Panasonic drives. There will be no more connections for Sony or Mitsumi drives.

➤ **Sound Blaster 16 MultiCD with Advanced Signal Processing** This card comes with a special chip: the Advanced Signal Processing (or ASP) chip. This chip adds special effects such as surround-sound. It also enables the sound card to compress and decompress sound files stored on your hard drive, which saves hard drive space. This option also comes with the advanced set of software, including HSC InterActive.

Again, Creative Labs will likely rename this model when it phases in its cards with IDE connections for your CD-ROM drive and stops offering connections for Sony or Mitsumi drives.

➤ **Sound Blaster 16 SCSI-2** This package includes a Sound Blaster 16 and a SCSI-2 adapter for connecting your CD-ROM drive to your computer. This is useful if your CD-ROM drive doesn't connect to the other Sound Blaster cards. This option also comes with the advanced set of software.

➤ **Sound Blaster 16 SCSI-2 with ASP** As the name implies, this is almost the same package as the previous one in this list, except it includes the ASP chip.

Chips Ahoy!
You can add the ASP chip later. You can save money now and buy the Sound Blaster without the ASP chip and upgrade later after you've won the lottery. Read Chapter 20 to learn more about adding the ASP chip.

Other Points of Interest

Creative Labs also sells Sound Blasters as part of multimedia upgrade kits. Since this chapter is to help you select precisely the Sound Blaster you want, I don't want to go into too much detail about those products. Just remember the multimedia upgrade kits come with the basics, including a Sound Blaster and speakers. Then, depending on the specific option, you get a wide variety of different software options.

Here's one other bit of hardware you might be interested in: the Wave Blaster II. This is a so-called daughterboard for Sound Blaster 16 cards and a few cards created by other vendors that are built identically to the Sound Blaster 16. In simple terms, you plug the Wave Blaster II into the existing sound card. The result produces wave-table synthesis sounds like the AWE32. This is useful if you already own a 16-bit FM synthesis card and want to inexpensively upgrade to wave-table synthesis. Wave Blaster doesn't work, however, with the Value Editions.

If you have any questions about any of these packages, here's Creative Labs' sales hotline number: 800-998-5227.

The Least You Need to Know

Sound Blaster sound cards come with a variety of options.

➤ You can still buy 8-bit Sound Blasters. The Sound Blaster is a mono 8-bit card and the Sound Blaster Pro is a stereo 8-bit card. Since 8-bit cards are becoming obsolescent, we won't cover them in this book.

➤ The AWE32 is Creative Labs' most advanced sound card because it features wave-table synthesis. It comes in two packages: the Value Edition and the standard package. You get a few more on-card capabilities for advanced uses in the standard package and more advanced software.

➤ There are several Sound Blaster 16 options, ranging from the Value Edition to a version with an advanced SCSI-2 CD-ROM interface. Besides including more software, the advanced versions of Sound Blaster 16 cards also include a chip, called the Advanced Signal Processing (ASP) chip, that enables you to add special effects to sounds.

Part 2
Down and Dirty: Installing Sound Blaster

Imagine this: You are installing Sound Blaster, the top of your computer is off, and high-tech electronic stuff is scattered throughout the room. You're lost, you don't know what to do, and the entire experience is starting to feel... expensive.

Here's what you should do. Read this part of the book. You'll learn how Sound Blaster works in your PC, how to install Sound Blaster 16 and AWE32, and how to connect all the other pieces that make sounds. You'll also learn how to make Sound Blaster work in Windows and how to change your configuration. Best of all, you'll learn how to troubleshoot if problems occur.

If you ignore this section and an installation nightmare occurs, don't come running to me!

Chapter 6

Read This Before Installing (PLEEEEESE!)

In This Chapter

➤ Open 'er up and install Sound Blaster

➤ Irksome IRQs—and how they can ruin your day

➤ Those darned DMAs—they'll ruin your day, too

Most children eventually learn that sometimes before you play, you must work. So it is with Sound Blaster: before you listen, you must install.

I've installed a number of sound cards and I give Creative Labs credit for making installation relatively simple. *Relatively* is the key word here—given the nature of PCs and operating systems such as DOS and Windows, you'll never experience utter simplicity.

This part of the book describes how to install Sound Blaster hardware and software. Before you start, read about some of the basics such as opening up your computer and the tools you'll need. Learn how your PC operates and how those things impact the Sound Blaster installation. I don't mention these things because I have an overriding need to be boring or technical. Au contraire—I like to think of myself as a witty, bon vivant type of guy.

Knowing a few basics about how your PC works will help you breeze through the installation process. It also will help you fix many of the problems that can occur after installation.

Staring Down the Terrible Trio

Well, it's time to take the long view again. In Chapter 3, I mentioned that making all the components in a PC work together was something of a miracle in arbitration.

Much of the credit goes to system software; some is built into your computer, and some comes in the form of your operating system such as DOS. But there's more to it than that.

The next three sections describe three critical bits of information you need to know as you install your Sound Blaster—and most other cards (circuit boards) you add into your computer. These items help the system software do its work.

I call these three items the terrible trio because a problem with any one of them can bring your system to a screeching halt. You *will* be tested on the terrible trio. I won't do the testing, though—Sound Blaster will. Conflicts and system crashes occur if you don't understand these three items. You'll only pass the test called installation if you pay attention now.

Know Your Address

Random-access memory, or RAM as it's called in the computer biz, plays a critical role in how well your computer functions. Virtually every part of your computer, whether it's hardware or software, requires it. These hardware and software pieces use RAM to temporarily store bits and pieces of information.

I/O Base Address The specific chunk of your computer's random-access memory used by a hardware device such as your Sound Blaster card. Just like a row of suburban tract houses, each device must have its own address.

Hardware such as your Sound Blaster card requires specific chunks of memory. If another piece of hardware or software uses that chunk of memory, one or both of the items can malfunction or your system can crash.

This reserved chunk of memory is called an *I/O base address*. I/O refers to the expression *input/output*, which refers to how information enters and leaves your computer. Examples of input devices are keyboards and joysticks. Examples of output devices are printers and monitors.

The temptation to think of I/O base addresses like the address of homes and businesses is irresistible and reasonably accurate. If you get in a taxi cab and give the driver an address, he should know how to get you there.

Similarly, when it's time for your Sound Blaster—or most other add-in devices in your computer—to act, your computer, and particularly your computer's central processing unit, needs to know where to send instructions. If it knows your Sound Blaster's base I/O address, there isn't any problem.

I've been in cities where there are many similarly named and addressed streets. (How many Peachtree Streets are there in Atlanta, anyway?) When that happens in a computer—if two devices have the same address—your computer becomes confused and can crash. Or perhaps neither device will work.

When you install Sound Blaster, the installation program assigns a free I/O base address to the sound card. It actually does this for the card itself and for the joystick/MIDI port. If one of these addresses overlaps the address of another device, you can have problems.

Now that you understand how I/O base addresses work, you can handle I/O address problems and see they're relatively simple to fix, as you'll learn in Chapter 12. If you're still struggling with I/O addresses, make sure you have the phone number for the Creative Labs tech support staff, in case you have a problem while installing your Sound Blaster. Now aren't you glad you're starting to learn this propeller-head stuff? But wait—there's more.

DMAs, Please

Like kids, computer devices such as sound cards are always vying for attention. In this case, computer devices are competing for the attention of various other resources in your computer. One of the most sought-after of these resources is your system's RAM. Just like a room full of kids whining for their mommies at the same time, chaos would ensue if all the devices were trying to grab the same chunk of RAM at the same time.

The solution is *direct memory access channels*, or DMA channels. These are specific pathways your computer system assigns to each device. As with I/O base addresses, the Sound Blaster installation program assigns a DMA channel to the sound card at the time of installation.

Direct Memory Access (DMA) Channel No, this isn't a cable channel that helps you remember things better. It's the direct pathway to RAM used by a device such as your Sound Blaster. If more than one device uses the same DMA channel, malfunctions can occur.

Most PCs have eight DMA channels, so when conflicts occur, you must switch that device to another channel. With Sound Blaster, as you'll learn in Chapter 12, you use either the installation program or a program called DIAGNOSE to change the DMA channel Sound Blaster uses.

Excusing IRQs

Writers love to stretch metaphors, similes, and the like to the breaking point—and here goes. Imagine a sixteen-screen multiplex theater, in which each theater holds 300 people. Say all sixteen movies are extremely popular and they start and end at precisely the same times.

That means most of the 5,000 people try to jam in and out of sixteen theaters at the same time. The stress on the ticket counter and on the doorways into the theaters would bring the system to a halt. Now, multiply that problem by millions and you'll have some idea about the stresses your computer must sort out. That's because your computer—and particularly your computer's central processing unit (CPU)—sorts out and processes millions of instructions per second.

These instructions may be from software asking your Sound Blaster to play a sound, or it may be a CD-ROM shooting information through the CD-ROM interface to your video adapter and to your monitor to play a video. The CPU is the device that must route all these instructions to and from the appropriate device.

This brings us to *interrupt requests*, or IRQs for short. These are, in effect, priority numbers assigned to devices in your PC such as your Sound Blaster. When the CPU gets an instruction, it examines the IRQ of the device that sent it. If the device's IRQ number is high enough, it will briefly interrupt what it's doing and process that device's instructions.

Interrupt Request (IRQ) This is a priority number assigned to a device such as your Sound Blaster. This priority number helps your computer's central processing unit sort out the flood of data being sent to it by your Sound Blaster and all other devices in your computer.

Like DMA channels and I/O base addresses, your Sound Blaster (and many other devices in your PC) has its own IRQ number. PCs usually have sixteen IRQs, but many of them already are spoken for by devices such as your keyboard and communications ports.

This means that IRQs are in high demand. If two devices have the same IRQ and try to operate at the same time, you'll inevitably get a malfunction. As often as not, that malfunction will be a system crash. That's why the IRQ of your Sound Blaster is so important. As with I/O base addresses and DMA channels, the Sound Blaster installation program assigns an IRQ number to the sound board.

It's distressingly simple to assign the same IRQ to two devices. You may, for example, add a device after you install your Sound Blaster and give it the same IRQ as your Sound Blaster.

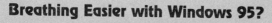

Breathing Easier with Windows 95?

Supposedly, problems like IRQ, DMA channel, and I/O base address conflicts will go away with the introduction of the Windows 95 operating system. That's because a part of Windows 95 is Plug and Play. In theory, Plug and Play means Windows 95 and add-in cards such as Sound Blaster work together to automatically determine the correct settings. At this writing, though, it's too soon to tell how well this system will function. At the very least, it will require all the add-in cards in your computer to be compliant with Plug and Play. At this writing, few are. Read Chapter 11 to learn more about how Sound Blaster works with Windows 95.

As with DMA channels and I/O base addresses, you can change your Sound Blaster's IRQ—or that of the conflicting device. In Chapter 12, we'll discuss in greater detail how to adjust the IRQ, DMA channel, and I/O base address on your Sound Blaster card.

Getting Ready to Install

Chapter 7 is about installing Sound Blaster 16 and Chapter 8 is about installing the AWE32. However, I'm an efficient guy. There are certain things that are the same for installing both cards.

The next few sections explain some of the things you need to do before installing your sound card. Specifically, I'll tell you which tools you'll need and how to open up your computer to perform the installation. If you haven't done it before, it can be scary to think about taking the top off your computer and rooting around inside. But you needn't worry—just read this section and you'll be all right.

The Right Tools

It's a stereotypically male thing to like tools. However, to those of you who don't fit this stereotype, be glad that you won't need many tools for installing your Sound Blaster. Here's the list:

➤ Flat head and Phillips head screwdrivers

➤ Tweezers

➤ Maybe needlenose pliers

Say No to Magnetism Make sure the screwdrivers you use aren't magnetized. Magnetized screwdrivers often are handy, but you don't want to put anything magnetic near your computer. That's because magnetism can ruin the information stored on your hard drive.

Zap! You're It! Usually, if you have some static build-up and touch your computer, nothing bad will happen, but sometimes, bad things do happen. I accidentally zapped my computer a couple of years ago and had to reset one type of its system software, called BIOS, from scratch.

Pretty short list, huh? I'll describe what you'll use each of those tools for in the next several chapters.

Take It Off

No matter which Sound Blaster you install, you'll start by taking off the top of your computer. This procedure varies from computer to computer, but it always starts with this: turn off your computer and, just to be extra safe, unplug it.

You're still not done with the electrical thing even after taking those precautions. While standing next to your computer, you must discharge any static electricity that may be clinging to you. Do this by touching something metal—I use a nearby lamp—before you pop the top of your computer.

The next part is where you'll use the screwdriver. Typically, there are screws that connect the top of the computer case to the rest of the computer. You'll need to remove these screws and then remove the top. Generally, you do this by sliding the case backward a bit and then by lifting the front end.

This is a good time to look at the documentation that came with your computer to learn more about your computer's particular case. Some cases are more complex than others; you can find yourself pulling and yanking to no avail if yours is one of the complicated types. Reading the documentation will save you this difficulty.

After you take the top off your computer, place it where it won't get dusty, kicked, or otherwise mutilated. I once accidentally punted the top of a computer and, after that, it never fit right. I hate it when that happens.

Playing the Slots

Now, take a look inside your computer. If you're not familiar with how the insides of computers look, it may be confusing at first. Sometimes, the documentation that accompanies computers will show a picture or diagram of your computer's innards and tell you the names of each part.

Look for the motherboard. It's easy to find: the *motherboard* is the large green circuit board that takes up most of the bottom of the computer (or the vertical plane if you have a tower case).

Next, look for free slots. *Slots* are the places in your motherboard into which you plug devices such as your Sound Blaster. The easiest way to look for slots is to take a quick look at your Sound Blaster card, and then look for cards that look like it. Sure, add-in cards such as your video adapter or CD-ROM interface have very different jobs to do than Sound Blaster, but they look similar.

There are several different types of slots. There are 8-bit slots, which are the shortest slots. 16-bit slots are longer. If yours is a new computer, it may not have any 8-bit slots. However, it may have slots that look different from either 8-bit or 16-bit slots.

Different Types of Slots

The different types of slots handle data differently. 8-bit slots handle data 8 bits at a time (a bit is the smallest unit of measure for computerized data). These old slots have been around since the beginning of desktop PCs. A 16-bit slot handles data—you guessed it—16 bits at a time, which, obviously, is faster. Slots like PCI slots are faster because they handle data 32 bits at a time. They're also designed for greater efficiency.

Depending on your computer and its design, other types of slots such as PCI slots or VL-Bus slots may be present. Some computers may also have EISA slots or, if yours is an older IBM computer, Micro Channel slots. Again, your PCs documentation should have a diagram showing you the different types of slots.

For installing Sound Blaster, don't worry about all these other types of slots. Sound Blaster only plugs into 16-bit slots, so you'll need to find a free one. If you peer into your computer and don't see an available 16-bit slot, chances are you have other add-ins cards in your computer that are using them. If this is the case, you have only two options (besides doing without your Sound Blaster, that is):

➤ Pull out the other add-in cards placed in 16-bit slots and see if any of them are 8-bit cards—8-bit cards do fit into 16-bit slots. If that's the case, pull the 8-bit card out and place it in an 8-bit slot.

➤ Determine if you can live without one of the add-in cards already in one of your 16-bit slots. If so, yank it out and put it on the shelf. For example, perhaps you have an older sound card already in your computer that, obviously, you won't need after installing Sound Blaster.

Yank That Old Sound Card

If you have another sound card in your computer, I strongly urge you to yank it out. There's no reason for having two sound cards in your PC and, in many cases, neither will work right if the other is present.

You pull cards out of their slots by first making sure that they are not screwed in to the frame of the computer. The screw-ins are discussed in the next section. Then you use gentle but firm force to pull the card straight toward you.

Think Before You Pull

One important caution before you start pulling cards out of your computer: don't pull anything out of your computer unless you know for certain what you're pulling. It seems obvious, but any professional technical support technician will tell you this goof happens all the time.

Get on the (Back) Plane

The thing about add-in cards such as your Sound Blaster is you often want to plug things into them. For example, after you've installed Sound Blaster, you'll want to plug speakers or headphones into it.

The back of an adapter—called the *backplane*—is the part that sticks out of the back of the computer. Put differently, there's a rectangular hole in the back of your PC filled by the backplane of your card. Each hole corresponds to an add-in slot.

This is a long explanation for a simple task. Before you insert your Sound Blaster, first take off the little plate, called a backplane plate, that covers the hole when no card is installed. With the plate removed, the back of your Sound Blaster will be exposed out the back of the computer so you can plug in your speakers.

This is another job for your screwdriver. Carefully unscrew the screw that holds down the backplane plate and remove the screw. Do this carefully because it is extremely easy to drop the screw into the bowels of your computer. Then lift the backplane out of the system.

You don't want to drop a screw in your PC for several reasons. First, you'll want to use that screw to secure your Sound Blaster to the computer. Also, screws rattling around in your PC are nothing but trouble—they can cause grief such as short circuits.

If you do drop the screw securing the backplane plate into your PC, use a tweezers to retrieve it. If that doesn't work, try using a needlenose pliers. If that still doesn't work, I suggest lifting your computer, turning it upside down and gently shaking. That's not a very elegant way to do things, but it's effective.

The Least You Need to Know

In the next two chapters, we'll dive into the installation process in earnest. In this chapter, though, you took the steps necessary to start the installation process. Specifically, you learned about:

➤ How to safely remove the cover of your PC.

➤ The slots into which you insert your Sound Blaster.

➤ Interrupt requests (IRQs), DMA channels, and I/O base addresses, which help keep all the flow of data from devices such as Sound Blaster.

➤ The malfunctions that can occur if you have conflicting I/O base addresses, DMA channels, or IRQs.

Know—And Install—Your Sound Blaster 16

In This Chapter

➤ How Sound Blaster 16 is special

➤ Installing the software

➤ Making sure it works

The moment of truth has arrived—if the sound card you bought is a Sound Blaster 16. It's time to install your sound card. If you bought an AWE32, skip this chapter and go right to Chapter 8, which describes installing that card.

If you just dive into installation without knowing what you're doing, it can be a painful process. However, the last few chapters provided information that should simplify matters. They described how sound cards work, how to prepare for installation, and about problems such as IRQ or DMA channel conflicts that prevent sound cards from working.

In this chapter, you will learn about some specific qualities of your Sound Blaster 16. Then, at last, you can get down to the real nitty-gritty: installing it.

Note, though, this chapter is *not* about fixing problems that occur after installation or fine-tuning your installation. For information about diagnosing and fixing problems, read:

➤ Chapter 10 about how Sound Blaster works with Windows.

➤ Chapter 12 if you need to change your settings.

➤ Chapter 13 for general troubleshooting.

➤ Chapter 14 about troubleshooting in Windows.

About Sound Blaster 16

The next few sections provide a guided tour of your Sound Blaster 16. You will become familiar with your card, which should further simplify installation and troubleshooting. If, however, you want to cut right to the chase and install your card, skip these sections.

What This Baby Can Do

Your Sound Blaster 16 has some powerful capabilities, beginning with the capability to play either 8-bit or 16-bit stereo sounds with sampling rates as high as 44.1KHz. Those specifications are quite common—most 16-bit sound cards can match them. However, Sound Blaster 16 has some capabilities that many other sound cards don't. Those capabilities include:

➤ **Advanced signal processing** Depending on which package of Sound Blaster 16 you bought, yours may include an advanced signal processing (ASP) chip (this is an extra-cost option). If your needs are simple and your budget is small, the ASP chip may be overkill, but if you want to squeeze the most sound out of your Sound Blaster, the ASP chip is an excellent addition.

The ASP chip enables you to add special effects such as the reverb effect. It also has one other capability: It helps compress and decompress the sound files it's playing. Waveform files require a lot of disk space; the capability to automatically compress the files means they take less disk space.

➤ **Virtually perfect compatibility** Sound Blaster has become a de facto standard for sound cards. As a result, software vendors make sure that their software works with it.

Virtually every other sound card on the market boasts of being "Sound Blaster compatible." Put differently, that means they'll work with most software (such as games) that are tested with the Sound Blaster. Practically, however, total compatibility is elusive—in my experience, other sound cards sometimes are not Sound Blaster compatible and don't work with some games. You'll never have that problem with your Sound Blaster. By definition, it is compatible.

➤ **CD-ROM interface**   No matter what model Sound Blaster 16 you buy, it has at least one built-in interface to which you can connect a CD-ROM drive. Some Sound Blasters have an interface that only works with drives from Panasonic and Creative Labs. Other versions have interfaces that also work with Sony and Mitsumi CD-ROM drives.

The Sound Blaster 16 SCSI-2 has a single CD-ROM interface but, as the name implies, it's a SCSI-2 interface. Because this is a standardized interface, you can connect virtually any CD-ROM drive to it. You also can connect any other SCSI device, such as a SCSI hard drive, to it.

➤ **Four watts per channel amplification**   All sound cards have built-in amplification, but Sound Blaster's has a bit more amplification oomph than many other sound cards. Sound Blaster provides four watts of amplification per channel; most other cards provide only between two and three watts. The benefit is that speakers without their own power supply play louder and more clearly.

Even more useful, the regular Sound Blaster 16 package is one of the few sound cards I've seen that has a dial on the card for altering volume. That means if you don't use self-amplified speakers (and I strongly believe you should), you'll have adequate power and volume and you also can adjust the volume.

➤ **Software selectable DMA channels and IRQs**   This means you can change DMA channels and IRQs using software that comes with Sound Blaster. This is becoming an increasingly common capability, but it still is far from universal. Without this capability, you must pull the card out of your computer and adjust jumpers on the card by hand—a clumsy, time-consuming process.

What's on the Card

In this section, you'll become acquainted with the Sound Blaster 16 card. Specifically, let's focus on the backplane of Sound Blaster—that's the part that sticks out of the back of your computer and with which you will interact most frequently.

Looking at the backplane of the card, there are two plug-in jacks, an adjustment thumbwheel, another plug-in jack, and a plug-in port. From the top, those items are:

➤ **Line in**   This is where you plug in an external device such as a tape player or audio CD.

➤ **Mic in**   As the name implies, this is where you plug in your microphone for recording sounds.

➤ **Thumbwheel adjuster**   This is for adjusting volume. Note, though, that it only adjusts the volume of sound generated with the Sound Blaster's built-in amplifier. It doesn't adjust volume for sound amplified by your speakers' built-in amplifier.

➤ **Spk Out**   This is where you plug in your speakers.

➤ **Joystick/MIDI port**   Technically, this a MPU-401 MIDI port. This is where you connect your game controller. It's also where you would attach external MIDI devices, such as a synthesizer.

Now, turn the card so that the circuits face you. There's a lot of stuff on the card; I'll list only two of the more important points of interest.

➤ **CD-ROM interface connectors**   These are located on the left side of the card. Depending on the model of Sound Blaster you bought, there may be one connector or three. I'll talk more about using these guys in Chapter 9.

➤ **CD in connector**   This is located at the top of the card, close to the backplane. This is a four-prong connector. If your CD-ROM drive is an internal model, you must connect a cable, which should be included with your drive, between the back of the drive and this connector.

The Moment of Truth: Sound Card Installation

The moment of truth is approaching. It's time to start thinking seriously about installing your Sound Blaster. Before you do, make sure your PC meets these minimum requirements and has at least 4M of free hard disk space to accommodate the included software. If disk space is at a premium, you needn't install all that software. You'll learn how to selectively install Sound Blaster programs later in this chapter.

After all this build-up, actually inserting Sound Blaster 16 into your computer is something of an anticlimax. The first step is to open up your Sound Blaster box and become familiar with what's inside. For installation, the pieces we are most concerned with are:

➤ The sound card itself, which you should leave safely tucked in its static-free plastic bag until you absolutely need it.

➤ The software disks for installing Sound Blaster. The next section deals with installing software.

➤ The *Getting Started* guide that comes with Sound Blaster.

Next, make sure you read Chapter 6, which describes in detail how to get your computer ready for Sound Blaster. To briefly review that process:

➤ Turn off and unplug your computer.

➤ Take the top off your computer.

➤ Find a free 16-bit slot for your Sound Blaster.

➤ Unscrew the backplane plate for that slot and remove the plate. Store the plate someplace out of the way, like in the box in which your computer came. Put the screw aside for later; you'll use it to fasten down your Sound Blaster.

Now, insert the Sound Blaster into a free slot. To do that, rest the bottom of the card, which has gold-plated strips on it, on the top of the slot. Then, use firm force and push the card straight down into the slot. You may need to jiggle the card slightly forward and aft to coax it into the slot.

When sliding the card into its slot, don't be afraid to use firm force but don't use brute force. If the top edge of the card looks like it isn't perfectly horizontal, the card isn't seated in the slot firmly—give it a bit more pressure.

Do It Again

If the card absolutely refuses to go in its slot, it may be snagged on something else in your computer. Specifically, the backplane of the sound card may be snagging the back of the computer, or the card may be snagging a neighboring card.

After you properly seat your card, plug in your computer and start it—but don't put the top back on yet. Now it's time to install the software needed to make your Sound Blaster work. That's what the next section is about.

Going for a Drive

This chapter assumes that the only thing you're installing is your Sound Blaster card. If you also are installing your CD-ROM drive at the same time, this is a good time to skip ahead to Chapter 9 and read about the connections between your drive and your Sound Blaster. Then, return to this chapter.

Next, connect your speakers to the backplane of your Sound Blaster. Jump ahead to Chapter 9 for details.

Installing the Sound Blaster Software

Installing the hardware wasn't so hard, was it? Before you use Sound Blaster, however, you must install the software that makes it run.

That isn't difficult, either. Sound Blaster's installation program automatically makes changes to your system that enable Sound Blaster to work. It also installs two types of software. One type is basic software for fine-tuning your Sound Blaster configuration. The other type of software are the extras that allow you to do things such as edit sound and music files.

The next several sections walk you through the software installation process.

Getting Started in the Software Biz

Remove the installation floppy disks from the special envelope that holds them in the Sound Blaster box. To begin installing software, place the "Installation" disk in your floppy drive. This may be your A: drive or B: drive, depending on which floppy drive on your system works with disks of the same size as the "Installation" disk, which is usually a 3.5-inch disk.

Next, switch to that drive by typing **A:** at the DOS prompt (or **B:**) and then pressing **Enter**. Then, at the DOS prompt (A:\> or B:\>), type **INSTALL** and press **Enter** again.

This loads the Sound Blaster installation program. It greets you with the first installation screen.

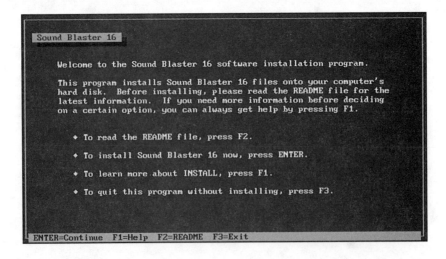

The initial Sound Blaster install screen.

To continue with installation, press **Enter**. However, the installation program also gives you the option to exit out of installation or to learn more about it. If you continue with the installation, the second installation screen gives you two options: you can perform a Full Installation or a Custom Installation.

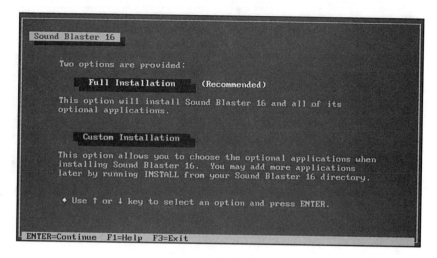

Choosing your installation option.

The Full Installation option automatically installs all files. If you select that option, the installation begins and you need to follow on-screen instructions, such as placing new floppy disks in your drive.

The Custom Installation option adds a screen that lets you select which software to install. This is useful if disk space is at a premium or you don't want to use specific applications that come with Sound Blaster.

Getting Specific

If you choose the Custom Installation option, the first Custom Installation screen appears. This is where you select the specific applications you want to install.

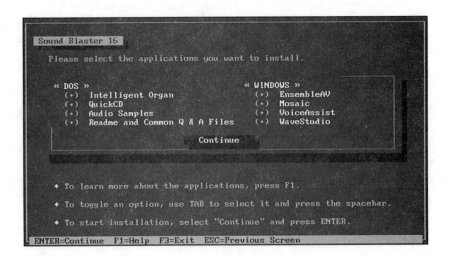

Selecting custom installation options on the first Custom Installation screen.

Use the up or down arrow keys on your keyboard to select the option you want; then press **Enter**.

In the first Custom Installation screen, items currently selected for installation have a dot to their left. To eliminate the dot, press **Tab** until the cursor is below the dot of the item you want to deselect. Then press **Spacebar**. The dot disappears and the installation program won't install that option. If you change your mind, press **Spacebar** again and the dot reappears.

When you finish selecting all the items you want, press **Tab** until the **Continue** button is highlighted. Then press **Enter**, and the installation process continues.

The next screen appears whether you selected Custom Installation or Full Installation. In this screen, you tell the installation program the directory in which you want to place Sound Blaster files and the drive from which your PC boots. This also leads to a screen in which you tell Sound Blaster which, if any, CD-ROM drive you are installing.

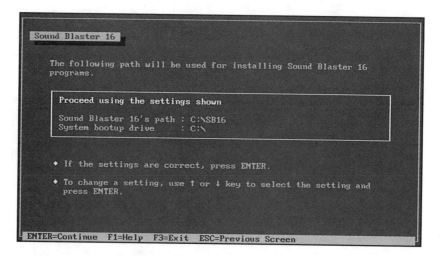

Selecting drives and paths.

Depending on which model of Sound Blaster you are installing, the **Proceed using the settings shown** area of the screen may change as you set:

➤ The drive and path for Sound Blaster files.

➤ The drive from which your computer boots.

➤ The drive and path of your Windows files.

➤ The type of CD-ROM drive you are installing.

Most computers boot (start up) from the C: drive. Unless yours is the rare exception, don't change that option. Also, by default, the installation program places all Sound Blaster files in a directory called C:\SB16. Again, there probably isn't any reason to change that setting. Similarly, unless you are certain that your Windows directory is different from the one listed, don't change that setting.

If you are installing one of the CD-ROM drives that Sound Blaster supports at the same time you are installing your sound card, select that drive from the list. If you are not installing a drive or are installing another type of drive, select **None**.

To move between the options on this screen, use the up and down arrow keys. Notice the installation program highlights the option you select.

If you want to change a setting, highlight that option and press **Enter**. You then change the setting in the next screen that appears. When you finish, press **Enter**. After you make all the changes you want, highlight the line in the screen that says **Proceed using the settings shown** and press **Enter** again.

Next, you'll see a screen in which you set items such as IRQs, I/O port addresses, and the like for your Sound Blaster. You learned about these little demons in Chapter 6. If you've forgotten, I urge you to re-read that chapter. Also, remember to read Chapter 11 about Windows 95 to learn how that operating system helps resolve these conflicts.

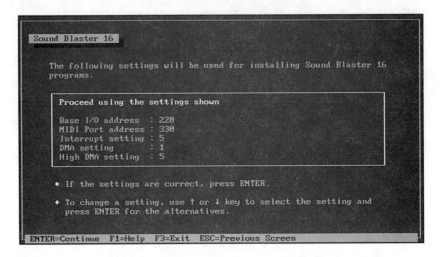

Setting port addresses, DMAs, and more.

It's possible there are conflicts between these settings and those used by other devices in your computer, such as an internal modem. However, usually, the default settings don't result in conflicts.

If you are certain that a conflict exists, this is the place to change the settings. You may not know about conflicts yet; for now, don't change the current settings. You can return to this screen later to change the settings, as we'll discuss in Chapter 12. Press **Enter** to continue with the installation process.

At this point, the installation program copies files to your hard drive. You need only follow on-screen directions about changing disks.

When all the files are installed, Sound Blaster tells you about changes it made to your DOS startup files. These two files, AUTOEXEC.BAT and CONFIG.SYS, contain instructions that DOS automatically executes when your computer first starts. Press **Enter** to continue.

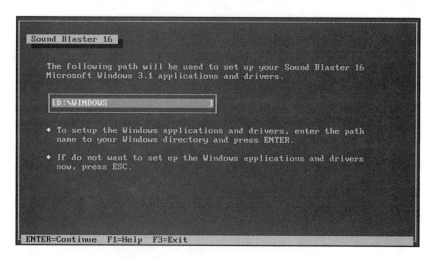

```
┌─────────────────────────────────────────────────────────────────┐
│ Sound Blaster 16                                                  │
│                                                                   │
│   The following lines will be added to your system files:         │
│                                                                   │
│   C:\AUTOEXEC.BAT file:                                            │
│   >> SET BLASTER=A220 I5 D1 H5 P330 T6                             │
│   >> SET SOUND=C:\SB16                                             │
│   >> SET MIDI=SYNTH:1 MAP:E                                        │
│   >> C:\SB16\DIAGNOSE /S                                           │
│   >> C:\SB16\SB16SET /P                                            │
│                                                                   │
│   C:\CONFIG.SYS file:                                              │
│   >> DEVICE=C:\SB16\DRV\CSP.SYS /UNIT=0 /BLASTER=A:220             │
│   >> DEVICE=C:\SB16\DRV\CTSB16.SYS /UNIT=0 /BLASTER=A:220 I:5 D:1 H:5 │
│   >> DEVICE=C:\SB16\DRV\CTMMSYS.SYS                                │
│   >> FILES=40   (If it is less than 40 or does not exists)         │
│                                                                   │
│                                                                   │
│   ♦ To continue, press ENTER.                                     │
│                                                                   │
│ ENTER=Continue  F1=Help  F3=Exit                                  │
└─────────────────────────────────────────────────────────────────┘
```

Sound Blaster tells you about changes to be made to your startup files.

Next, the installation program sets up Windows to work with Sound Blaster. First, it asks you to confirm the directory in which Windows is installed.

```
┌─────────────────────────────────────────────────────────────────┐
│ Sound Blaster 16                                                  │
│                                                                   │
│    The following path will be used to set up your Sound Blaster 16 │
│    Microsoft Windows 3.1 applications and drivers.                 │
│                                                                   │
│    ┌─────────────────────────────────────────────┐               │
│    [D:\WINDOWS                                    ]               │
│    └─────────────────────────────────────────────┘               │
│                                                                   │
│    ♦ To setup the Windows applications and drivers, enter the path │
│      name to your Windows directory and press ENTER.              │
│                                                                   │
│    ♦ If do not want to set up the Windows applications and drivers │
│      now, press ESC.                                              │
│                                                                   │
│ ENTER=Continue  F1=Help  F3=Exit                                  │
└─────────────────────────────────────────────────────────────────┘
```

Setting your Windows directory.

If you know that the directory listed on-screen is wrong, change it in the text box. Delete characters with **Backspace**, and then type the correct directory. If the listed Windows directory is correct, or after you make your changes, press **Enter** to continue.

No Escape!

At this point, you can press **Escape** if you don't want to set up Windows to run with your Sound Blaster. I strongly recommend against this, even if you rarely use Windows. That's because Windows programs offer some of the best sound and multimedia opportunities.

After you press **Enter**, the installation program begins copying the files Sound Blaster needs to work in Windows. It may also ask if you want to replace specific files that already are in your Windows directory with the version of the same files that comes with the Sound Blaster card.

These files are necessary for Sound Blaster to work. Most often, they are updated versions of files that Windows already installed. By using your arrow keys, select:

➤ **Backup**   Tells the installation program to replace the existing file but to make a copy of it.

➤ **Skip**   Skips this part of the process entirely. This, in effect, keeps the original file in your Windows directory.

➤ **Proceed**   Replaces the file without backing it up.

Here's a good rule of thumb: replace any existing files with the ones that Sound Blaster provides, but select the **Backup** option. Creative Labs tested the files that come with Sound Blaster to make sure they work with the sound card. The existing files, which were probably loaded when you installed Windows, probably were not tested with Sound Blaster.

During this process, the installation program also makes changes in some critical Windows-related files to make sure that Sound Blaster works in Windows. Specifically, it alters your WIN.INI and SYSTEM.INI files. Remember how your AUTOEXEC.BAT and CONFIG.SYS files contain instructions that DOS automatically executes when you start your computer? Similarly, WIN.INI and SYSTEM.INI contain instructions that execute whenever you start Windows.

After setting up Sound Blaster to work with Windows, the installation process is complete. Note, though, that before you can listen to Sound Blaster, you must restart your computer. If you press **Enter**, you return to the DOS prompt. But if you press **F10**, your computer restarts and, if all went well, you can use Sound Blaster.

Makin' Sure It Works

Notice that I included the phrase "if all went well" in the last sentence. Usually, all does go well, but sometimes it doesn't. To test that everything works as it should, use an included utility called DIAGNOSE.

To use this utility, switch to your Sound Blaster directory which, by default, is C:\SB16. Do that by first typing **C:** and pressing **Enter**. Then type **CD \SB16** and press **Enter**. At the prompt for that directory, type **DIAGNOSE**, which displays the first screen of the Sound Blaster 16 diagnostic utility.

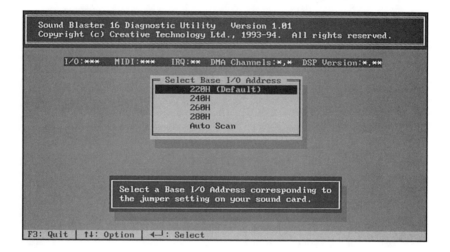

Diagnosing your system.

This utility diagnoses:

➤ Base I/O address

➤ MPU-401 MIDI Port

➤ IRQ

➤ Low DMA, the DMA channel needed to play 8-bit sounds

➤ High DMA, the DMA channel needed to play 16-bit sounds

For each diagnostic, select an option and press **Enter**. For example, the first diagnostic is for base I/O address. Select one and DIAGNOSE will tell you if it's available. If you're not sure, select **Auto Scan** and press **Enter**. When each test is finished, the next text appears on-screen automatically.

At the end of the process, you can make sure that both sound and music are playing. The DIAGNOSE utility displays screens in which you can check both 8- and 16-bit sounds on both the right and left channels. Then it lets you test to make sure that MIDI music plays in both channels.

Use the arrow keys to select the precise test you want, and then press **Enter.** You should hear sound from your speakers. If your speakers are properly connected and the volume is turned up adequately but you don't hear sounds, you still have an IRQ, DMA channel, or base I/O address conflict. Run DIAGNOSE again and try a different mixture of settings.

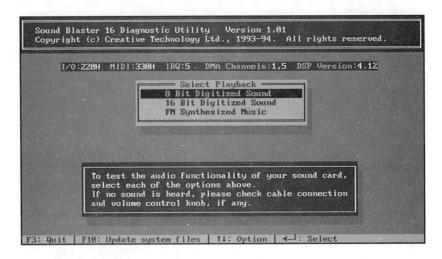

Testing Sound Blaster.

Even if everything is functioning correctly in the DIAGNOSE utility, you aren't out of the woods yet. That's because this utility doesn't diagnose whether your Sound Blaster works in Windows. I'll discuss Windows and the potential problems you can encounter there in Chapter 10. Chapter 11 discusses Windows 95.

Remember that you saved the screw that was used to tighten down the backplane plate? If you are not connecting a CD-ROM drive to the CD-ROM interface on your Sound Blaster, use that screw to fasten down Sound Blaster to the chassis of your computer. If you are going to use your Sound Blaster's CD-ROM interface, hold on to that screw until after you complete that process (see Chapter 9 for a discussion on hooking everything up to your Sound Blaster, including your speakers and your CD-ROM drive).

Consult your PC's documentation to help you put the cover back on your PC. Another reminder: fill out and mail in your registration card so you can get technical support.

The Least You Need to Know

In this chapter, you learned about your Sound Blaster 16 and how to install it in your computer.

➤ Sound Blaster 16 has many advanced capabilities, including the capability to add special effects like reverb to sound files.

➤ Most of your interaction with Sound Blaster 16 is with its backplane, which includes plug-ins for speakers, a microphone, and a volume control.

➤ The software installation program sets up your Sound Blaster to work in Windows and DOS.

➤ After installation, make sure everything works—in DOS, at least—with the DIAG-NOSE utility.

Chapter 8

Know—And Install—Your Sound Blaster AWE32

In This Chapter

➤ Why AWE32 sounds terrific

➤ Software installation made simple

➤ Testing to make sure it works

If you aren't quivering in anticipation by now, you're made of ice. Here you bought what many consider to be the best sound card available, the Sound Blaster AWE32, and it's nearly time to install it.

First—a reality check. To paraphrase airline cabin attendants, "The destination of this chapter is to help you become acquainted with your AWE32 and to install it. If yours is another destination, such as installing a Sound Blaster 16, now is a good time to switch to Chapter 7."

If your new sound card is an AWE32, however, hold on for a fun ride. By the time you finish this chapter, you'll be much more intimate with your AWE32; you will have installed it and you'll be ready to use it.

About Your AWE32

The Sound Blaster 16 is an excellent FM synthesis sound card, but the Sound Blaster AWE32 is a way cool, outta-sight sound card. Its wave-table synthesis capabilities produce superb MIDI playback since it plays back actual digital samples of sound. Also, it has options that enable you to tweak the card and the sounds it creates.

The next couple of sections help you become better acquainted with your Sound Blaster AWE32.

Takin' AWE32 Out for a Spin

Let's look at some of the AWE32's capabilities. This baby starts with the same capabilities as the more advanced Sound Blaster 16 card with the Advanced Signal Processing (ASP) chip. That means that it:

➤ Is a standard; it works with virtually all software.

➤ Is "backward compatible," which is a fancy way of saying it plays standard 8-bit and 16-bit sound and FM synthesis MIDI files.

➤ Has the Advanced Signal Processing (ASP) chip that enables you to easily add effects such as the reverb effect. It also enables you to save disk space by compressing sound files and decompressing them as you use them.

➤ Has CD-ROM interfaces (in the standard edition) for Sony, Mitsumi, Creative, and Panasonic CD-ROM drives.

The above points are a solid feature set that, in themselves, surpass many other sound cards. However, to these basic features, Creative Labs added:

➤ A digital signal processor (DSP) that, among other things, speeds up the playback of sounds. Note that the DSP is not part of the new Sound Blaster 32 package.

➤ The ability to upgrade from the standard 512K of on-board RAM to as much as 28M of on-board RAM. While the standard amount of RAM is sufficient for most users, adding RAM enables serious sound aficionados and MIDI musicians to add additional sound samples. You can set AWE32 to do this automatically whenever you start Windows, as you'll learn in Chapter 17. Learn more about adding sound samples in Chapter 23.

What's on the Card

Now it's time to become acquainted with your AWE32 on a slightly more intimate basis. Let's take it out of its protective plastic wrapper and look at it.

Sturdy but Sensitive

Even though they're jam-packed with electronic gizmos, sound cards are solid critters that don't break easily. Still, when handling your sound card, it's probably best to hold it by its top and bottom edges or by the silver backplane plate.

First, face the card toward you so you see all the circuitry. Let me point out several points of interest that we'll talk about in more detail in other parts of the book:

➤ **The CD-ROM interfaces**   Those are the plug-ins all the way on the left side of the board as it faces you. Learn how to plug a CD-ROM drive into those plug-ins in Chapter 9.

➤ **Memory expansion slots**   These are where you plug in more on-board memory. These are located just above the CD-ROM interfaces. Read Chapter 20 to learn about adding more memory.

➤ **The CD-ROM connector**   If yours is an internal CD-ROM drive, you must connect a cable from the back of the drive to this four-pin connector. The connector is at the top of the card near the backplane, or toward the right as you look at the card. Read Chapter 9 to learn more about connecting your CD-ROM drive.

Next, turn the card and look at the silver backplane. There are four plug-in jacks and an adapter. From the top, those connectors are marked as:

➤ **Line in**   For connecting devices such as a cassette player or audio CD player. This is handy for recording sounds from those sources.

➤ **Mic out**   Where you connect your microphone.

➤ **Line out**   For connecting self-powered speakers. It does not use the AWE32's built-in amplifier, which you won't need if your speakers have their own amplifier.

➤ **Spk out**   For connecting speakers that aren't self-powered. This makes use of the AWE32's built-in amplifier.

➤ **Joystick**   For connecting either your joystick or a MIDI device such as a synthesizer.

The Moment of Truth: AWE32 Card Installation

We're close. In a moment, we'll install your AWE32. First, make sure your PC has at least 4M of free hard disk space to accommodate the included software. That's a bare minimum. To install all the included software, you need about three times that much, at least for the AWE32's standard edition. If disk space is tight, you can selectively install Sound Blaster programs—you'll learn how later in this chapter.

Inserting your AWE32 into your computer is the easy part. So let's get started. Open your AWE32 box and take a look inside. Initially, you need:

➤ The sound card itself.

➤ The software disks for installing AWE32. The next section of this chapter deals with installing software.

Next, reread Chapter 6, which describes how to get your computer ready for Sound Blaster. To briefly review:

➤ Turn off and unplug your computer. We don't want this to be a shocking experience.

➤ Take the top off your computer.

➤ Find a free 16-bit slot for your Sound Blaster. Note this must be a full-length slot. Your AWE32 is a long board, and, given differences in PC construction, there may not be enough space inside your PC to accommodate it.

➤ Unscrew the backplane plate, remove it, and store it someplace safe, like in the box in which your computer came. Put the screw aside—you'll need it later.

Now, it's time to insert the AWE32 into a free slot. Rest the bottom of the card, which has gold-plated strips on it, on the top of the slot. Then, using firm force, push the card straight down into the slot. You may need to jiggle the card slightly forward and aft to coax it into the slot. Don't be afraid to use firm force—cards and computers are tougher than you might expect. However, don't do your Godzilla imitation, either. (Chapter 7 includes a figure that shows an example of inserting a new card into your computer. Refer to that figure if you've never inserted a card before and want to see how it's done.)

One hint that your card isn't inserted correctly is that its top edge won't be perfectly horizontal. If that's the case, give it a bit more pressure until it is firmly in the slot.

Unsnagging Your Sound Blaster

If the card absolutely refuses to go in its slot, it may have snagged on the backplane of the computer or on the card in the next slot.

Next, plug in your speakers. If they're self-powered, plug them into the Line out jack. If not, plug them into Spk out. When you finish, plug in your computer and start it. You haven't finished, however. Next, let's switch our attention to installing the software needed to make your AWE32 work.

All This and CD-ROM, Too?

This chapter only discusses Sound Blaster installation. If you also are installing your CD-ROM drive at the same time, this is a good time to skip ahead to Chapter 9 and read about that process. When you finish, return to this chapter to learn how to complete the installation process.

Installing the Software That Comes with the AWE32

The AWE32 comes with two types of software. One type of software works behind the scenes so your sound card works in both Windows and DOS. The other type of software is the applications for getting the most enjoyment out of your sound card.

AWE32's installation program installs both types of software. The next two describe the installation program.

Remove the installation floppy disks from the special envelope that holds them in the Sound Blaster box. To start the installation process, place the appropriately labeled "Installation" disk in your floppy drive. This may be your A: drive or B: drive, depending on which floppy drive on your system works with disks of the same size as the "Installation" disk, which is usually a 3.5-inch disk.

Switch to that drive by typing **A:** (or **B:** if that's appropriate), and then pressing the **Enter** key. Then, at the DOS prompt (which looks like **A:\>** or **B:\>**), type **INSTALL** and press the **Enter** key. You will see the opening screen of the Sound Blaster AWE32 installation program.

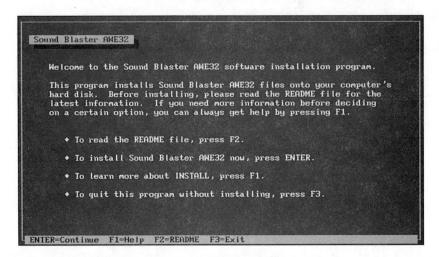

The opening installation screen.

Your options at this screen are to:

➤ Press **F2** to read a special file with last-minute updates to the documentation. This information usually is somewhat technical, but it's worth reading just to stay up to date.

➤ Press **Enter** to continue with installation.

➤ Press **F1** to learn more about the installation process.

➤ Press **F3** to exit the installation program.

If you press **Enter** to continue, the Installation program displays its next screen that gives you two options: Full Installation and Custom Installation. Full installation installs the AWE32 software plus all applications. Custom installation, however, lets you install only the applications you want.

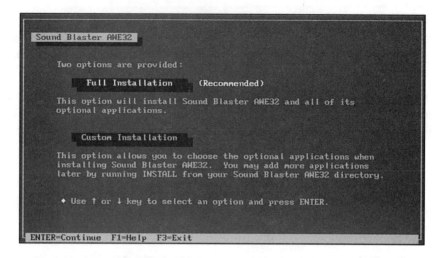

Deciding on the type of installation.

To move between the two options, use the up and down arrow keys on your keyboard. When the option you want is highlighted, press the **Enter** key.

If you choose the Custom Installation option, you will see a screen asking you to select the applications you want to install.

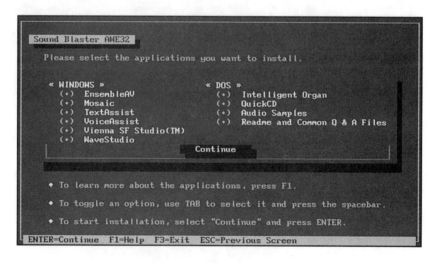

Deciding which applications to install.

Applications that are ready to be installed have a dot next to them. To deselect an application so it isn't installed, move to that application with either the up or down arrow key or the **Tab** key. Then press the **Spacebar** key and the dot disappears. If you change your mind, press the **Spacebar** key again and the dot reappears.

If you aren't sure what an application does, highlight its name; then press the **F1** key for an explanation. Press the **ESC** key to leave that screen to return to the custom installation screen. After selecting the applications you want to install, press the **Tab** key until **Continue** is highlighted and press **Enter** to continue the installation.

AWE32 Installation Specifics

Now things start getting specific. The installation program asks if you want to set up your system so that the AWE32 works in DOS automatically.

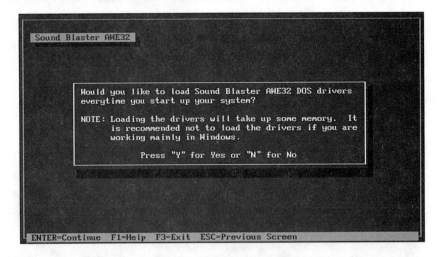

Deciding whether to automatically load AWE32 in DOS.

The screen notes that loading the software to run AWE32 in DOS requires some memory (about 40M of RAM, to be exact). It also suggests that, if you work primarily in Windows, you not load them automatically each time you start your computer. Press **Y** for "Yes" or **N** for "No" to make your choice and continue the installation.

Playing in DOS

The option to set up your system so AWE32 automatically works in DOS is a bit misleading. If you select No, your sound card still will work in virtually all circumstances in DOS. If you answer Yes, you can use the Play utility from the DOS prompt to play sounds and music and also program the Advanced Signal Processing (ASP) chip from the DOS prompt. Unless these are important options to you—and for most of us they aren't—I suggest selecting **No** at this screen.

Whatever you decide, the next screen offers the opportunity to confirm and, if necessary, change the following:

➤ **Sound Blaster AWE32 path**   The drive and directory in which the installation program places Sound Blaster files. The default is C:\SB16.

➤ **Microsoft Windows path**   The drive and directory in which Windows is installed. In most cases, that path is C:\WINDOWS.

➤ **System bootup drive**   The drive from which your computer boots. That drive is almost always the C: drive.

➤ **CD-ROM drive connection**   The CD-ROM drive, if any, that you connect to your AWE32 card.

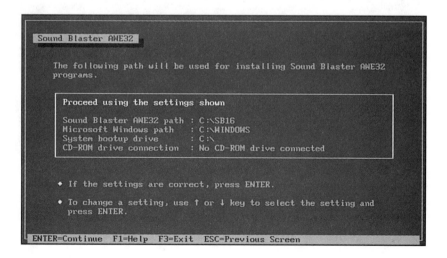

Setting your paths.

Chances are you won't change any of the first three settings. If you do, however, use the up or down arrow keys to highlight the setting you want to change, and then press **Enter**. Another screen appears in which you change the setting, such as by typing the new drive and path. When you finish changing a particular setting, press **Enter** to return to the screen listing all the settings.

Don't Touch That Path The default drives and paths are standard and chances are you won't need to change them. In fact, I strongly recommend against making any changes unless you are absolutely certain you know what you're doing.

The final selection, **CD-ROM drive connection**, pertains only if you are connecting a supported CD-ROM drive to your AWE32 card. Select this option and press **Enter** to view a screen from which you select the appropriate CD-ROM drive.

If you are connecting your CD-ROM drive to a CD-ROM interface other than Sound Blaster, select the **No CD-ROM drive connected** option. Also select that option if you will connect a CD-ROM drive to your AWE32 card later; you can rerun the installation program then and change this setting.

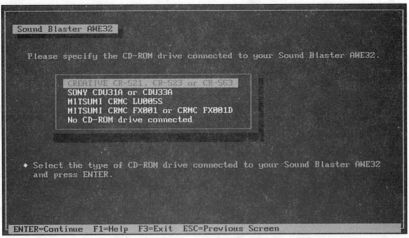

Selecting a CD-ROM drive.

When you finish making changes, use the up and down arrow keys to highlight the top line, **Proceed using the settings shown**. Then press **Enter**.

Next, a screen shows settings for your base I/O address, the address of the MIDI port, your IRQ, and both low and high DMA settings. Low DMA is for playing 8-bit sounds and high DMA is for playing 16-bit sounds. Read Chapter 6 for a refresher on what these items are.

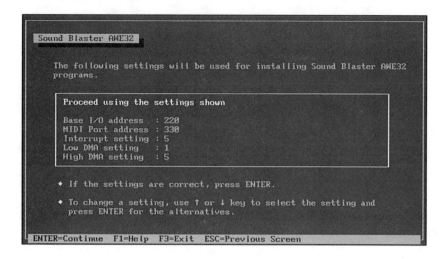

Setting port addresses, DMAs, and more.

You may need to change these settings—at some point. For now, unless you are certain that there is a conflict with another device and you know what you're doing, leave them alone. You'll learn more about changing these settings in Chapter 12.

If you know for certain that a setting conflicts with another device in your PC and you want to change it, use the arrow keys or **Tab** key to highlight that setting. Then press **Enter**. From the ensuing dialog box, change the settings and press **Enter** again.

When you finish setting these options, use the arrow or **Tab** key to highlight the top line, **Proceed using the settings shown**. Then press the **Enter** key. Now, the installation program copies files to your hard drive. Sit back and relax; you need only follow the on-screen instructions for inserting new disks into your drive. When the installation program finishes installing files, it displays a screen advising you of changes that will be made to certain files on your computer. Note that, depending on which option you chose during installation, the screen you see may be different from this one.

```
┌─────────────────────────────────────────────────────────────┐
│  ┌──────────────────────┐                                    │
│  │ Sound Blaster AWE32  │                                    │
│  └──────────────────────┘                                    │
│                                                              │
│     The following lines will be added to your system files:  │
│                                                              │
│   C:\AUTOEXEC.BAT file:                                      │
│     ▶ SET BLASTER=A220 I5 D1 H5 P330 E620 T6                 │
│     ▶ SET SOUND=C:\SB16                                      │
│     ▶ SET MIDI=SYNTH:1 MAP:E MODE:0                          │
│     ▶ C:\SB16\DIAGNOSE /S                                    │
│     ▶ C:\SB16\AWEUTIL /S                                     │
│     ▶ C:\SB16\SB16SET /P /Q                                  │
│                                                              │
│   C:\CONFIG.SYS file:                                        │
│     ▶ DEVICE=C:\SB16\DRV\CSP.SYS /UNIT=0 /BLASTER=A:220      │
│     ▶ DEVICE=C:\SB16\DRV\CTSB16.SYS /UNIT=0 /BLASTER=A:220 I:5 D:1 H:5 │
│     ▶ DEVICE=C:\SB16\DRV\CTMMSYS.SYS                         │
│     ▶ FILES=40  (If it is less than 40 or does not exists)   │
│                                                              │
│     ◆ To continue, press ENTER.                              │
│                                                              │
│  ┌───────────────────────────────────────┐                  │
│  │ ENTER=Continue  F1=Help  F3=Exit       │                 │
│  └───────────────────────────────────────┘                  │
└─────────────────────────────────────────────────────────────┘
```

Sound Blaster tells you about changes to be made to your startup files.

This screen is merely informative; it tells you how the setup program will change your AUTOEXEC.BAT and CONFIG.SYS files. These files are sometimes called *startup files* because they contain instructions that DOS automatically executes whenever you start your computer. In this case, the installation program alters these files with instructions needed to run your AWE32 in DOS. You can't alter the information in this screen, so just press **Enter** to continue.

Doin' Windows

The installation program then sets up your Windows environment to work with the AWE32. First, the installation program asks if you want Texto'LE to be your default text editor when you are in Windows.

This is a strange option. In Windows, you sometimes will need a simple text editor, which is like a scaled-down version of a word processor. For most people, Windows Notepad, which comes with Windows, is the default editor.

If you select **Yes** whenever you use File Manager to open a file with the .TXT file extension name, texto'LE loads instead of Windows Notepad. This is a decent editor that works with the TextAssist program so it can actually speak the words you type. Read Chapter 18 for more information.

This is kind of like moving, in a small way, to the paperless office. Instead of text documents that you print, you create voice documents. This sounds neat, but it's not always practical—often you need to type words, not speak sounds. As a result, chances are you'll select **No**.

Certain files are necessary to run AWE32 in Windows; some were installed when you installed Windows, some weren't. The AWE32 installation program next examines your system to see if these files are present. If the files aren't present, the installation program installs them. If they are present, you will see a series of screens that gives you the option to replace the files.

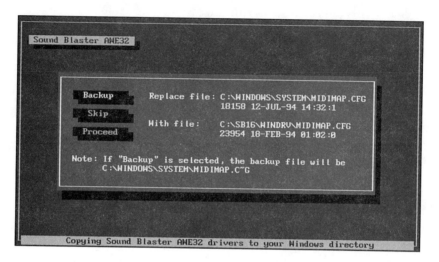

Selecting to replace certain Windows files.

The installation program asks if you want to replace the file currently on your disk with the file that comes with the AWE32. My suggestion: do it. Creative Labs has tested the sound card with these specific files, so chances are that everything will work the way it should.

Your three options in screens like this are:

➤ **Backup**, which installs the AWE32 version of the file but creates a backup copy of the existing file.

➤ **Skip,** which skips the process. This leaves the currently installed file on the disk.

➤ **Proceed**, which installs the AWE32 file and doesn't back up the old file.

> **Don't Forget Windows 95!** The discussion about Windows here refers only to Windows 3.1 and Windows for Workgroups. If you are using Windows 95, skip ahead to Chapter 11.

I suggest using the Backup option. Finally, the installation program examines and, if necessary, alters files that Windows needs when it starts up. Specifically, it changes WIN.INI, SYSTEM.INI, and CONTROL.INI. These files contain commands that are executed when you start Windows.

Finishing the Process

At last, the installation process is complete. Before using your Sound Blaster card, though, you must reboot your computer. The final screen gives you the option of returning to the DOS prompt by pressing **Enter** or rebooting your computer by pressing **F10**.

Note that you aren't finished with the installation—at least if you're a Windows user. The first time you load Windows, Sound Blaster automatically creates a program group called AWE32. It may also create program groups for other software you chose to install during the installation process, such as Text Assist. The program groups will contain icons for all the installed applications.

Depending on whether you are installing the standard AWE32 or the Value Edition, you also may have to install some additional software. Specifically, the installation program doesn't install Cakewalk Apprentice and HSC InterActive, which come with the standard edition, so you must do that separately. I'll tell you how in Chapters 19 and 23.

Making Sure AWE32 Works

Just because you put the card in your computer and then installed the software doesn't mean you're home free. Nope—life often isn't that simple.

As a result, let's do some testing to make sure that, so far at least, everything works as it should. To diagnose your AWE32 installation you'll run the DIAGNOSE program. First, switch to your Sound Blaster directory, which, by default, is **C:\SB16**. To do that:

1. Type **C:** and press **Enter**.

2. Type **CD \SB16** and press **Enter**.

3. Type **DIAGNOSE** and press **Enter** again.

You will be greeted by an opening screen. After you clear that screen, you will see screens that diagnose conflicts and, if necessary, change the:

➤ Base I/O address

➤ MPU-401 MIDI Port

➤ IRQ

➤ Low DMA, the DMA channel for playing 8-bit sounds

➤ High DMA, the DMA channel for playing 16-bit sounds

Also, the DIAGNOSE utility tests to make sure the random-access memory (RAM) on your AWE32 works correctly. Note, though, that this test isn't available for the Sound Blaster 32.

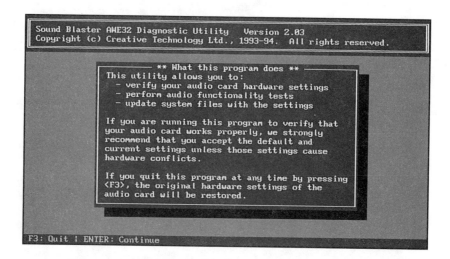

Diagnosing your system.

For all screens except the RAM test, the DIAGNOSE utility displays a series of settings. For example, when testing the base I/O address for the audio card, you can test several different addresses for conflicts. Select a setting and press **Enter**. If that setting (such as a simple IRQ) is available, DIAGNOSE makes the setting permanent and automatically displays the next screen.

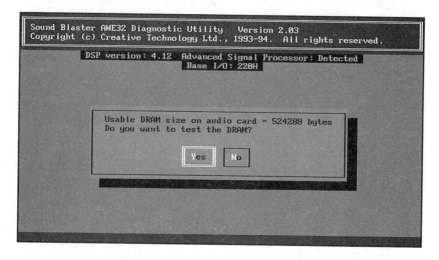

Diagnosing AWE32's RAM.

If the currently assigned address is free, the utility tells you so; if not, you must test another address. If the next address you test for is free, the utility assigns it to your AWE32. You also can select auto-scan to have the DIAGNOSE utility look for a free address and assign it automatically.

By contrast, the RAM test is merely diagnostic; it tells you if the on-board RAM is functioning. If it isn't, you should return your card or have it serviced.

After diagnosing and, if necessary, changing your settings, you can run some tests to make sure you hear sounds and music.

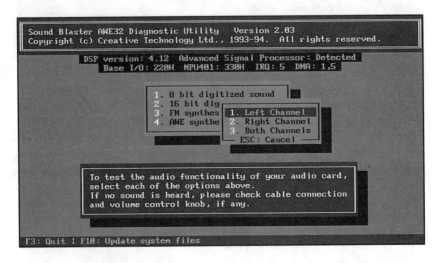

Testing Sound Blaster sounds and music.

You can test to see if your Sound Blaster plays back 8-bit and 16-bit WAV files, FM synthesized MIDI files, and wave-table synthesized files (which Sound Blaster calls *AWE synthesized sound*). You also can test to see if Sound Blaster plays back on each channel, or speaker.

When testing, you should hear sounds or music coming out of the appropriate speaker. If you don't, chances are you have an IRQ, DMA channel, or base I/O address conflict. If you do have a conflict, fix them by repeating the diagnosis and testing procedures. Even if everything is functioning correctly in the DIAGNOSE utility, you aren't out of the woods yet. That's because this utility doesn't diagnose whether your AWE32 works in Windows. I discuss Windows and the potential problems you can encounter there in Chapter 10.

Now let's finish up—I know you're eager to use your Sound Blaster. If your CD-ROM already is attached or if you aren't installing one now, use the screw that previously held down the backplane plate to screw down the sound card. Then put the top back on your computer. If you aren't quite sure how to do that, consult your PC's documentation.

The Least You Need to Know

In this chapter, you learned about your Sound Blaster AWE32's capabilities and how to install it. You learned that:

➤ The AWE32's wave-table synthesis capabilities enable it to play MIDI music more realistically than standard FM synthesis playback.

➤ The AWE32 includes special chips for adding special effects and speeding up the playback of sounds.

➤ The installation program enables you to set IRQs and DMA channels.

➤ The installation program installs the software needed to make AWE32 work in Windows and DOS and the applications that help increase your enjoyment of AWE32.

➤ The DIAGNOSE utility makes sure your AWE32 settings are correct.

Chapter 9

Connecting All the Pieces

In This Chapter

➤ Getting connected

➤ Getting SCSI

➤ About CD-ROM

Sound cards bring out the kids in us. So it wouldn't surprise me if, like a kid on the way to an amusement park, you're getting impatient and want to start playing.

The last two chapters told you how to install the Sound Blaster 16 and the AWE32. Well, we're almost there. There are only two things—and maybe three—left to do:

➤ Connect all the basic pieces, such as your MIDI instruments and joystick.

➤ Connect your CD-ROM drive to your Sound Blaster.

Because we live in an imperfect world, the third thing you may need to do is change your configuration and troubleshoot. Read Chapter 12 about changing your Sound Blaster configuration, Chapter 13 about general troubleshooting, and Chapter 14 for troubleshooting in Windows.

The Easy Connections

First, let's do the easy part: connecting the stuff such as your microphone. After you install Sound Blaster, walk around to the back of your PC, and look at the Sound Blaster's backplane. It contains several plug-in jacks; the number and name of the jacks varies according to your board. There also is a joystick/MIDI adapter.

The jacks look like the jacks on, say, your Walkman where you plug in your headphones. The joystick/MIDI adapter looks similar to the other adapters on the back of your PC. Plug your devices into the following places, as appropriate. The names as imprinted on the back of your Sound Blaster might be slightly different.

➤ **Line in**   For connecting devices like a cassette player or audio CD player. This is handy for recording sounds from those sources.

➤ **Mic**   Where you plug your microphone.

➤ **Line out**   For connecting self-powered speakers to the AWE32. It does not make use of the AWE32's built-in amplifier, which you won't need if your speakers have their own amplifier.

Feeling (Self) Powerful

If you have self-powered speakers (ones that use batteries or an AC adapter) and the AWE32, use the **Line out** jack; you'll get better sound quality. If you use self-powered speakers and use the **Spk out** jack, the sound card amplifies the sound, and then the speakers amplify the sound. This double amplification degrades sound quality.

➤ **Spk out**   For connecting speakers. This jack uses the sound card's internal amplifier; it also is used for headphones.

➤ **Joystick**   For connecting either your joystick or a MIDI device such as a synthesizer. Attach the end of the cable coming from the device to this port. Then, with a screwdriver, tighten down the connection.

If you don't connect a CD-ROM drive, put the cover back on your PC and take Sound Blaster out for a spin. Play a game or any program that makes sound or plays music. If everything works fine—great! If not, read Chapter 12 on fine-tuning your Sound Blaster configuration and Chapters 13 and 14 on troubleshooting.

Know Your CD-ROM Drive

Sound cards and CD-ROM drives go together like horses and carriages, love and marriage, and all the other things that are well-matched. Many of the most interesting applications that use sound come on CD-ROM.

That, of course, explains why many versions of Sound Blaster cards come with built-in CD-ROM interfaces. In the rest of this chapter, you'll learn how to connect your CD-ROM to Sound Blaster cards. You'll also learn some of the ins and outs of CD-ROM drives and CD-ROM interfaces.

Now, A Word from Our Sponsors About CD-ROM Drives

CD-ROM is a storage medium just as your hard drive is a storage medium. However, there are some important differences.

For one thing, your hard drive is a *magnetic medium*. That is, the drive consists of magnetized platters. You store data by placing computerized information on the platters in specific patterns. Hard drives have mechanisms that both read the magnetic patterns and place information on the drive in specific patterns.

By contrast, CD-ROMs are an *optical medium*. In simple terms, CD-ROMs store data as a series of microscopic pits on the CD-ROM disc. A laser shoots light onto the disc and a sensor determines whether there is a reflection; the pattern of pits discerned in this way defines the data.

So what's the big hoo-raw about CD-ROM? In a single word: capacity. A CD-ROM stores a lot of stuff—about 650M worth of digital stuff, to be exact. That's why, from the beginning, CD-ROMs were popular for large text databases such as government regulations and laws. CD-ROMs also are natural for multimedia since many multimedia items, like videos and sound files, require a lot of disk storage space.

Magnetic Media This refers to the most common method of storing digital data. It involves creating specific magnetic patterns that represent data on a magnetic medium such as a hard or floppy disk. The disk both creates these magnetic patterns and reads them back.

Optical media Media such as a CD-ROM that uses light to discern patterns of tiny pits etched into the media. Those patterns determine the data.

What Once Was Big...

Interestingly, 650M doesn't seem like much storage capacity anymore—many PCs come standard with hard drives bigger than that. One of the technical challenges of the near future is developing CD-ROMs that both work with the current crop of drives and hold considerably more than 650M.

CD-ROM Interface This is the intermediary between your CD-ROM drive and the rest of your computer. It routes information from your CD-ROM to the proper place in your computer.

Small Computer System Interface (SCSI) The longtime standard for CD-ROM interfaces. However, SCSI isn't limited to CD-ROM drives. You also can use SCSI adapters for connecting other devices such as SCSI-compatible hard drives and tape backup devices to your computer.

SCSI? What's SCSI?

The CD-ROM holds the data and the CD-ROM drive reads the data. But a third piece—called the *CD-ROM interface*—acts as an intermediary between the disc, drive, and the rest of your computer.

For example, if the CD-ROM you are using says it's time to play a sound effect, the CD-ROM drive transmits the sound effect file to the CD-ROM interface. The CD-ROM interface routes that information to the appropriate place, such as your computer's central processing unit and your sound card.

Usually, CD-ROM interfaces are separate add-in adapters that require their own IRQs, DMA channels, and base I/O addresses. Using Sound Blaster's built-in CD-ROM interface saves all the hassle of adding another adapter card to your system. For years, the standard interface for connecting CD-ROM drives to the rest of your computer has been the *Small Computer System Interface,* or SCSI for short. Yes, it's pronounced "SCUZ-zy."

The SCSI standard has evolved; currently, the most widely accepted version is called SCSI-2. Commonly, you add SCSI to your system by inserting a dedicated SCSI adapter to your PC. These are useful if you want peak performance and if you have other SCSI devices such as a SCSI hard drive.

The problem is that SCSI adapters are finicky to install. However, if your needs are simple, Creative Labs has simplified matters in two ways. First, it offers one package, called the Sound Blaster 16 SCSI-2 that, as the name implies, includes an on-board SCSI-2 adapter and the software you need to make it work.

That, in itself, greatly simplifies matters. However, many Sound Blaster cards also come with on-board proprietary SCSI adapters, or adapters that only work with specific CD-ROM drives. Those drives are from Creative (which are identical to drives by Panasonic), Sony, and Mitsumi.

The main disadvantage of the proprietary SCSI adapters on Sound Blaster cards is that they move data a bit slower than more standardized SCSI adapters. Also, you can attach multiple SCSI devices to a single, standardized SCSI adapter, but you can only attach a single device to your Sound Blaster's proprietary adapters.

> **I Have an IDE**
> Increasingly, a different type of interface is being used for CD-ROM drives. That interface is the IDE interface that also is used for your hard drive. While often a bit slower than SCSI drives, an IDE interface also is simpler to set up and use. Over time, Creative Labs will be phasing out its on-board SCSI adapters and replacing them with IDE adapters.

Still, Sound Blaster's SCSI options are quite handy. The built-in adapters are less finicky about things such as IRQ and DMA channels than stand-alone adapters, so you're likely to have fewer conflicts. The rest of this chapter describes how to connect a CD-ROM drive to your Sound Blaster's built-in CD-ROM interface.

I'm Feeling Connected (CD-ROM-wise)

Let's focus on using the proprietary adapters to connect Sony, Creative, Panasonic, or Mitsumi CD-ROM drives to your Sound Blaster. A section later in this chapter describes how to connect other types of drives to the Sound Blaster 16 SCSI-2 sound card.

Let's start at the beginning.

➤ Turn off and unplug your computer.

➤ Take the top off your computer.

➤ If you've already installed your Sound Blaster card, take it out of your computer. If you haven't installed it, take it out of its packaging.

> **An Inside Job**
> You only can connect an internal CD-ROM drive to your Sound Blaster's proprietary CD-ROM interface. Internal drives fit inside your computer like a hard or floppy drive. If yours is an external drive, which resides outside your computer, you must buy and use a separate SCSI adapter.

➤ Make sure that your CD-ROM drive works with the CD-ROM interfaces on the Sound Blaster card. That's not a problem if you have a card with a SCSI-2 adapter—virtually every drive works with that.

You can't install your drive to the proprietary CD-ROM connectors unless it's a Creative, Panasonic, Sony, or Mitsumi drive. Chances are high that any drive from those manufacturers will work, but to make sure, read your Sound Blaster's *Getting Started* guide. It lists the specific CD-ROM drive models with which your Sound Blaster works.

Using the Proprietary Adapter

I'm assuming that you already installed your internal CD-ROM drive in your computer. There are many sources of help for installing CD-ROM drives such as (WATCH OUT! Here comes a shameless plug!) *The Complete Idiot's Guide to Multimedia.*

Let's start by holding your Sound Blaster in your hand. The circuitry should be facing you and the backplane should be to your right. Now comes your introduction to *jumpers*. Jumpers are a common way of making settings on hardware cards such as your Sound Blaster. A jumper consists of two prongs and a plastic *jumper block*, sometimes called a *shunt*, that fits over the prongs.

Pay Attention!
Before you pull your sound card out of your computer, make sure you unplug everything, such as your speaker wire and joystick, from the back. This is a small boo-boo, but it's one that, to this day, I make repeatedly.

All Sound Blaster 16s and AWE32s except the Value Editions and the Sound Blaster 16 SCSI-2 have a bank of four jumpers in the lower left corner of the card. The jumpers are marked as follows:

➤ Other

➤ Mit (for Mitsumi)

➤ Sony

➤ Cre (for Creative Labs and Panasonic)

By default, the jumper block is over the prongs marked Cre. If yours is a Creative (or Panasonic) drive, leave it there. If yours is one of the other drives, carefully pull the jumper block off the Cre prongs, put it over the appropriate prongs and push down gently so it seats firmly.

The Right Tools

If you have tiny, slender fingers, you should be able to move jumper blocks around without any tools. Those of us who are a bit more, uh, ham-handed benefit greatly from using a tweezers or needlenose pliers for this task.

What, you may ask, is an "Other" drive? This is a bit strange, but there is no known use for the "Other" jumper. Perhaps Creative Labs put it there on the assumption that, in the future, they would support other drives.

Next comes two more connections. You need to stand near your opened computer for these connections. First, you connect a ribbon cable from the connect in the back of the CD-ROM drive to the appropriate CD-ROM connector on your Sound Blaster. The CD-ROM connectors on the card are marked, but the print on the card is small, so you may need to squint a bit to find it.

The ribbon cable should come with your CD-ROM drive. Snap the cable first into the back of the CD-ROM drive and then into the correct adapter on the sound card. Don't worry about which end goes where; the cables only fit on the end in which they are supposed to be connected.

If you have the cable connected the wrong way, your CD-ROM drive won't work. Some ribbon cables have one edge marked differently than the other—typically it's marked in red. You must plug that edge into the first pin of the connector. Usually, that pin is marked but sometimes it's not. The result is that if things don't work, you may need to experiment with different ways of connecting the ribbon cable until everything works correctly.

Getting the Jump on Lost Blocks

It's easy to lose *jumper blocks*—they're tiny suckers. Therefore, you might want to sit on the floor with a piece of white paper underneath the sound card so if a jumper block drops, it's easy to find. If you lose the jumper block inside your computer or in your carpet, you must go to your local electronics store and get a new one.

Next, connect the sound cable that goes from the back of the CD-ROM drive to the sound card. This cable has four prongs at each end. The Sound Blaster plug-in is in the upper right part of the card. This cable is necessary for your internal CD-ROM drive to play sounds.

What to Connect

Note that if you have an external CD-ROM drive and you are using another SCSI adapter (on a separate adapter card), you needn't connect the sound card. However, if you are using a third-party SCSI adapter and an internal drive, you still must connect this audio cable.

Insert the Sound Blaster into a free 16-bit slot without breaking either the ribbon cable or the sound cable connections. Then, run your Sound Blaster's installation program—even if you've done so before. To review how to run the installation program and select the proper CD-ROM drive, read Chapter 7 for Sound Blaster 16 and Chapter 8 for AWE32 installation instructions. If you still run into problems, read Chapter 13 for troubleshooting tips.

More Technical Jargon

The installation program installs software called *drivers*. A driver is a small bit of software that helps your hardware and software work together. Two drivers are installed: one that works specifically with your CD-ROM drive and another, called MSCDEX, which is more generic and helps your CD-ROM drive work with DOS.

To review installation instructions, note that in the installation screen in which you set the drive and path for Sound Blaster files, there also is an option for selecting a CD-ROM drive. Highlight that option and press **Enter.**

Then, select your specific drive in the ensuing dialog box and continue with the installation process. This tells the installation program to install the appropriate software and make changes to your AUTOEXEC.BAT and CONFIG.SYS files so your CD-ROM drive can operate.

After you run the installation program, your drive should run. *Should*, however, is a big word. If you run into problems, jump ahead to Chapter 13 about troubleshooting.

Connecting to the SCSI-2

The other option for connecting your CD-ROM drive to your Sound Blaster is the Sound Blaster 16 SCSI-2 package. This includes a standardized SCSI-2 adapter built into the Sound Blaster card. This is a good option if yours isn't a Sony, Mitsumi, Creative, or Panasonic drive. You can connect virtually any internal CD-ROM drive to it and, with a bit of effort, you can connect external CD-ROM drives.

What If...
Unfortunately, Creative Labs doesn't offer a built-in SCSI-2 adapter as part of the AWE32 card. If you need a generic SCSI-2 adapter and want the wave-table synthesis of the AWE32, you must buy the SCSI adapter separately.

The ribbon cable and sound cable connections are the same with the Sound Blaster SCSI-2 as they are for the Sony, Mitsumi, Creative, or Panasonic drives. Jump back to the previous section of this chapter for the low-down on how to do that. Then, switch back to the next section to learn more about installing the software.

Be Adaptable

When you buy a Sound Blaster 16 SCSI-2, it won't work with external CD-ROM drives (ones that aren't contained within the case of your PC). There are, however, adapter kits available to make it work with external drives. These are available from a number of mail-order firms and cost about $30. One vendor that carries these kits is Cables to Go (call 800-225-8646).

SCSI-2 Finishing School

You're back? Everything hooked up okay? Good. Now let's move on to installing the software. Unlike using your Sound Blaster with a Sony, Mitsumi, Creative, or Panasonic drive, the SCSI-2 adapter has a separate installation program.

Place the disk labeled Adaptec EZ-SCSI in your floppy drive. I'll assume that the floppy drive is the A: drive, but yours may have a different letter, such as B:.

From the DOS prompt, type **A:INSTALL.EXE**. You are greeted with an opening screen; press **Enter** to continue with installation. The installation program scans your system for any SCSI adapters and lists them in the second screen of the SCSI installation program.

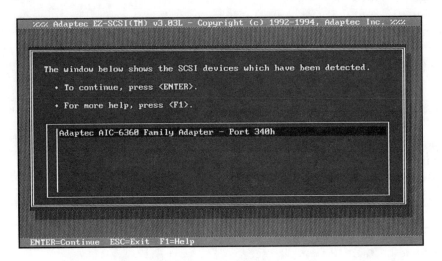

Scanning for SCSI.

Unless your system has a previously installed SCSI adapter, only one item is listed on this screen. If more than one adapter shows up on this screen, I urge you to either remove the other SCSI adapter or to use it. Multiple active SCSI adapters are a sure ticket to IRQ and DMA channel hell. At any rate, select the SCSI adapter and press **Enter**. The installation program asks which directory you want to install the SCSI files in; the default is C:/SCSI.

The installation program then starts installing the files needed to work with your SCSI-2 adapter. When the installation program finishes, the final screen appears telling you the installation program will make some changes to your CONFIG.SYS startup file.

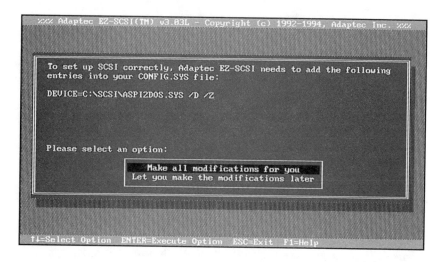

Changing your startup file.

Again, unless you have an overriding need to change the default, select **Make all modifications for you** and press **Enter**. The installation saves your old CONFIG.SYS file as CONFIG.BAK. This backup is useful if you stop using either your CD-ROM drive or the SCSI-2 adapter.

Making Sure It Works

After completing installation, you must reboot your computer before any changes take effect. After you do that, the easiest way to see if your CD-ROM drive is working is to switch at the DOS prompt to the CD-ROM drive. In most cases, your CD-ROM's drive letter is the one after your last hard drive letter. For example, if your last drive letter had been C:, type **D:** and press **Enter**.

Next, put a disc in the drive. From the DOS prompt for that drive, type **DIR**. You should see a listing of files from your CD-ROM drive scroll on your screen. If you see that, you're all set. If you don't, read Chapter 13 about troubleshooting. If you get really stumped, it may not be Sound Blaster's fault. That means you must contact your CD-ROM vendor's technical support staff.

The Least You Need to Know

This chapter described how to connect stuff to your Sound Blaster card.

➤ You connect your speakers, headphones, joystick, and external devices such as tape decks into the back of your Sound Blaster.

➤ Most Sound Blasters (except for Value Edition versions) contain adapters for Sony, Mitsumi, Creative, and Panasonic CD-ROM drives.

➤ The Sound Blaster 16 SCSI-2 contains a generic SCSI adapter for all other CD-ROM drives.

➤ Installing a CD-ROM drive requires you to connect two cables between the drive and the Sound Blaster.

➤ You also must install software to make the CD-ROM drive work, a process that occurs during the general Sound Blaster installation—for most drives.

➤ For the Sound Blaster SCSI-2, you install software separately from the general Sound Blaster installation procedure.

Chapter 10

Doing
Windows 3.11

In This Chapter

➤ Going for a driver

➤ Mapping your trip with MIDI Mapper

➤ The supposed MPC standard

Okay—let's get the obligatory, obvious Windows joke out of the way first. Yes, Sound Blaster does Windows, but sometimes, doing Windows is easier said than done. Getting sounds to play in Windows 3.11 and Windows for Workgroups requires a whole rigmarole that you needn't go through in DOS.

The good news is that your Sound Blaster's installation program takes care of this rigmarole—usually. The bad news is that it doesn't always work and you may need to make some adjustments. This is important because most of the software that comes with Sound Blaster is Windows software. Also, some of the best games and multimedia titles work in Windows.

This chapter describes the parts of Windows you need to know about to get sound. As with most of the other chapters in this part of the book, the goal here is to provide the knowledge to fix problems and optimize performance.

If you installed your Sound Blaster and everything seems to work fine in Windows, you can skip this chapter. For now. However, read on if you get no sound, or if the sound you do get in Windows somehow isn't right. This chapter provides background and Chapter 14 provides specifics about fixing sound problems in Windows.

The 10-Cent Windows Tour

Most people don't like DOS. Operating systems should make managing files and performing other housekeeping tasks simple, but this operating system's interface is stark, cryptic, and generally unsatisfying to use. You must remember stupid stuff; for instance, if you want to see all the files in a directory side by side instead of in a single column, you type **DIR /W** or **DIR \W**.

Here it is—the mid-1990s—and DOS is still with us. Finally, though, its days are numbered with the release of Windows 95. Chapter 11 discusses using Sound Blaster with Windows 95.

Even Microsoft understood early on that DOS had severe limitations. As a result, about ten years ago, it introduced Windows. Windows wasn't an operating system in its own right (although Windows 95 is). Rather, it works with DOS to cover up DOS' shortcomings.

The idea behind Windows was similar to the idea behind the Macintosh. That is, people respond better to a graphical environment in which you see and point at things rather than type cryptic commands. This means that, in a word processor, you highlight a word and click on a button and—voilá—that word is boldfaced. It seems intuitive and natural to most of us today, but this is a relatively recent innovation that met with surprising resistance at first.

Windows 95 Advanced Tips

In theory, Windows 95 will be an operating system in its own right and won't suffer from Windows' and DOS' limitations. However, since so many users currently depend on DOS and Windows, Windows 95 must be "backward compatible." In other words, it must run with your current software. This means there will, indeed, be some of the same old limitations in Windows 95—otherwise it won't run our old, limited DOS and Windows programs.

Windows covers up many of DOS' most glaring shortcomings. For example, it handles memory much better than DOS alone. And, starting with recent versions, it handles multimedia—and particularly sound—much better.

The Windows Multimedia Revolution

Although Windows 1.0 was released more than ten years ago, it wasn't until the release of Windows 3.1 that Windows became adept at playing sounds—or other multimedia for that matter. It was in that version that Microsoft added what technical propeller-heads worldwide call *multimedia extensions*. These additions help Windows work with sound.

The next few sections talk about the parts of Windows that help your Sound Blaster work. Read on if you want to learn to fix and fine-tune how Sound Blaster works in Windows. If you don't read on, hey—I'll live. But when things break down, you'll come running back, believe you me.

Driving Your Drivers

The things that drive sound in Windows are... *drivers*. Drivers are little bits of software that help hardware (such as Sound Blaster) and your software (Windows and your games or multimedia titles) work together.

Windows loads most Windows drivers automatically whenever it starts. In order for that to happen, drivers must be noted in several files. Most notably, the WIN.INI and SYSTEM.INI files contain many instructions for loading a wide variety of drivers and other software automatically.

The Sound Blaster installation program installs the relevant drivers on your hard disk. As you'll learn in the next section, Windows provides a way to check if drivers are indeed present, to add them if they aren't, and to delete them when they no longer are needed.

After placing the drivers in the correct place on your hard drive (typically in your \WINDOWS and \WINDOWS\SYSTEM directories), the installation program changes the files (such as WIN.INI and SYSTEM.INI) to automatically load the drivers. But various things can happen to cause your Windows sound configuration to crash.

Driver A little bit of software that's kind of like an arbitrator. It gets your hardware (such as Sound Blaster) and software (such as your multimedia titles) to work together. A number of drivers are necessary for Windows to work correctly with Sound Blaster. (Most driver files have the .DRV and .SYS file name extensions.)

Crashes Can Ruin Your Day

One thing that can ruin your Windows sound configuration is a system crash while you are playing a sound or music file. Or the installation program for another piece of hardware or software could alter your WIN.INI and SYSTEM.INI files in a way that the Sound Blaster drivers no longer load properly. Both problems have happened to me—the latter occurs more frequently than you would suppose.

Even though Chapter 14 is the chapter for troubleshooting Windows-related problems, here's a quickie hint now. When things go wrong with your Windows sound capabilities, the easiest solution often is to simply rerun the Sound Blaster installation program. While time-consuming, this seems to often fix things. If you're reading this chapter because you encountered a problem, I probably just saved you a lot of time. You're welcome.

Be a Control Panel Freak

If I were a drill sergeant, I'd probably scream something like: "THIS IS WINDOWS CONTROL PANEL. IT IS YOUR FRIEND. IT ALSO CAN KILL YOU!"

Since I'm (usually) a mild-mannered writer, I'll simply say that the Control Panel is a centralized place in which you tweak many different parts of Windows' innards, including items that relate to how sound plays.

By default, you open Control Panel by first opening the Main program group in Windows Program Manager, and then double-clicking the **Control Panel** icon. You also can run Control Panel by selecting **File** from the main Program Manager window; then **Run**. In the Command Line text box of the Run dialog box, type **C:\WINDOWS\CONTROL** and click **OK**. Control Panel looks like a Program Manager program group window that contains a number of different icons.

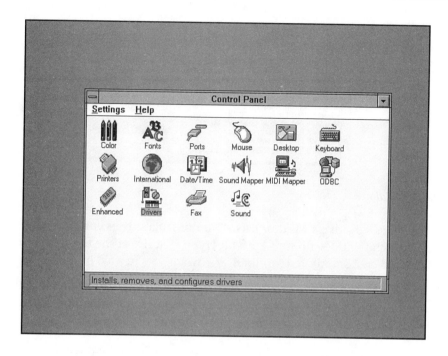

Windows Control Panel.

There are two important Control Panel icons:

➤ **Drivers**   Contains access to all the drivers needed to run Sound Blaster in Windows (as well as other multimedia-related drivers).

➤ **MIDI Map**   Where you go to make sure your MIDI configuration is working correctly.

Drivers... and More Drivers

The Drivers dialog box lists all installed multimedia drivers. Many of the drivers in this dialog box are about music and sound, but many aren't. There also are drivers that affect how Windows plays videos and animations. From the Drivers dialog box, you can install more drivers, delete drivers, and in some cases, fine-tune already-installed drivers.

To display the Control Panel, first double-click the **Main** program group in Program Manager. In that program group, double-click the **Control Panel** icon.

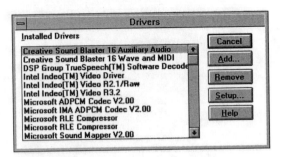

The Drivers dialog box.

The Installed Drivers window lists all multimedia drivers currently used by Windows, although their descriptions are a bit cryptic. Notice at the top of the Drivers dialog box figure (taken from my system) there are two drivers needed by Sound Blaster.

The Sound Blaster installation program installed its drivers automatically. Chances are that all the other drivers also were installed during some other process, such as when you installed Windows or some other bit of hardware or software.

Installing That Sucker

Simply having a driver stored on your hard disk does not mean it's installed to run in Windows. If the Drivers dialog box doesn't list the driver, it won't work in Windows, even if it's on your hard disk. Installing Windows drivers is one of the things that installation programs such as the one for Sound Blaster do.

If your Sound Blaster is an AWE32, you must have all the following listed in the Drivers dialog box:

➤ Creative Sound Blaster AWE32 MIDI Driver

➤ Voyetra/Sound Blaster SuperSAPI FM Driver

➤ Creative Sound Blaster 16 Auxiliary Audio

➤ Creative Sound Blaster 16 Wave and MIDI

➤ MIDI Mapper

➤ Timer

➤ [MCI] CD Audio (if you are using a CD-ROM drive)

102

➤ [MCI] MIDI Sequencer

➤ [MCI] Sound

If you have a Sound Blaster 16, the following drivers must be listed:

➤ Voyetra/Sound Blaster Super SAPI FM Driver

➤ Creative Sound Blaster 16 Auxiliary Audio

➤ Creative Sound Blaster 16 Wave and MIDI

➤ MIDI Mapper

➤ Timer

➤ [MCI] CD Audio (if you are using a CD-ROM drive)

➤ [MCI] MIDI Sequencer

➤ [MCI] Sound

Note that there also are other drivers listed in the dialog box unrelated to Sound Blaster. The ones I listed are only the ones needed to run Sound Blaster.

➤ The Add button is for adding new drivers. You typically won't need to do this, at least for Sound Blaster. That's because Sound Blaster's installation program does this for you. You may, however, sometimes need to add drivers required by Windows. If that's the case, click **Add** and follow on-screen instructions. You will need your Windows installation disks to do this, though.

➤ The Remove button, as the name implies, is for removing drivers. Be careful—once removed, the drivers are gone, gone, gone. To repeat one of the rules: don't remove anything unless you know what you're doing.

➤ The Setup button is for setting up, or fine-tuning specific drivers. Not all drivers give you the ability to set them up so the button may be unavailable, or grayed out. Or in the case of Sound Blaster drivers, clicking the button merely displays a window telling you what version your driver is.

Your Sound Blaster driver version.

The driver version number is useful information when you are talking with Creative Labs' technical support. Often, older drivers malfunction in certain situations; that's why vendors like Creative Labs regularly release newer drivers. If yours is an older driver, one solution to your problem may be to get a newer driver. A Creative Labs technical support technician can brain this out with you and, if necessary, help you obtain a newer driver.

Rules of Thumb for Drivers

Here are a couple of rules of thumb when dealing with Windows multimedia drivers:

You should only have drivers installed for one sound card. If you see drivers with names that resemble a sound card you once had in your system, you may have problems and need to delete them. But a subrule of thumb (or a rule of subthumb?) is that you shouldn't delete the driver until you run into problems.

Don't delete a driver unless you are certain about what you are doing. Ever. It is highly unlikely, if something goes wrong later, that you'll figure out the problem is an accidentally deleted driver. Nope. If that's your problem, it will turn into one of those unsolved mysteries they show on television.

Are you getting the feeling that this Windows driver business is confusing and potentially dangerous to mess around with? Join the club. Read Chapter 13 on trouble-shooting to learn which are which and how to correct the situation if certain drivers aren't present.

Check Your MIDI Map

There are 128 general MIDI "instruments" and 64 drum sounds your Sound Blaster can play. The MIDI file tells your Sound Blaster which notes to play. However, in Windows, another piece is required—a MIDI map—to direct the instructions in the MIDI file to Sound Blaster's on-board synthesizer and to Windows. The MIDI map is kind of like the road map you take with you on a car trip, except it's for MIDI music.

The Sound Blaster installation program automatically installs and loads the proper MIDI map. For the most part, this isn't something about which you need be concerned. For the most part, that is. But—and I'll cover this in more detail in Chapter 14—problems hearing MIDI sounds may be caused by your MIDI map. If that is a problem, you'll undoubtedly get acquainted with the MIDI Mapper dialog box, which you can view by double-clicking the **MIDI Mapper** icon in Control Panel.

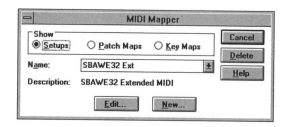

MIDI Mapper.

What's important here are *setups*. You can have many different setups for each sound card; each works best under a different set of circumstances.

To view the available setups, click the **Setups** radio button. The names of all the setups are listed in the Name drop-down box. If you click the down arrow, you will see that Sound Blaster installs a variety of setups. For example, there are several setups available for my AWE32.

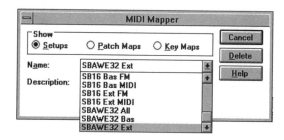

Different Sound Blaster AWE32 setups.

Here's a bit of preventive medicine: if MIDI files currently sound like they should, open up your MIDI Mapper dialog box and write down the current setup name. Don't lose it. When things go wrong, it is possible that somehow your setup was accidentally changed and you must revert to the one that currently works.

Which Is It? MIDI or WAV?

If you aren't sure whether you are hearing MIDI sounds or waveform sounds, use the EnsembleMIDI utility that comes with your Sound Blaster card. This utility plays MIDI files, which have the .MID file extension name. To play WAV files, use the EnsembleWAVE utility. Learn how to use both these utilities in Chapter 16.

What about the other two options in the MIDI Mapper dialog box: Patch Maps and Key Maps? Don't worry about them. Musicians use these for creating MIDI music and, for now, they aren't important to our discussion, which is oriented toward fixing problems.

MPC: Standards Aren't Always Your Friends

I can't leave the discussion of sound in Windows without talking about the Multimedia PC (or MPC) standard. Even if you're relatively new to computing, you probably have seen the MPC logo on software such as CD-ROM titles.

The MPC standard—and its shiny logo—was the brainchild of the so-called Multimedia PC Marketing Council. This is a group of multimedia software and hardware vendors who realized that consumers, and vendors for that matter, didn't understand what was required to create and run multimedia in Windows. This was several years ago when, with the addition of multimedia extensions, it became apparent that Windows would become a primary platform for multimedia titles.

Multimedia PC (MPC) This is supposedly a standard. It was developed by multimedia hardware and software vendors to tell you what software and hardware —including sound cards— you need to successfully run multimedia on your PC. It's not much help, though; the current "standard" is barely acceptable for many of today's multimedia titles.

The very first standard this group developed was truly laughable; it included a minimal 386 computer, an 8-bit sound card, and a single-spin CD-ROM drive. Even several years ago when this reputed standard was developed, such a PC was woefully inadequate for most multimedia titles. Many people, particularly consumers who got stuck buying these underpowered but "official" PCs, howled that the standard was causing more damage than it was solving.

So, the MPC Council put on their thinking beanies again and went back to work. The so-called Multimedia PC Level 2 standard, which still is in effect, is a bit more realistic but also out of date. It calls, among other things, for a minimum of a 486 computer, a double-spin CD-ROM drive, and a 16-bit FM synthesis sound card such as the Sound Blaster 16.

So what's with the MPC logos? That MPC logo on software simply means the software runs on a minimally configured system that meets the MPC standards. If you own a Sound Blaster 16 or AWE32, that part of your system, at least, meets the standard. However, that doesn't really say much. If your entire system minimally meets the MPC Level 2 standards, you still may get old while waiting for multimedia files to load or videos to play. In other words, take this standard with a grain of salt.

The Least You Need to Know

This chapter introduced you to the elements of Windows needed to make your Sound Blaster work.

➤ You must install a variety of software called drivers in order for your Sound Blaster to work in Windows. Sound Blaster installation takes care of this automatically.

➤ You also must use an appropriate MIDI map to make sure you can play MIDI music in Windows. This is another thing Sound Blaster installation takes care of.

➤ Even though Sound Blaster's installation program takes care of drivers and MIDI maps, things still can go wrong. When they do, you must use the Drivers and the MIDI Mapper dialog boxes in Windows Control panel.

➤ The MPC standard states the minimum hardware and software requirements for running multimedia in Windows. A 16-bit FM synthesis card such as Sound Blaster 16 is the minimum sound card according to this specification.

It's Windows 95 Time (at Last!)

Windows 95 reminds me of going to summer camp as a kid—it took forever for that special time to arrive and, inevitably, it was a little disappointing after all the build up.

At last, Windows 95 is indeed here and, for the most part, it's good news for Sound Blaster users. It makes installing and setting up Sound Blaster much easier, and it also makes it simpler to fine-tune how you play sounds and music.

In this chapter, you'll get an overview of the still brand-spanking new operating system and what it means for Sound Blaster users.

Windows Ninety-What?

Check it out—this book has many chapters about installing and troubleshooting Sound Blaster in DOS and in Windows 3.11 and Windows for Workgroups. It has one chapter about Windows 95. One major reason for this is Windows 95 is much easier to deal with for Sound Blaster users than DOS and the old Windows. Why?

Well, let's take a (very brief) stroll down memory lane. MS-DOS is an arcane operating system with roots more in the '70s than in the '90s. When Microsoft initially developed DOS, the last thing on its mind was handling the sophisticated sound and music we expect from Sound Blaster. In fact, the initial release of DOS was developed a couple of years before adoption of the MIDI standard.

Microsoft developed Windows to cover up some of DOS's technical shortcomings and to provide a more user-friendly alternative to DOS' techno-weenie interface. Versions of Windows before Windows 95 don't replace DOS, however. Rather, they run along with DOS.

Like DOS, Windows initially couldn't handle sounds and music. Eventually, though, two things happened. First, Creative Labs started selling Sound Blasters that worked around many of Windows' (and DOS') shortcomings. Second, Microsoft released Windows 3.1, which included some jury-rigged methods of handling sound. Those methods are the subject of Chapter 10.

Windows 95 replaces both DOS and older versions of Windows. Instead of being a cover-up for DOS, it is an operating system in its own right. That means, instead of being jury-rigged, Microsoft built Windows 95 from the ground up for music, sound, and other multimedia. That makes it much easier to install Sound Blaster cards and to adjust and troubleshoot them. That's what the rest of this chapter is about.

Installing Sound Blaster in Windows 95

First the good news about installing Sound Blaster in Windows 95: *Plug and Play*. This refers to a new method of installing add-in cards that eliminates those pesky IRQ, DMA channel, and base I/O address conflicts.

Plug and Play
You plug in your sound card, and then play your sounds and music. With Windows 95, it's just about that easy if you have a Plug and Play-ready Sound Blaster and computer.

With Plug and Play, Windows 95 keeps track of all IRQs, DMA channels, and base I/O addresses. It automatically adjusts those settings to avoid conflicts when you install the card. Sound exciting?

Well, it *will* be, when the rest of the world is ready for Plug and Play. In the next section, there's more details about a Plug and Play installation. You'll learn that it takes special hardware and special system software to make Plug and Play work. Because it will take a while for the world to convert to Plug and Play, I also describe installing Sound Blaster into Windows 95 without Plug and Play.

Pluggin' Along with Plug and Play

The bad news about Plug and Play isn't too bad. That news is that, before you enjoy the brave new world of simple hardware installation Plug and Play promises, your system must be ready.

First, your PC's Basic Input/Output Services (a.k.a. BIOS) must support Plug and Play. BIOS is system software; it works behind the scenes to control how information enters your computer (called *input*) and how it leaves your computer (called *output*).

Getting the right BIOS may or may not be simple, depending on your PC. It will be simple if you bought your computer since, say, mid-1995. That's about the time when PC vendors started including Plug and Play-ready BIOS in their PCs.

It will be relatively simple if you bought your computer after about mid-1994. That's when PC vendors started using so-called flash BIOS. With flash BIOS, you can upgrade your BIOS by using a simple software installation program that you get from your PC vendor. If your BIOS isn't Plug and Play-ready and if your PC doesn't have flash BIOS, the only solution is to replace a chip on your computer's motherboard that includes the BIOS. This is best done by a service professional. To get the skinny on your system's BIOS, call your PC vendor.

Besides having the right BIOS, you also must use a Plug and Play-compatible card. At this writing, Creative Labs had not released their Plug and Play Sound Blasters, but they were about to.

If you do have a Plug and Play-compatible card, installation becomes wonderfully simple:

1. Turn off your computer and take the top off (see Chapter 6 to learn more about doing this).

2. Insert the Sound Blaster card.

3. Start your PC and Windows 95. Open the Control Panel by clicking the **Start** button. Then select **Settings Control Panel**. The Windows 95 Control Panel loads.

4. In Control Panel, double-click the **Add New Hardware** icon. This displays the Add New Hardware Wizard, which walks you through the process of making sure that Windows 95 correctly selects IRQs, DMA channels, and base I/O addresses for your Sound Blaster.

Meet the Wizard

Windows 95 is full of Wizards. A Wizard is a series of dialog boxes that walks you through specific tasks such as adding a new sound card. Wizards are great because they simplify even complex tasks.

5. In the second screen of the Add New Hardware Wizard, choose to either have the Wizard automatically detect already-installed hardware or to install a specific piece of hardware. It doesn't matter which you choose. But if you select **Install Specific hardware**, make sure to select **Sound, video and game controllers** from the window. When you finish, click the **Next** button.

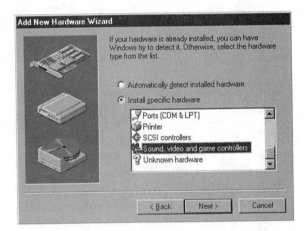

Selecting the type of card to install.

6. If you select that option, in the next dialog box, select **Creative Labs** from the Manufacturer's window and your model from the Models window.

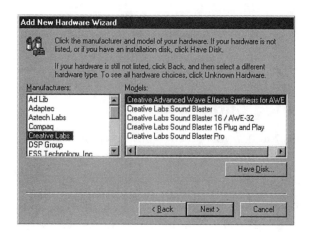

Selecting your specific card.

7. Then, follow the rest of the Wizard's instructions, clicking **Next>** to move to each successive dialog box. From here on, the process is even simpler than installing software.

Speaking of which, when you finish installing the hardware, you still must install the software that goes with your Sound Blaster. To do that, either follow the instructions that come with your sound card or read Chapter 7 of this book about installing Sound Blaster 16 or Chapter 8 about installing AWE32.

There is, however, one difference with installing for Windows 95. Depending on your version of Sound Blaster, you either install the software from within Windows 95 or, more likely, from the DOS prompt. However, with Windows 95, you get to the DOS prompt differently than you do with DOS and older versions of Windows. With Windows 95, you must restart your computer by clicking the **Start** button in the lower left corner of your Windows 95 desktop and then selecting **Shut Down**. In the shut down dialog box, select **Restart the Computer in MS-DOS Mode**. This reboots your computer and leaves you at the DOS prompt.

Movin' Away from DOS

In Windows 95, you don't do much at the DOS prompt. It's primarily there so you can do stuff such as run DOS installation programs. It also is important to game players since many of the best games developed in recent years are DOS games.

There is one more method of getting to the DOS prompt, which I describe in the next section. Once at the DOS prompt, install the software as described in Chapters 7 and 8.

Doing Without Plug and Play

If you read Chapters 7 and 8, you already know most of what you need to know about installing Sound Blaster without Plug and Play. To repeat, you turn off and unplug your computer, take the top off, and insert your Sound Blaster card. Then, install the software as described in those chapters. It all works about the same as installing Sound Blaster into a DOS system.

Temporary Leave You can temporarily leave Windows 95 and go to the DOS prompt and then quickly return. However, do not select this option when installing your Sound Blaster software. Rather, go through the shut down procedure before you install the software.

As I mentioned at the end of the last section, however, there is one difference. Left to its own devices, Windows 95 doesn't stop at the DOS prompt; it goes right into Windows. However, you must install your Sound Blaster hardware from the DOS prompt.

If you are in Windows 95, follow the instructions in the last section about restarting your computer and going to the DOS prompt. If you are just starting up your computer, however, you also can get to the DOS prompt without first starting Windows 95.

Making an Old Installation Work

What if you installed Sound Blaster before you install Windows 95? This is the most simple installation of all—you probably needn't do anything. If yours is an AWE32, however, there may be one small and easily correctable glitch. If your MIDI playback sounds bad, chances are Windows 95 is using the driver that plays back FM synthesis sound, not the driver for wave-table synthesis sound. If that's the problem, a section later in this chapter describing the multimedia settings in the Windows 95 Control Panel helps you correct it.

At one point early in the process, you will see an on-screen message that says **Starting Windows 95**. The very moment you see that message, press the F8 key. Do it quickly; if you wait too long, you'll miss your chance and Windows 95 will load.

If you press **F8** soon enough, however, you will see a menu with a variety of start-up options. Select the option to go to the DOS command prompt. When you do, install the Sound Blaster software.

Controlling Sound Blaster in Windows 95

If you are accustomed to wrestling with Sound Blaster settings in previous versions of Windows, you'll love Windows 95. Its sound and music controls are simple-to-understand and concise.

First, click the **Start** button in the lower left corner of your Windows desktop. In the ensuing menu, select **Settings** and then **Control Panel**. Windows 95 displays the Control Panel.

The Windows 95 Control Panel.

Unlike the Windows 3.11 and Windows for Workgroup Control Panels, it doesn't take a rocket scientist to figure out how to handle sound and music in Windows 95. If you look at the Control Panel, you'll see an icon called Multimedia. There are no surprises here... double-click the **Multimedia** icon and Windows 95 displays the Multimedia Properties dialog box.

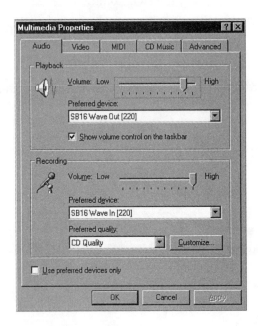

The Multimedia Properties dialog box.

This is a tabbed dialog box. That means it has tabs across the top; clicking a tab leads to a tab about a specific subject. The next few sections describe the tabs that are relevant to Sound Blaster.

The Audio Low-Down

The first of the sound and music-related dialog boxes is the Audio tab. This is for setting Sound Blaster to play digital audio files such as WAV files.

Remember the Drivers dialog box in the old Windows discussed in Chapter 10? If you don't remember, consider yourself lucky. A visit to that dialog box is like a visit to the principal's office—you only go there if there's a problem and the result of the visit can be painful. But things are easier in Windows 95 in the Audio tab. The Audio tab (shown in the preceding figure) is a simple way to set up drivers and volume for Sound Blaster. It has two sections: Playback and Recording.

At the top of the Playback section is the Volume slider bar. This is the master control for digital audio playback. It works like the master level setting in Creative Mixer, as described in Chapter 15.

Beneath the Volume slider bar is the Preferred device drop-down list. This is where you select the primary driver for playing back digital sounds. It's pretty straightforward: if there is more than one option, select the one that sounds most like your sound card.

In Case of FM Synthesis...

The Preferred devices drop-down list is a good place to come if, after initially installing Windows 95, your AWE32 only plays FM synthesis MIDI. If that's the case, chances are Windows 95 automatically selected the FM synthesis driver instead of the driver for wave-table MIDI playback. To correct the problem, simply switch drivers in the drop-down list to the AWE32 playback driver.

The last item in the Playback area is a check box called Show volume control on the taskbar. If you check this, you can change the volume simply by clicking an icon on the taskbar at the bottom of the Windows 95 desktop. My strong suggestion: activate the check box for placing a volume control icon on the taskbar.

When you do, a speaker appears on the taskbar at the bottom of your Windows 95 desktop. If you double-click the volume icon, the Windows 95 Volume Control dialog appears, in which you can change volume. I will describe this dialog box in a later section.

The first two parts of the Recording area are similar to those in the Playback area. The Volume slider bar sets master recording levels, and Preferred device sets the driver for recording with your Sound Blaster.

The Preferred quality drop-down list sets your personal preferences for recording WAV files. Your options are:

➤ CD Quality, which is the default. This is recording at a sampling rate of 44,100Hz in 16-bit stereo.

➤ Radio quality refers to recording at a sampling rate of 22,050Hz in 8-bit mono.

➤ Telephone quality refers to recording at 11,025Hz in 8-bit mono.

You can customize and redefine those preferences by clicking the **Customize** button. This leads to the Customize dialog box.

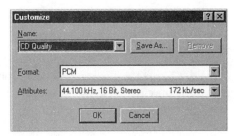

Customizing recording preferences.

In that dialog box, select a compression format in the Format drop-down list. This list provides the names of the different methods of compressing sound files. PCM is the default, although Soundo'LE supports only IMA ADPCM. Sound Blaster, however, can play sound files compressed with any of the options.

When you select the format and the attributes, click the **Save As** button and give your new type of recording preference a name in the ensuing dialog box.

Save Separate Settings

In most cases, you won't need to customize these settings. If you do, make sure to save any customizations as a separate setting rather than changing the three default preferences that come in the drop-down list.

When you finish the Customize dialog box, click **OK** to return to the Audio tab.

The final option in the Audio tab is the Use preferred devices only check box. This limits your programs to using only the preferred devices that you selected in this tab. Don't activate this check box unless you have a strong reason. Put differently, only make this selection if your software absolutely requires the use of a Sound Blaster. That's rare software—even the software that comes with Sound Blaster works with virtually any sound card.

If you change any options, click **Apply** when you finish to put the changes into effect.

Getting Set for MIDI

The MIDI tab of the Multimedia Properties dialog box is where you select the precise way you want Sound Blaster to play back MIDI. It's also where you add a new MIDI instrument to your Sound Blaster. To get to the MIDI tab, double-click the **Multimedia** icon in the Windows 95 Control Panel.

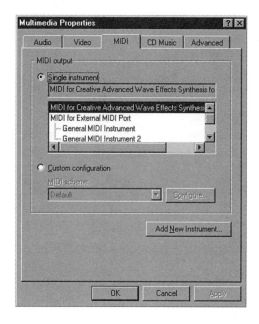

The MIDI tab in Windows 95 Control Panel.

Select the specific "instrument" that will play back MIDI music. I put the word *instrument* in quotes for a couple of reasons. First, in this case, the term *instrument* may well refer to your Sound Blaster card. For example, in the previous screen, the selected instrument was **MIDI for Creative Advanced Wave Effects Synthesis for AWE32**.

In reality, this "instrument" is the synthesizer chip located on my AWE32 card. Each sound card has at least one synthesizer chip and the AWE32 has two, one for wavetable synthesis and another for FM synthesis. However, you also can play back MIDI through an actual instrument such as a synthesizer.

If you activate the **Single instrument** radio button, you will see a list of all installed instruments registered with Windows 95 that play MIDI sounds. If you are like most AWE32 users and your primary use is playing games and listening to sounds and music, select **MIDI for Creative Advanced Wave Effects Synthesis for AWE32**. If you are like most Sound Blaster 16 users, select **MIDI for Internal OPL2/OPL3 FM Synthesis**. OPL2/OPL3 refers to the chip on your Sound Blaster for FM synthesis MIDI playback.

Activating the **Custom Configuration** radio button is like using the MIDI Mapper in older versions of Windows as described in Chapter 10. As I cautioned you in that chapter, don't mess with this unless you're a serious MIDI musician and you want to precisely fine-tune how you create and play back MIDI.

If you click the **Configure** button, you will see the MIDI Configuration dialog box.

The MIDI Configuration dialog box.

In that dialog box, you can assign a different instrument to play on each of the 16 channels available for MIDI. By comparison, if you select the **Single instrument** option described previously (and which I strongly recommend for most users), the instrument you select plays back automatically on all channels.

So if you must experiment (or if you're a MIDI musician), in the MIDI Configuration dialog box, highlight a specific MIDI channel, and then click the **Change** button. In the ensuing dialog box, select the instrument for that channel in the **Instrument** drop-down list. Click **OK** and repeat the process for the other channels, as you desire. If you change any options, click **Apply** to put the changes into effect.

Adding a New Instrument

Even a casual MIDI musician may get his hands on a new instrument. Adding the instrument to Windows 95 is extremely easy; you start the process from the MIDI tab described in the previous section.

First, connect the instrument to Sound Blaster's MIDI port. Then, click the **Add New Instrument** button in the MIDI tab of the Multimedia Properties dialog box. This starts a Wizard that walks you through the simple process of adding the instrument.

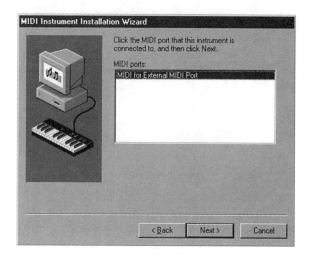

Adding a new instrument.

In most ways, adding an instrument is like adding a new sound card as described previously in this chapter. Simply follow the instructions in the Wizard, giving the instrument the name of your choice in the appropriate area.

When you finish, your new instrument is part of the Windows 95 environment. This means you can do things such as set that instrument to play back MIDI music instead of your Sound Blaster. Or you can create chains of MIDI instruments for using a sequencer to manage and create complex MIDI compositions. For MIDI musicians, this new power and simplicity makes Windows 95 worth the price of admission.

Playing Audio CDs

It's hardly a new trick to be able to play your audio CDs on your CD-ROM player. You could do that easily enough with older versions of Windows. In the Multimedia Properties dialog box, the CD Music tab sets up the capability to play audio CDs.

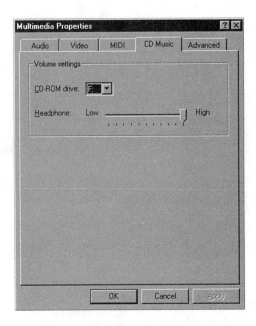

The CD Music tab.

The tab is quite straight forward. In the **CD-ROM drive** drop-down list, you select the letter of your CD-ROM. With the Headphone slider bar, you select the volume for the music playback. If you change any options, click **Apply** when you finish to put the changes into effect.

Multimedia Odds and Ends

Windows 95 also comes with several small applications aimed directly at multimedia, some of which relate to sound and music.

To access the applications, click the **Start** button in the lower left corner of the Windows desktop. Select **Programs**, **Accessories**, and then **Multimedia**. In the menu that appears, there are a number of small applications that come with Windows 95 you can start:

➤ **CD Player** Plays audio CDs. This is the Windows 95 equivalent of EnsembleCD, described in Chapter 16.

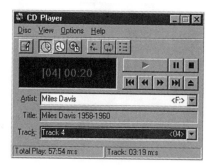

The Windows 95 CD Player.

This utility has about the same capabilities as EnsembleCD, including the capability to develop playlists of specific tracks you want to hear.

➤ **Media Player**   An update of the utility of the same name in older versions of Windows. This utility plays virtually all types of multimedia, including digital sounds, MIDI files, video, and animation.

For more precise control over the playback of sounds and music, however, I suggest using EnsembleMIDI and EnsembleWAVE that come with your Sound Blaster. For example, Media Player doesn't support the use of playlists as do the Sound Blaster utilities. Read Chapter 16 for more information about those programs.

➤ **Sound Recorder**   An updated version of the utility by the same name in previous versions of Windows. This is a relatively underpowered WAV recorder and editor compared to Creative WaveStudio, which comes with many versions of Sound Blaster. Read Chapter 22 to learn more about Creative WaveStudio.

➤ **Volume Control**   A simple mixer that enables you to adjust volume and balance for all types of music and sound play back. This dialog box doesn't have as many capabilities as Creative Mixer, which I will describe in Chapter 15, however, Volume Control is much more convenient, so I'll describe it in the next section.

Mixing in Windows 95

Windows 95's Volume Control dialog box is great if you dislike fumbling around in the various folders and program groups looking for the Creative Mixer.

To use Volume Control, double-click the speaker icon on the right side of the task bar. Note, however, that for this icon to be visible, you must have selected that option in the Audio tab in the Multimedia dialog box in Control Panel.

You also can load Volume Control by clicking the **Start** button and then selecting **Programs**, **Accessories**, **Multimedia**, and **Volume Control**.

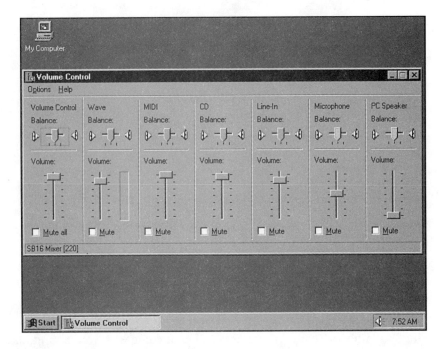

The Windows 95 Volume Control.

The Volume Control dialog box works pretty much like Creative Mixer: there are slider bars for volume and balance for all the various sound devices such as MIDI, WAV files, and audio CDs. Like Creative Mixer, the left-most control is a master control.

You can fine-tune the Volume Control dialog box by opening the **Options** menu and then clicking **Properties** to display the Properties dialog box.

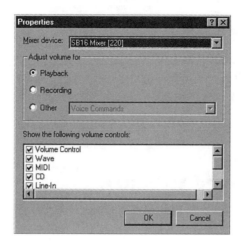

Fine-tuning Volume Control.

The selections in the Properties Dialog box are:

➤ **Mixer Device drop-down list**   Where you select the specific MIDI device you want to control.

➤ **Adjust volume section**   Where you select the items you want the Volume Control dialog box to control. The options are Playback, Recording, and Other (which you select from a drop-down list). If you change any of these settings, the appearance of the dialog box changes slightly.

➤ **Show window**   Where you select the controls you want visible. To display a specific control, click it so a check appears next to it. To eliminate the display of a specific control, click to eliminate the check.

There are several things not available in Volume Control that are present in Creative Mixer. Specifically, Volume Control has no meters or gauges to graphically show you playback levels. Nor does Volume Control include the extensive recording settings and the automatic gain controls that Creative Mixer has. Still, for sheer convenience for setting playback volume, you can't beat Volume Control.

A Very Nice Touch

Changes you make in one mixer show up in the other mixer. This sort of communication between software was sorely missing in previous versions of Windows. It's just one more example of how Windows 95 is easier to deal with for playing and recording sound and music.

The Least You Need to Know

This chapter introduced you to the ins and outs of installing and fine-tuning Sound Blaster in Windows 95.

➤ If you have a Plug and Play-ready Sound Blaster and your PC is ready for Plug and Play, you need not worry about IRQ, DMA channel, or base I/O address conflicts.

➤ Installing Sound Blaster without Plug and Play is very similar to installation with older versions of Windows.

➤ The controls for Sound Blaster are simpler to understand than they were for older versions of Windows and are focused in the Multimedia section of the Control Panel.

➤ Windows 95 comes with a variety of small applications, such as a mixer and a player for sounds and music. In general, the equivalent products that come with Sound Blaster provide more power.

Change Your Mind, Change Your Configuration

So there you are, using your Sound Blaster, happy as a clam. Games, edutainment titles... you name it. Your computer is one happy, noisy, musical piece of high-tech wizardry.

Then... boom. One day it doesn't work. Chances are, it's time to change your configuration. More specifically, it's time to change your IRQ, DMA channel, or base I/O address for either the card itself or the joystick/MIDI port that's part of the card.

Sure, you thought you were finished with all this stuff after you ran the Sound Blaster installation program. In the computer world, unfortunately, nothing is forever. This chapter tells you how to change your configuration.

Switching IRQs and DMA Channels

An IRQ or DMA channel conflict can ruin your day. At best, it causes a part of your computer such as your Sound Blaster to malfunction. At worst, it causes your computer to crash. You say you don't remember what these little monsters are? Read Chapter 6 for a refresher.

Worse still, unless you are accustomed to dealing with such conflicts, you may not immediately understand what the problem is. You could become baffled and think your sound card is broken. Or you could just give up and not use your computer, turning your multi-thousand dollar machine into a beige room decoration.

There's a good chance, however, that if your system crashes or Sound Blaster fails to work properly, it's a DMA channel or IRQ conflict. That's particularly true if everything worked fine after installing Sound Blaster; then you install something else such as an internal modem, and things stop working as they should. The modem causes, by far, the most common problems for nonbusiness users.

In the next two sections, read how to prevent and diagnose these problems, and then how to fix them when they occur.

Learning the Score: Using MSD

Information is power. I've already said it several times in this book and I'll probably say it again before I'm done. Here's a good example.

Say you successfully installed your Sound Blaster card, but in a month, you install an internal modem. And a month or a year later, you must install another card, say a video capture card for collecting videos you shoot with your camcorder.

There's a fair-to-middlin' chance that, as you add new items to your PC, you'll encounter IRQ and DMA channel conflicts. You can do things the common, but inefficient, way and experiment with IRQs and DMA channels when you install the modem and video capture card, hoping to find a combination that works. This, however, is time-consuming and frustrating.

Instead, put knowledge to work with a couple of tips. First, keep a list of all IRQs, DMAs, and base I/O addresses that you use. Whenever you install a piece of hardware that adds to or otherwise changes the settings, change your list.

Remember... So You Can Play

Here's another reason you should write down your IRQs and DMAs: games. The setup programs of many games require you to specify which sound card you are using and what its IRQ, DMA, and base I/O addresses is. These items are easy to forget—unless you write them down.

Also, learn about a useful little software tool that comes with recent versions of DOS called *Microsoft Diagnostics*, or MSD. While far from perfect, MSD can help you learn more about your system, including figuring out which IRQs are spoken for.

Use MSD from the DOS prompt. Switch to your DOS directory, which typically is C:\DOS. Type **CD \DOS**. Then type **MSD** and press **Enter**. The initial MSD screen lists all the different types of information the utility provides.

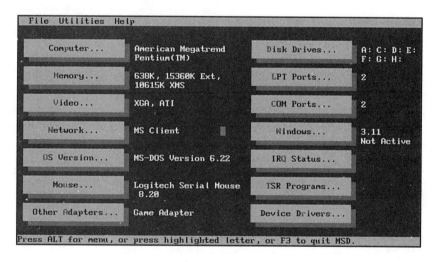

The Microsoft Diagnostics (MSD) opening screen.

For now, we're just interested in seeing which IRQs are in use. So click the **IRQ Status** box with your mouse or press the **Q** key. MSD displays the IRQ Status screen.

```
 File  Utilities  Help
═════════════════════════════ IRQ Status ═════════════════════════════
   IRQ  Address    Description       Detected         Handled By
   ───  ───────    ───────────       ────────         ──────────
    0   0D38:0543  Timer Click       Yes              SAVE.EXE
    1   D1B4:1923  Keyboard          Yes              Block Device
    2   0AE6:0057  Second 8259A      Yes              Default Handlers
    3   0AE6:006F  COM2: COM4:       COM2:            Default Handlers
    4   EC02:009E  COM1: COM3:       COM1: Logitech Seria???
    5   0AE6:009F  LPT2:             Yes              Default Handlers
    6   0AE6:00B7  Floppy Disk       Yes              Default Handlers
    7   0070:06F4  LPT1:             Yes              System Area
    8   0AE6:0052  Real-Time Clock   Yes              Default Handlers
    9   F000:EF5A  Redirected IRQ2   Yes              BIOS
   10   0AE6:00CF  (Reserved)                         Default Handlers
   11   0AE6:00E7  (Reserved)                         Default Handlers
   12   0AE6:00FF  (Reserved)                         Default Handlers
   13   F000:EF63  Math Coprocessor  Yes              BIOS
   14   0AE6:0117  Fixed Disk        Yes              Default Handlers
   15   0AE6:012F  (Reserved)                         Default Handlers

                              ┌────────┐
                              │   OK   │
                              └────────┘

 IRQ Status: Displays current usage of hardware interrupts.
```

Checking IRQs with MSD.

Yup, the screen is a bit of a mishmash. Check out the leftmost column that lists the IRQs and the fourth column from the left that tells whether MSD detected that the IRQ is in use.

MSD won't, alas, tell you there is a conflict. It will, however, point out that another device is using a specific IRQ. Say an adapter for your scanner is using an IRQ that you also assigned to Sound Blaster. MSD will tell you that the scanner already is assigned to that specific IRQ. So, if you're searching for a free IRQ, look down the column with the heading **Detected**. If there isn't an entry in that column, the specific IRQ is probably free.

Here's one important bit of information about IRQs: conflicts only cause problems if you try to use both devices assigned to the same IRQ at the same time. So, say IRQ 5 is reserved for your second parallel port. If you don't use that port, you can safely use IRQ 5 for your Sound Blaster.

When you finish MSD, press **F3** to exit. This obviously can be very useful information. I strongly suggest that you run this utility before you either change your Sound Blaster's IRQ or before you install another piece of hardware that requires an IRQ. It can save you much time and hassle.

Pay More, Get More

If you're willing to spend the money, there are utilities available that do a better job of detecting and reporting available IRQs. For example, PC Tools for Windows and The Norton Desktop for Windows both contain such utilities that, frankly, I prefer to Microsoft Diagnostics. But MSD does have this going for it: you can't beat the price.

Making the Change

All the preparation work in the world can't shield you from the fact that, eventually, you'll have to change your Sound Blaster's settings.

The good news is that you can change your Sound Blaster's IRQ or DMA channel with software. That means you won't have to take the top off your computer and take your Sound Blaster card out to make the adjustment. You must do that for changing the addresses, however, as you'll learn later in this chapter.

The bad news is that setting IRQs and DMA channels still can be a matter of hit or miss if you're not prepared. Remember that there are a finite number of IRQ and DMA channels from which to choose. If your computer is like mine, virtually all the IRQ settings are taken, as are many of the DMA channels. I taught you to use MSD in the last sections of this book in an effort to avoid the hassle of try-this, try-that IRQ settings.

Another bit of bad news is that while DOS comes with MSD to help you find available IRQs, there is no such included utility to help you find DMA channels. The silver lining, however, is that DMA channels aren't in nearly as much demand as IRQs, but you still may need to experiment to find an available one that works.

This problem of finite DMA channel and IRQ choices is compounded by the fact that your Sound Blaster only lets you use a few of those settings. Part of this limitation is due to sheer practicality; many settings are automatically taken by other parts of your computer. For example, IRQs 3 and 4 are already taken by your communications port, so Sound Blaster won't even let you use them.

Depending on your Sound Blaster model, there are two ways to change your DMA channel and IRQ address:

➤ The DIAGNOSE program for DOS that came on the install disks for your Sound Blaster.

➤ The Sound Blaster Configuration program for Windows.

The easiest of the lot is the Sound Blaster Configuration program for Windows. To use it, start Windows (by typing **win** at the DOS prompt and pressing **Enter**) if it isn't already started. Double-click the **Sound Blaster** program group icon to open its group window. Double-click the icon that says **SB Configuration**. You will see the Sound Blaster Configuration program on-screen.

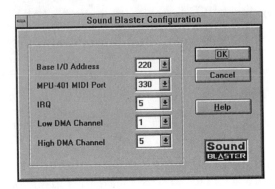

Configuring Sound Blaster in Windows.

With this program, changing configuration is a simple matter of selecting the DMA channel or IRQ you want from the drop-down list. When you finish, click **OK**. Then you must exit Windows and reboot your computer.

My Choice Is...

While Sound Blaster Configuration is simpler to use, I prefer using DIAG-NOSE. That's because after changing settings, you must reboot your computer. With Sound Blaster Configuration, you must unload Windows and reload it after you reboot, two steps you don't have when using DIAGNOSE.

132

To use DIAGNOSE, at the DOS prompt, switch to your Sound Blaster directory, which by default is C:\SB16. To do that, type **CD\SB16** and press **Enter**. Type **DIAGNOSE** and then press **Enter**. As you might recall from Chapters 7 and 8 in which we installed Sound Blaster, the DIAGNOSE program tests for errors and conflicts in your settings and helps you change them. Read those chapters for a quick refresher on this Sound Blaster Utility.

After the initial greeting screens, DIAGNOSE gives you the chance to change your base I/O address and the address for your joystick/MIDI port. Move through those screens by highlighting the currently selected settings and then pressing **Enter**. Next you come to the IRQ setting screen.

If It Ain't Broke... It seems obvious, but it's worth repeating. Don't change IRQ or DMA settings—and particularly don't change address settings—unless you absolutely must. Exhaust other troubleshooting options, as discussed in Chapters 13 and 14, before you change these settings.

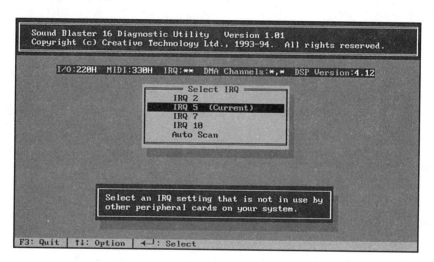

Setting IRQs in DIAGNOSE.

If you have a conflict, select **Auto Scan**. This looks for free IRQ addresses and selects one. After you finish setting the IRQ address, the next two screens are for the low DMA channel (for playing back 8-bit sounds) and the high DMA channel (for playing back 16-bit sounds). If necessary, try the same procedures for the two DMA channel selections. Note that the high and low DMA channels can be the same, if necessary.

When you finish changing the settings, go through the testing procedure for 8-bit, 16-bit, and FM synthesis sound (and, if yours is an AWE32, wave-table synthesized sound). If everything works as it should, press **F10**. This updates all your system files and you should be ready to go.

Changing Your Address

While switching an IRQ or a DMA channel is relatively simple, switching base I/O addresses for the Sound Blaster or for its MIDI/joystick port is something of a rigmarole.

It's a rigmarole for two reasons. First, it's not quite as easy to tell if you have an address conflict as it is to determine if you have an IRQ or DMA channel conflict. For example, there are no handy little utilities such as MSD to tell you.

Second, while you use software to change IRQ or DMA channel conflicts, you must fix address conflicts the hard way: you pull the card out and change the setting with a jumper. The good news is that if you suffer a malfunction, the chances are much greater the problem is an IRQ or DMA channel conflict than an address conflict.

Got It?

Let me clarify a confusing part of this process. You use Sound Blaster Configuration or DIAGNOSE to change your IRQs and DMA channels without touching your Sound Blaster card. However, both programs give the impression that you can use them to change base I/O addresses. It's not that simple, though. You must change addresses on the card itself, as described in the next sections. However, you *also* must make the same changes in one of the programs. Doing so changes the contents of the DOS and Windows startup files (such as AUTOEXEC.BAT and SYSTEM.INI) to reflect the changes you made to the card.

Roll Up Your Sleeves Again...

So let's start. Before you change settings, have a clear idea of what your settings are and what you are changing them to. If you didn't write down the addresses, run the DIAGNOSE program; it tells you the current settings. In each of the diagnostic screens, as described in Chapters 7 and 8, the current setting has the word **(Default)** next to it.

Next, turn off your computer and unplug everything from the back of Sound Blaster, such as speakers. Pop the top of your computer and pull out your Sound Blaster card. Chapter 6 tells you how to do this safely. For safety sake, though, here's just one reminder: turn off your computer's power and unplug it.

Now comes the tricky part. You must change jumper settings on your card. *Jumpers* are a series of prongs. To create a specific setting, you either place a plastic jumper block—sometimes called a shunt—over the prongs or remove the jumper block.

In broad strokes, here are the steps:

1. Make sure you write down the current address settings. You may need to revert to them later.

2. With the card in your hand, locate the appropriate jumpers for switching base I/O addresses either for the card or for the joystick/MIDI port.

   Note that next to each jumper is a cryptic set of letters. These help you confirm that you are using the correct set of jumpers. I'll mention these letters as appropriate.

3. Confirm the address as currently set by the jumper. I'll describe the address options a bit later.

It's Not the End of the World If you change a DMA channel or IRQ with software and get it wrong, it's not the end of the world—it's easy to change back with software. But I strongly urge you to not muck around with base I/O addresses unless you confirm with somebody like Creative Labs' technical support department that such changes will solve your problem. That's because changing addresses is a more complex process than changing DMA channels or IRQs.

4. Move the jumper blocks as appropriate to set a new address.

   Here are some tips about changing jumper blocks.

   ➤ When you place the jumper block over the jumper's prongs, push the block straight down on the prongs and press down firmly.

   ➤ If the setting requires you to take the jumper block off the jumper, don't actually take it all the way off; place the jumper block on a single prong. This has the same effect as taking it off entirely, but you won't lose the jumper block and then have to hunt for it when you need it again.

   ➤ Be careful about handling jumper blocks. They're tiny little critters and are easy to lose. If you have fat fingers like yours truly, you might want to use a tweezers or even a needlenose pliers to take the jumpers off and put them on.

Sound easy? Well, it can be frustrating. When changing base I/O addresses, make sure to have your *Getting Started* guide open in front of you. Breathe deeply and stay calm—this stuff can be confusing.

The next two sections describe how to change the jumpers to specific settings on the Sound Blaster 16 and the AWE32.

Jumpers on the Sound Blaster 16

The first task is to locate the appropriate jumpers on the sound card. I'll describe the location of the jumpers, but it's easier to visualize if you look at both the sound card itself and the *Getting Started* guide that came with your sound card. That guide has a diagram of your sound card and shows the locations to which I am referring.

➤ **Sound Blaster 16 jumpers for changing the base I/O address of the sound card itself.** These jumpers are the bottom two jumpers of a set of five jumpers—the other three are unrelated to this task. You can find this jumper set in about the center of the card, when viewing it from left to right, and about a third of the way up from the bottom of the card. On the card, these jumpers are marked IOS0 and IOS1.

➤ **Sound Blaster 16 jumper for changing the base I/O address for the MIDI/ joystick port.** This is a single jumper located at the top of a set of seven jumpers— again, the other jumpers in the set are not relevant to this task. You can find this jumper set is located near the bottom of the card, about a third of the way over from the left hand edge. On the card, this jumper is marked MSEL.

First, here's how to change the base I/O address for the audio card. The default address is 220H, which means that both jumper blocks are on their jumpers. The other options are:

➤ **240H**, in which the bottom of the two jumpers has the jumper block covering it, but the top one doesn't.

➤ **260H**, in which the top of the two jumpers has the jumper block covering it, but the bottom doesn't.

➤ **280H**, in which neither jumper has a jumper block covering it.

Here's how to change the base I/O address for the MIDI/joystick port. The default setting is 330H, which means the jumper is covered by the jumper block. The alternative setting is 300H, in which the jumper is *not* covered by the jumper block.

When you finish changing addresses, replace the card and put the top back on your PC. But you aren't finished yet. You still must run DIAGNOSE or Sound Blaster. There, you input the changes that you made and those programs, in turn, alter your startup files like AUTOEXEC.BAT and SYSTEM.INI.

AWE32 Address Jumpers

First, locate the appropriate jumpers on the sound card. I'll describe the location of the appropriate jumpers, but do yourself a favor and also look at the sound card itself and the *Getting Started* guide. That guide has a diagram of your sound card and shows the locations to which I refer.

All the jumpers you need for this operation are located in a block of six jumpers. This block is two jumpers wide by three jumpers high. It is located about two thirds of the way from the left side of the card and about one third of the way from the bottom (the bottom is the part with the gold connectors).

Specifically, we're interested in:

➤ **The jumpers for the base I/O address of the card itself.** These are the top right jumper in the block and the jumper directly below it. They are marked IOS0 and I0S1.

➤ **The jumper for the address of the joystick/ MIDI port.** This is the jumper on the bottom right of the block of jumpers. This jumper is marked MSEL.

➤ **The jumper to enable or disable the joystick port.** This is the jumper on the bottom left of the block of jumpers. On the card, this jumper is marked JYEN.

Take a Second Look Caution is in order when locating the block of jumpers. That's because the AWE32 has a similar looking block of six jumpers located at the bottom of the card and to the left of the jumpers that I'm describing. That's why it's helpful to view the diagram of your card in the *Getting Started* manual.

Here's how to change the base I/O address for the card itself. The default is 220, which means both jumper blocks are on the jumpers. The other options are:

➤ **240H**, in which only the bottom of the two jumpers has a jumper block on it.

➤ **260H**, in which only the top of the two jumpers has a jumper block on it.

➤ **280H**, in which neither jumper has a jumper block on it.

For the MIDI port, you have only one option. By default, the address is 330H and the jumper block is on the jumper. To switch to address 300H, take the jumper block off.

The joystick port is, by default enabled, which means you are able to use the port. When enabled, the jumper block is on the jumper. To disable the joystick port, take the jumper block off the jumper.

Do This Last

Only disable the joystick if, through trial and error, you discover the conflict is with the joystick port. This is unlikely to happen, but it is possible. If you resort to this option, however, you will be unable to use a joystick or attach a MIDI device to your computer.

When you finish changing addresses, put the card back in the computer and put the top back on. Finally, run either DIAGNOSE or Sound Blaster Configuration to make sure the changes you made are reflected in your startup files such as AUTOEXEC.BAT and SYSTEM.INI and to make sure your Sound Blaster is working properly. Also, it's a good idea to write down your new settings in your manual or someplace safe.

The Least You Need to Know

So, you think you're not a techno dweeb? Ha! In this chapter, you learned:

➤ You can use the DIAGNOSE and the Sound Blaster Configuration programs to change your IRQ and DMA channels.

➤ You also can use utilities such as Microsoft Diagnostics, which comes with recent versions of DOS, to help you determine which IRQs are in use and which aren't.

➤ To change the base I/O addresses for your sound card or the MIDI/joystick port, you must pull the card out and manipulate on-board jumpers.

➤ Only change jumpers if you are certain what's required after exhausting other possibilities and talking with Creative Labs' support personnel.

➤ Even after you change jumper settings, you still must run either DIAGNOSE or Sound Blaster Configuration to make sure those settings are saved as part of your startup files such as AUTOEXEC.BAT.

Shooting Trouble—
A General Guide

If you are reading this chapter, you're either a dweeb wannabe, a glutton for technical punishment, or you are in the throes of a technical snafu.

If you suffer from the first two problems, there are places where you can get help. If yours is the third problem, however, you've come to the right place. In this part of the book, you learned how to successfully install your Sound Blaster, how to connect all the pieces, and how to fix the most common problems.

In this chapter and the next, you'll dive into troubleshooting mode. This chapter provides general troubleshooting while Chapter 14 focuses on getting you up and running in Windows. I can't guarantee that you'll fix every problem, but you can fix many of them.

Good luck, pardner.

Some Basic Tips

Let's start with some basic solutions. These are what I call head-slappers. That's because they often are so obvious that, after you solve the problem, you'll slap your head and wonder how you could be so dumb.

These solutions are obvious, perhaps. But as any support technician will tell you, it's these obvious solutions that solve a majority of the problems.

So, if you are having problems with Sound Blaster, first make sure that:

➤ **Your sound card is firmly seated in its slot.** To do that, turn off and unplug your PC, take the cover off (details about this process are in Chapter 6), and push the card firmly into its slot. You needn't pretend this is a bench press or other body-building exercise, but do push firmly. If you feel the card move farther down into the slot, you probably found your problem. If not, keep looking.

➤ **The speakers are correctly connected to the sound card.** First, make sure the plug-in is in the correct jack. Read Chapter 7 to learn about the jacks in the back of your Sound Blaster 16 and Chapter 8 to learn more about the jacks on your AWE32. Then, make sure the jacks are firmly seated.

➤ **The batteries in your self-powered speakers still have juice.** Also, your self-powered speakers should be plugged in if you use an AC adapter.

➤ **Make sure you set the volume high enough to hear.** If you use self-powered speakers, turn the volume up on the speakers. If you use a Sound Blaster 16, turn the volume up using the thumb-wheel on the backplane of the sound card. Or if you aren't hearing anything in Windows, use Creative Mixer (described in Chapter 15) to turn the volume up there. Sure, you'll feel like a goof if this turns out to be your problem. But—hey—at least this problem is simple to fix.

Can't Hear?
If you plug speakers that aren't self-powered into the Line Out jack on an AWE32, you won't hear any sound. That's because the Line Out jack doesn't make use of the AWE32's on-board amplifier. If your speakers aren't self-amplified, make sure to plug them into the Spk out jack.

Power to the Speakers

Self-powered speakers, which are the most common type used with PCs, have a built-in amplifier you use instead of your sound card's built-in amplifier. How do you determine if your speakers are self-powered? Self-powered speakers have volume controls on the speakers themselves.

➤ **You know where the problem is occurring.** Is the problem only in DOS or only in Windows? Does it only occur when playing a specific game? This bit of knowledge obviously narrows the source of the problem. If the problem only occurs in Windows, skip to the next chapter. Otherwise, read this chapter.

Finally, here's my omnibus, usually-works solution to Sound Blaster problems: reinstall Sound Blaster. This resets your system to a pristine state of Sound Blasterness. Alas, this solution doesn't work all the time, but it does work more often than not. If these little tips don't solve the problem, keep reading.

The Three Monsters : IRQs, DMA Channels, and Addresses

When it comes to severe problems such as crashes, the most common cause is the Three Monsters: IRQ, DMA channel, or base I/O address conflicts.

These conflicts can occur between your Sound Blaster and existing hardware when you first install your sound card. Or they can occur after you install Sound Blaster but then install a new bit of hardware such as an internal modem or a video capture card.

In Chapter 12, you learned how to fix IRQ, DMA, and base I/O address conflicts. Here are some hints and symptoms proving your sound card has such a conflict.

➤ These conflicts tend to show themselves soon after you install a new bit of hardware. You won't wait long for them to appear.

➤ A typical symptom of a DMA channel and base I/O address conflict is that some piece of equipment stops working. However, sometimes your system crashes.

➤ A typical symptom of an IRQ conflict is that your system crashes. However, sometimes the symptom is that a specific piece of hardware stops working.

➤ Of the three problems, the most likely to occur is an IRQ conflict. The least likely problem is a base I/O address conflict.

➤ You typically *won't* get symptoms such as poor sound quality or buzzing in your speakers; things either work or they don't. It's not a matter of things working poorly.

If you get a conflict, read Chapter 12. Fixing these problems isn't always pleasant but it's necessary.

Before You Change...

I want to emphasize yet again that before you start changing base I/O addresses, assume your problem is an IRQ or DMA channel conflict. Those problems are both more common and are simpler to solve since you don't have to take your Sound Blaster out of your computer. I also suggest getting an outside expert opinion, such as talking to a Creative Labs technical support technician before you start changing base I/O addresses.

Another thing to remember: just because you solve one conflict, it doesn't mean you are done. Nope, often installing a new bit of hardware causes multiple conflicts. Don't be surprised if this happens.

Here's one more snaky problem that can occur with these conflicts. Sound Blaster only gives you a limited number of options for changing IRQs, DMA channels, and base I/O addresses. It's possible that none of the options will work because they all are in use by other bits of hardware. When that occurs, you must change the settings on the other hardware—hopefully, that hardware provides you with additional options.

Plug and Play... and Away!

If you are all set up for Windows 95, none of these problems may occur. That's because Windows 95 supports Plug and Play. If you run it and if your computer and Sound Blaster are Plug and Play-capable, conflicts are automatically resolved with no effort on your part. Read Chapter 11 for the low-down on this modern miracle.

Games with No Sound

I wish all problems were as simple as this one. You go out and buy the game of your dreams. It's full of action, suspense, and witty dialog that only a few people, like yourself, are smart enough to fully comprehend. You install the game, anxiously, load it and... nothing. Zero sounds. Nada.

Hopefully, you are able to resist the temptation to throw a brick through your monitor and, instead, start reading this section. Because, while this problem is frustrating, it also is simple to fix—usually.

The gist is this: most games—particularly most DOS games—have a separate setup program. You must tell that setup program which sound card you are using to play both music (MIDI files) and sound effects (WAV files). You also must tell it the DMA channels, IRQs, and base I/O addresses for your card.

The popular DOS game DOOM works this way, for example. As is typically the case, you must select the correct sound card settings (including IRQs and DMA channels) for both music and sound.

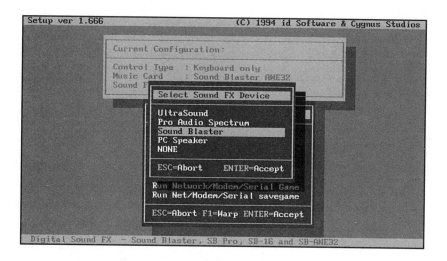

Setting up game sound in DOOM.

Usually, if you don't get sound in a specific game, this is the fix. However, every now and then, a game vendor doesn't know how to handle a specific sound card. That's less of a problem with Sound Blaster cards, which are the standard for sound cards, than it is with other cards. However, this still can be a problem with Sound Blaster, particularly if you use the AWE32. For example, one of my favorite games, Descent, has a setting for the AWE32, but in my version of the game (which is one of the earliest versions the vendor released), it doesn't work with the AWE32 and crashes.

The solution for this problem also is simple. Check with the game vendor to see if there is a more recent release of the program. If there is, the vendor should provide it for free or a nominal fee. Also, try other sound or music card settings. They often work. With Descent, I simply switched from the AWE32 setting, which caused the game to crash, to the General MIDI setting, which worked just fine.

Finally, setup programs for games often require you to list the Sound Card's IRQ, DMA, and base I/O addresses. If you change any of those items after you install the game, you may not get sound in your game. To correct this problem, simply use the game's setup program and provide the new settings for your sound card.

Memory Loss Problems

Before you installed Sound Blaster, you had plenty of memory. Now, when you load a DOS game, you get one of those nasty little messages saying you don't have enough memory.

Remember how the Sound Blaster installation program asked if you want to automatically load Sound Blaster in DOS whenever your computer starts? If I were a gambling man, I'd guess that if you have new memory problems, you answered that question **Yes**. This means your computer now automatically loads special Sound Blaster files that require about 40K of your system's RAM (random-access memory).

The kicker is that you'll rarely use those programs—a fact that the installation program or the Sound Blaster documentation doesn't explain. So, rerun the installation program and, this time, answer the question about automatic loading with a resounding **No**.

If that still doesn't solve your memory problem, it probably isn't Sound Blaster's fault; your computer probably just doesn't have enough RAM. One solution is to use a memory optimizer such as MemMaker, which comes with DOS 6.0 and later.

MemMaker, and other products such as Netroom and QEMM, are adept at rearranging how your programs use memory. The result is that more of the type of memory your games need is available. MemMaker isn't the most powerful of these programs, but it does come free with DOS. Read your DOS manual for instructions.

Seedy CD-ROM Problems

As you previously learned, Sound Blaster comes with a variety of interfaces for your CD-ROM drive. However, CD-ROM drives can be tricky little devils.

Here's a potpourri of CD-ROM problems and solutions:

➤ **Your internal CD-ROM works fine except you don't get any sound.** To get sound from an internal CD-ROM drive, you must connect a cable from the back of the drive to a four-pin connected at the top of the Sound Blaster card. If your CD-ROM drive works well but you don't get sound, chances are you either forgot to make this connection when you installed the drive or the cable came loose. Turn off your computer and attach—or re-attach—the cable.

➤ **You get erratic behavior from your CD-ROM drive.** Make sure you connected the ribbon cable firmly both in the back of the CD-ROM drive and your Sound Blaster's CD-ROM interface. Also make sure that you firmly connected the CD-ROM drive's four-color power supply cable. Read your drive's installation manual for more information about power supplies.

➤ **You installed the CD-ROM drive correctly but it doesn't have a drive letter.** This, essentially, renders your drive useless. The solution to this problem usually is simple. You need a special command in your CONFIG.SYS file called the LASTDRIVE command. On a separate line in that file, type:

LASTDRIVE=Z

This tells DOS to assign drive letters to all drives such as your CD-ROM drive after the last letter of your hard drive. In other words, if your only hard drive letter is C:, this command tells DOS to make your CD-ROM drive D:.

➤ **During startup, you see an error message saying no drive is connected.** If implementing the LASTDRIVE command doesn't work, check to see if MSCDEX is loaded in your CONFIG.SYS file. This is a necessary file, included both with DOS and, usually, with your CD-ROM drive. Typically, the software installation program that comes with your CD-ROM drive installs this required program. The command in your CONFIG.SYS file should read: **C:\DOS\MSCDEX**.

A related problem is that your version of MSCDEX doesn't work with your specific drive. This is a hard one to know about for sure. It can occur if your CD-ROM drive's installation program uses the version of MSCDEX that is in your \DOS directory, but that version is incompatible with your particular drive. The easiest way to check out this problem is to call your CD-ROM vendor's technical support staff.

Miscellaneous Hassles

Here are a few miscellaneous hassles that frequently occur:

➤ **Your old sound card worked fine, but your new one doesn't.** Did you remember to take out your old sound card? If not, do that now, then rerun Sound Blaster's installation program. It's possible to have two sound cards in your computer at the same time, but why would you do this? It's an invitation to trouble.

➤ **You just received some new MIDI files, but they sound horrible.** There's not much you can do about this one. Sometimes, MIDI composers create their masterpieces with one type of sound card, but the files don't sound good on another type of sound card. This is often a problem when composers create pieces for wave-table synthesis cards such as the AWE32 and you play them back on FM synthesis cards such as the Sound Blaster 16.

➤ **You followed all my advice and Sound Blaster *still* doesn't work. What gives?** Hey—I'm running out of patience, too. Here's one last thing to do: check your PATH statement.

145

The PATH statement is a command in your AUTOEXEC.BAT file. If a drive and directory, such as C:\SB16 are in the PATH statement, you need not switch to that directory to load a program located there.

Other software and hardware installation programs often change your AUTOEXEC.BAT file. Sometimes, those changes alter your PATH statement in such a way that your Sound Blaster path is no longer in the statement. So, let's fix it.

Switch to the C:\ prompt by typing **C:** and pressing **Enter**. Type **EDIT AUTOEXEC.BAT**. EDIT is a text editor included with DOS. Look through your AUTOEXEC.BAT file for a line that starts:

PATH=

After that line, there'll be a bunch of drives and directories, each of which ends with a semicolon. For example, a simple PATH statement might read:

PATH=C:\DOS;C:\SB16;C:\WINDOWS

If you don't see C:\SB16 in your PATH statement, position the cursor right after the equal sign and type it in. Make sure to put a semicolon after it. Then, save the file, exit EDIT, and reboot your computer.

Giving Up and Asking for Help

If the troubleshooting in this chapter and the next doesn't help, you'll have to give up the ghost and call Creative Labs for help. Before you call, make sure you can clearly articulate the problem you are facing. You should know the current IRQ, DMA channel, and base I/O address settings for the card. Also, create a list of the other add-in cards in your computer, such as an internal modem.

Creative Labs' technical support line's telephone number is 405-742-6655. If you'd prefer to fax, their number is 405-742-6633.

If you belong to CompuServe, you can get help there by typing **GO BLASTER**. Creative Labs also has its own computer bulletin board where you can ask for help. That number is 405-742-6660.

If you are looking for updated drivers and have access to the Internet, you can find them at Creative Lab's Internet FTP site. That address is ftp.creaf.com. NOTE: They don't have support on any other online services.

The Least You Need to Know

In this chapter, you learned about solving a variety of problems that can crop up with your Sound Blaster.

➤ Before you get too serious about problem solving, try the basics, such as making sure you connected everything correctly. This solves a surprising number of problems.

➤ Most serious problems such as crashes are the result of IRQ, DMA channel, and base I/O address conflicts.

➤ If a game doesn't play sound or music, the solution might be to use the game's setup program and select the correct sound card.

➤ If you install Sound Blaster and find your games don't have enough memory to run, you probably chose during installation to automatically load certain Sound Blaster files into memory. Rerun installation and choose **No** to that option.

➤ Often, CD-ROM-related problems are caused either by cables not being firmly hooked up or by necessary instructions that are missing from your CONFIG.SYS file.

Chapter 14

Troubleshooting Windows 3.11 Sound

> ## In This Chapter
>
> ➤ Driving your Windows drivers
>
> ➤ Know your SYSTEM.INI file
>
> ➤ Too much sound

There's sound, and then there's sound in Windows. Playing sound in Windows requires a correct installation. It also requires you to have correctly updated specific Windows-related files after installing Sound Blaster.

This chapter discusses what can go wrong with Sound Blaster when you are using Windows and how to fix it. First, though, I suggest you review Chapter 10, which describes how sound works in Windows.

Needed: Drivers

As you learned in Chapter 10, drivers drive sound in Windows. One common problem is that not all the drivers needed to run Sound Blaster in Windows are installed.

In Chapter 10, I listed all the drivers that should appear in the Drivers dialog box, which you access from the Windows Control Panel. If all the required drivers aren't present, you have problems. If you re-install those drivers, all should be copacetic. Sound simple? Sometimes it is, sometimes it isn't. That's because Sound Blaster installs some required drivers but not all. Some drivers are installed when you install Windows.

Jumping back to Chapter 10, review the lists of required drivers. I had one list for Sound Blaster AWE32 and another for Sound Blaster 16. The Sound Blaster installation program only installs drivers with the words **Creative** and **Voyetra**.

If one of the Sound Blaster drivers is missing, rerun Sound Blaster's installation program. If one of the other required drivers is missing, I still strongly suggest you rerun the Sound Blaster installation program; the driver could be on your disk but de-installed. Rerunning Sound Blaster's installation program sometimes re-installs it.

If that doesn't work, you must install the driver from scratch. To do that:

1. In the Main program group, double-click the **Control Panel** icon.

2. In Control Panel, double-click the **Drivers** icon.

3. In the Driver's dialog box, click the **Add** button. The Add dialog box appears.

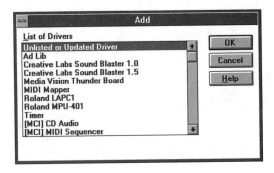

Adding Windows drivers.

4. In the Add dialog box, click the driver that is missing and click **OK**.

5. Often, the driver is on your hard disk but isn't installed to run in Windows. If that's the case, a dialog box informs you of that fact. Your options are to install a new version, install the current version (which is on your hard drive), or to cancel the installation process.

6. First click the **Current** button; this automatically re-installs the driver to work in Windows. Then, exit from the Drivers dialog box, and exit and restart Windows. Reload the Drivers dialog box from Control Panel. If the driver appears in the list, you're finished.

7. If the driver doesn't appear—or if the driver isn't on your hard drive—repeat the process, except click **New**. Follow on-screen instructions for placing the proper disk in your floppy drive.

Visiting Your INI-Laws

Just installing the correct drivers isn't necessarily enough. Nope, life often isn't that simple, particularly when it comes to Windows.

Those drivers must be duly noted in a file called SYSTEM.INI. This editable file, which is located in your \WINDOWS directory, lists drivers and scads of other instructions that automatically execute when you start Windows.

Your Sound Blaster's installation program should automatically change your SYSTEM.INI file to duly note all the appropriate drivers. Also, among other things, the process described in the previous section makes these changes to SYSTEM.INI.

Sometimes, other programs change your SYSTEM.INI file so that drivers don't load correctly. The easy solution (again!) is to re-install Sound Blaster. Most of the time, that solves the problem. If it doesn't and you want to do some further diagnostics, read the next two sections. They walk you through the process of changing your SYSTEM.INI file.

Firing Up Your SYSTEM.INI File

When you install hardware or software that works in Windows, chances are that the installation program alters the SYSTEM.INI file. In practical terms, that means that installing the latest, greatest Windows game could screw up your SYSTEM.INI file so Sound Blaster no longer works right. It happens more often than you'd think.

The contents of SYSTEM.INI are quite cryptic. The SYSTEM.INI file is broken up into sections, each of which begins with the section name in square brackets. This adds a tad of complexity to the problem: The driver must not only be noted in SYSTEM.INI, but it must be noted in the correct section.

Be Careful Out There In this section, I describe how to alter your SYSTEM.INI file if necessary. However, I strongly suggest that, before you begin tinkering, you exhaust other troubleshooting options and back up this file. Sometimes, if the changes discussed in this section aren't necessary, you'll need to revert to the original version of the file.

Before we dive into your SYSTEM.INI file, here are a couple of practical points to remember:

➤ Each section is likely to have many more lines than the ones listed here. I'm simply listing the lines that pertain to Sound Blaster.

➤ The Sound Blaster-related lines may not be located together in each section.

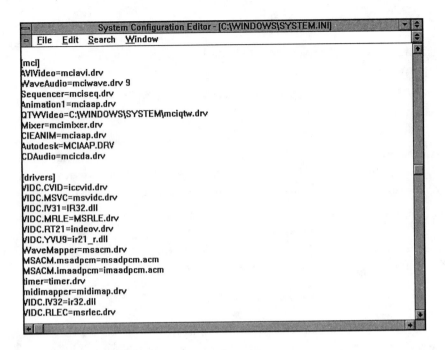

```
System Configuration Editor - [C:\WINDOWS\SYSTEM.INI]
 File   Edit   Search   Window

[mci]
AVIVideo=mciavi.drv
WaveAudio=mciwave.drv 9
Sequencer=mciseq.drv
Animation1=mciaap.drv
QTWVideo=C:\WINDOWS\SYSTEM\mciqtw.drv
Mixer=mcimixer.drv
CIEANIM=mciaap.drv
Autodesk=MCIAAP.DRV
CDAudio=mcicda.drv

[drivers]
VIDC.CVID=iccvid.drv
VIDC.MSVC=msvidc.drv
VIDC.IV31=IR32.dll
VIDC.MRLE=MSRLE.drv
VIDC.RT21=indeov.drv
VIDC.YVU9=ir21_r.dll
WaveMapper=msacm.drv
MSACM.msadpcm=msadpcm.acm
MSACM.imaadpcm=imaadpcm.acm
timer=timer.drv
midimapper=midimap.drv
VIDC.IV32=ir32.dll
VIDC.RLEC=msrlec.drv
```

This is a sample from my SYSTEM.INI file.

It's important that you know how to view and edit your SYSTEM.INI file. To do that, we'll use a utility that comes with Windows called SYSEDIT.

First, from Windows Program Manager, select **File, Run**. In the Command Line text box type **C:\WINDOWS\SYSEDIT**. Then click **OK**. (I'm assuming, of course, that C:\WINDOWS is your Windows directory. If it's different, use the correct directory instead).

The SYSEDIT program automatically loads your SYSTEM.INI file and other key files, including AUTOEXEC.BAT, CONFIG.SYS, and another key Windows file, WIN.INI. For now, let's worry only about SYSTEM.INI, which you can view by clicking its name in the cascading list of files in the SYSEDIT screen. You'll see a screen similar to the example of my SYSTEM.INI file.

The Guts of SYSTEM.INI

If you really want to feel like an idiot, try understanding all the lines in SYSTEM.INI. Few people do—even technical dweebs often become mystified.

It's really not important that you understand what the lines do. It's only important to understand that they issue commands when you start Windows. Often, those commands load drivers. If the command for loading a driver isn't present or was changed, the driver can't load.

When using SYSEDIT, to search for a section select **Search** from the menu, and then **Find**. In the Find dialog box, which appears next, type the name of the section header—which I'll supply shortly—including the squared brackets. Then, click **OK**. This should take you directly to the top of that section.

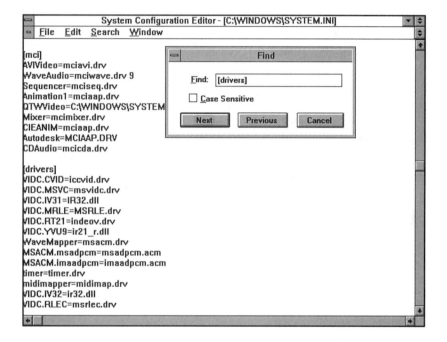

Finding a section of SYSTEM.INI.

If you can't find the section, that's probably the source of your problem. The solution to that problem is to rerun the Sound Blaster installation program (this solution is getting repetitive, but it really, really works).

If your Sound Blaster is an AWE32, look for the following sections and lines in your SYSTEM.INI file.

[boot]
drivers=mmsystem.dll msmixmgr.dll

[drivers]
Timer=timer.drv
Midimapper=midimap.drv
Aux=sb16aux.drv
MIDI=sbawe32.drv
MIDI1=sb16fm.drv
Wave=sb16snd.drv
MIDI2=sb16snd.drv
mixer=sb16aux.drv

[sndblst.drv]
port=220 (This is the base I/O address; yours may be different.)
int=5 (This is for your IRQ; yours may be different.)
dmachannel=1 (This is for your "low" DMA channel. Yours may be different.)
hdmachannel=5 (This is for your "high" DMA channel. Yours may be different.)
MIDIport=330 (This is for your MIDI port address. Yours may be different.)

[mci]
WaveAudio=mciwave.drv
Sequencer=mciseq.drv
CDAudio=mcicda.drv (This is only if you use a CD-ROM drive.)

If you have a Sound Blaster 16, you should see the following sections and lines:

[drivers]
Timer=timer.drv
Midimapper=midimap.drv
Aux=sb16aux.drv
MIDI=sbfm.drv
MIDI1=sb16fm.drv
Wave=sb16snd.drv
[sndblst.drv]
port=220 (This lists your sound card's base I/O address; yours might be different.)
int=5 (This is the IRQ; yours may be different.)
dmachannel=1 (This is the "low" DMA channel. Yours may be different.)
hdmachannel=5 (This is the "high" DMA channel. Yours may be different.)
MIDIport=330 (This is the MIDI port address. Yours may be different.)

154

[mci]
WaveAudio=mciwave.drv
Sequencer=mciseq.drv
CDAudio=mcicda.drv (This is only if you use a CD-ROM drive.)

Fixing Your INI File

Sheesh... this is starting to get a bit techie. You're probably thinking it's time to get out the propeller beanies. Hang in there, though. This is good stuff to know. Even if you call Creative Labs for technical support, there's a good chance they'll walk you through this stuff, too.

If either entire sections or specific lines are missing from SYSTEM.INI, there's a good chance you won't get sounds or music. Go through the entire section listed in brackets in your SYSTEM.INI file to make sure these lines are present.

If lines or sections aren't present in SYSTEM.INI, I first suggest that catch-all solution, rerunning the Sound Blaster installation program. If that doesn't work, go back into Windows, and restart SYSEDIT—it's time to edit SYSTEM.INI.

Use SYSEDIT like you would a word processor and add the lines or sections that are missing. If you edit a line, I suggest you retype the entire line and place a semicolon (;) at the beginning of the old line. This lets you keep the old line in the file for future reference; the semicolon tells Windows not to execute the contents of that line when Windows starts.

Here's another tip: if you see an obvious reference anywhere in your SYSTEM.INI file to a previously installed sound card, place a semicolon (;) at the beginning of that line. Again, that means that the line won't go into effect when Windows loads.

When you finish editing, select **File, Save**. Then, exit SYSEDIT, exit Windows and restart it.

Sound, but No Fury (or Music)

Here's a Windows hassle that I hate: you get sound but no music. Or music but no sound. Again, rerunning the Sound Blaster re-installation routine often is fruitful, but there may be yet another problem: drivers from previous sound cards.

Open up your Drivers dialog box from Control Panel, as described earlier in this chapter. Then look at the list of drivers for your particular Sound Blaster, as described in Chapter 10.

Make sure all the Sound Blaster drivers are installed; I listed the required drivers earlier in Chapter 10. If the required drivers aren't present, re-install Sound Blaster.

If the required drivers are in the list, one possible problem could be the presence of installed drivers from another sound card that once lived in your computer. Read the list of drivers in the Drivers dialog box and, if you see a driver with a name similar to your former sound card, remove it and restart Windows.

If that still doesn't solve the problem, you may not have the proper MIDI map loaded for playing MIDI. Read Chapter 10 to learn about MIDI maps. To reiterate, though, to change MIDI maps:

1. Start Windows Control Panel by double-clicking its icon in the Main program group.

2. In Control Panel, double-click the **MIDI Mapper** icon. The MIDI Mapper dialog box loads.

3. In the MIDI Mapper dialog box, click the **Setups** radio button.

4. Make a note of the MIDI map that's currently loaded; it's the one in the Name drop-down list. Try a different MIDI map by selecting it from the drop-down list. Sound Blaster installs a number of different MIDI maps; only select from the MIDI maps that have Sound Blaster in the name or that start with the letters SB.

4. Click **Cancel** when you finish.

5. Play a MIDI tune. You can do that using EnsembleMIDI, as described in Chapter 16.

Try as many MIDI maps as you want. If this doesn't fix the problem, revert to the MIDI map that was loaded when you started and continue troubleshooting.

Turn Up (or Down) the Volume

Sometimes when you load Windows, the sound volume is higher or lower than it was previously. This is likely to happen after you change installation settings.

The solution to this problem is simple. First, if you have self-powered speakers, make sure the volume setting is correct, the power is on, and the batteries are okay.

If that doesn't solve the problem, from the Sound Blaster program group in Windows, double-click **EnsembleMIDI** and start playing a MIDI song. For instructions about how to do that, read Chapter 16.

Next, also from the Sound Blaster program group, double-click the **Creative Mixer** icon. As you'll learn in Chapter 15, this small program is for changing things such as volume and recording levels.

Using your mouse, change the various levels until the volume suits you. When you finish, double-click the close bar in the upper right corner of Creative Mixer. Then, close EnsembleMIDI. Your volume changes should be permanent.

The Least You Need to Know

This chapter focused solely on problems that prevent Sound Blaster from working in Windows.

➤ Sound Blaster requires a number of Windows drivers to be loaded before it works in Windows.

➤ Those drivers must be listed in your SYSTEM.INI file. If they aren't, you must add them.

➤ Before making any changes to your SYSTEM.INI file, first rerun the Sound Blaster installation program. This often solves the problem.

➤ You also must load the correct MIDI map. This should be set during installation, but sometimes you must reset it in the MIDI Mapper dialog box.

Part 3
Using Sound Blaster Applications

Hey—you didn't just buy a Sound Blaster. A whole bunch of software came with it. Sure, you could ignore that software. But if you want to have a whole big bunch of fun, you'll learn how to use it. And that's what this book is about—having fun with Sound Blaster.

So in this part, you'll learn how to use included software to tweak your Sound Blaster card. You'll also learn how to speak to your computer—and have your computer respond.

This is cool stuff, so keep reading.

BRAD'S LIFE TOOK ON NEW MEANING WHEN HE DISCOVERED THAT HIS SOUNDCARD COULD MAKE **REALLY** DISGUSTING NOISES.

Chapter 15

Mixing Sounds in Sound Blaster

In This Chapter

➤ Why you should use a mixer

➤ Become a mixer master

➤ Customizing your mixer

The hard part is over—installing your Sound Blaster. Now the fun part begins—using your Sound Blaster.

Depending on which model you buy, Sound Blasters come with lots of software. This part of the book explains that software, how to start using it, and what to do with it. This chapter starts with one of the most basic, yet important, types of software: *mixers*. Mixers enable you to tweak Sound Blaster so it sounds exactly the way you want.

Mixing It Up: Using Your Mixers

Think of your stereo. In one way, Sound Blaster works like that. With your stereo, you choose whether to play the CD player or the radio. You also can select the volume, the balance between the right and left channels, and the level of bass and treble.

Mixer Software
Sounds like software for planning one of those famous mixer parties in college, however, mixer software for Windows and DOS enables you to determine volume levels and other settings for different types of audio such as MIDI files and sound effect files.

Well, that's what mixers do for Sound Blaster. For example, there will be times when you want to increase the volume of MIDI playback or decrease the volume of WAV file playback. Or you may want to change the balance of sound coming out of your speakers. Sound Blasters include utilities for both DOS and Windows that enable you to do just that. These are *mixer* utilities. Your Sound Blaster comes with the SB16SET mixer DOS and the Creative Mixer for Windows.

The rest of this chapter describes how to use the mixers that come with Sound Blaster to get precisely the right level of sound coming out of your speakers.

Why Mix?

One reason for using a mixer is that some programs have built-in controls for volume adjustment, and those adjustments become permanent when you finish with the program. Mixers enable you to return to your previous levels. Another reason is that some programs such as games don't have built-in sound level settings.

Getting Started: SB16SET for DOS

Let's start by taking SB16SET out for a spin. There are two ways to run SB16SET. You can:

➤ Type all mixer commands from the DOS prompt. These commands can be lengthy and difficult to remember. If you long to be a techno dweeb, this is the route to go, but I won't help you much; I prefer the next method.

➤ Load the SB16SET control screen, which is a simple-to-understand interface. In this interface, you change settings either with your mouse or with your keyboard.

To run the SB16SET control screen, switch to your Sound Blaster directory, which, by default, is **C:\SB16**. At the command prompt type **SB16SET** and press **Enter**. The following screen appears.

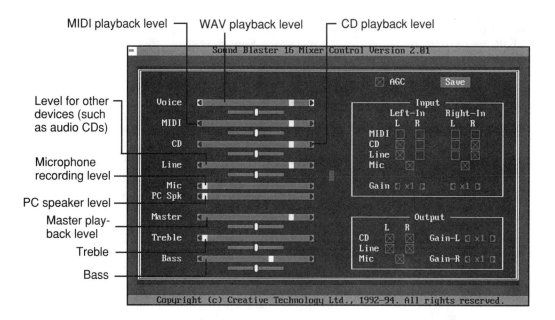

MIDI playback level ┐ WAV playback level ┌ CD playback level

Level for other
devices (such
as audio CDs)

Microphone
recording level

PC speaker level

Master play-
back level

Treble

Bass

The SB16SET control screen.

On the left side of the SB16SET screen, you can change the volume and balance for the various types of audio such as MIDI and CD-ROM. On the right side, you determine other input and output characteristics.

You can use both your keyboard and your mouse to control SB16SET. Using the mouse is faster and easier, but if you insist on using your keyboard to make settings, here's how:

What? No SB16SET? If you try to load SB16SET and get an error message, don't despair. Chances are you didn't load the drivers needed to run this utility. I will describe this problem (and, of course, the solution) in the "Don't Forget... " section later in this chapter.

➤ Use the **Tab** key to move either to the top setting on the left side of the screen or to cycle through all settings on the right side of the screen.

➤ To move to a specific setting on the left side of the screen, such as speaker volume, start at the top setting and use the up and down arrow keys. The setting you currently can change will blink.

➤ To adjust the setting, use the right and left arrow keys.

➤ For settings on the right side of the screen, move to the setting you want by pressing **Tab**. If the setting involves a check box, use the **Spacebar** key to toggle the check box on and off.

➤ Use **Tab** until you highlight the **Save** button. When it's highlighted, press **Enter** to save your changes.

Using the mouse is simpler:

1. For settings on the left side of the screen, position the mouse cursor over the item you want to adjust.

2. Hold down the left mouse button, and then move the mouse left or right to make the setting. For volume controls, left is softer and right is louder.

3. For settings on the right side of the window, click check boxes to activate or deactivate them.

Now... The DOS Settings

Now, on to the settings themselves. On the left side of the SB16SET window, you set volume, bass and treble levels, and for most settings, the balance between right and left speakers.

For example, you could set the bass level high on the right channel (channel refers to the sound that comes out your right or left speaker) and treble level high on the left channel. I use this as an example; in reality, this would be a goofy setting.

From the top, the settings on the left side of the SB16SET window are:

➤ **Voice**   Sets the volume level for WAV file playback. You set the balance for WAV file playback with the slider bar below this setting bar.

➤ **MIDI**   Sets the volume level for MIDI playback. You set the balance with the slider bar below the MIDI setting bar.

➤ **CD**   Sets the volume for an attached CD-ROM player. You set the balance with the slider bar below the CD setting bar.

➤ **Line**   The volume for an item such as an audio CD player that you plug into the Line in jack in the back of Sound Blaster. You set the balance with the slider bar below the Line setting bar.

➤ **Mic**   Sets the volume for a microphone. There is no balance control for this setting.

➤ **PC Spk**   Sets the volume for sounds that come through the built-in PC speaker. There is no balance control for this setting.

➤ **Master**   Sets the base levels for all the other settings. You still can fine-tune each setting individually after you set the master setting.

➤ **Treble**   Sets the level of treble. You set the balance below the Treble setting. Treble refers to how strong the higher pitched sounds are.

➤ **Bass**   Sets the level of bass. You set the balance below the Bass setting. Bass refers to how strong the lower pitched sounds are.

The settings on the right side are more arcane; it's rare that you would want to change them. There are, however, two settings about which you should know:

➤ **AGC**   Stands for automatic gain control. This automatically sets the amplification level to an optimal level when using a microphone.

➤ **Save**   As the name implies, saves any changes to your settings.

The other settings in the right side of the window determine how sound and music can come into Sound Blaster (known as input) and how sounds and music go out (known as output). The input options are MIDI, CD, Line (which is any device connected to the Line in jack), and Mic (which is for the microphone).

For each option, select a channel and subchannels. This can be confusing; you have a right and left channel option for both the right and left channels. I strongly suggest that you don't change the defaults.

You also can select a *gain* for input in each channel. Gain refers to how much Sound Blaster amplifies the sounds and music coming into your system. Again, I suggest not changing these settings; by default, the gain is at the maximum level.

The output options are for CD-ROMs, Line (which typically are your speakers), and Mic, which enables you to use Sound Blaster as an amplifier. Again, I strongly suggest that you don't make changes to these settings.

A Painless Gain   If you do change the gain, make sure the gain is equal for both the left and right channels. If they aren't, each speaker will play at a different volume.

After making any changes in SB16SET, remember to click the **Save** button. To exit SB16SET, click the **Control-menu box** button in the upper left corner of the program. To exit without saving, press the **ESC** key.

Don't Forget...

There are two important things to remember about the Sound Blaster mixers. First, using SB16SET in DOS does not change settings in Windows—or vice versa. Even if you find the perfect settings for DOS, you must do it all again for Windows.

Second, you must load the proper drivers before SB16SET can run. The Sound Blaster installation program asked if you wanted to load the sound card drivers for DOS every time you started your computer. This was a bit of a trick question—at least if you want to use the SB16SET mixer.

In general, the best answer for this question is No. That's because you don't need those sound drivers to hear sound in DOS; you only need the drivers to be able to adjust the sound levels. Another reason to select No is that these drivers require about 40K of precious system memory. So, if you said **No** during installation and now you want to use the DOS mixer, you must rerun installation and select **Yes**. Selecting Yes installs three drivers, two of which you need to run SB16SET.

Those two drivers are named CTSB16.SYS and CTMMSYS.SYS. The installation program places them on your CONFIG.SYS file. That means they automatically load whenever you start your PC. The conundrum is obvious: loading the drivers lets you use SB16SET but it chews up memory. A memory loss of 40K can mean the difference between playing a game or not.

Here's a solution. If you need SB16SET, re-install Sound Blaster and select **Yes** when the installation program asks if you want to run the drivers whenever you start your computer.

Now here's the beauty part: you can deactivate the drivers when you don't need them for tasks such as running SB16SET. To do that, at the DOS prompt for your C:\ root directory, type: **EDIT CONFIG.SYS** and press **Enter**. This loads the EDIT program so you can edit your CONFIG.SYS file.

Locate the lines that load the drivers. The lines start either with the words **DEVICEHIGH=** or **DEVICE=** and mention **CTSB16.SYS** and **CTMMSYS.SYS**. Before each of those lines, type **REM** and press the **Spacebar**. Save the file by opening the **File** menu and choosing **Save**; then reboot your computer by pressing **Ctrl+Alt+Del**. The REM command at the beginning of a line tells your system to ignore the command that follows. In other words, the drivers won't load.

When you need to run SB16SET, edit your CONFIG.SYS file again, this time removing the REM statements. It's a bit of a clumsy procedure, but it works.

Making It Sound Right in Windows

Creative Mixer, the mixer for Windows that comes with Sound Blaster, is similar to SB16SET, but it has some extra capabilities. Most notably, you can use Creative Mixer to set levels while music and sounds are playing. This is a handier way to set levels than the SB16SET mixer. With the DOS mixer, you set a level, exit the mixer, and then play music or a sound to see if the setting is correct. If not, you must repeat the process until it is.

To start Creative Mixer, double-click its icon (labeled Creative Mixer) in the Sound Blaster program group created by your Sound Blaster installation program.

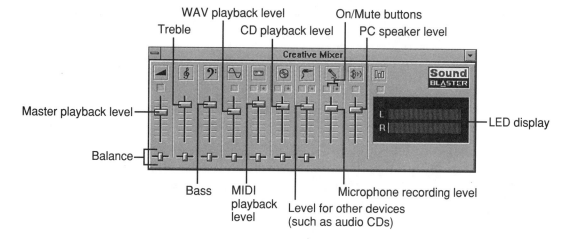

Creative Mixer for Windows.

To change a setting with your mouse you:

1. Move your mouse pointer over the appropriate slider bar.

2. Hold down the left mouse button.

3. Drag the slider bar to its new location. Moving it up increases the volume and moving it down decreases it. Moving the balance slider bar left or right changes the balance in the direction in which you move the bar.

Creative Mixer Settings

Now let's mix it up in Windows. When looking at Creative Mixer, from left to right, the settings are:

➤ **Master control**   This sets the base levels for all other sound level settings. You can fine-tune each setting individually after you set the master level.

➤ **Treble**   For setting the treble level. Treble refers to the higher pitches in the audio range.

➤ **Bass**   For setting the bass level. Bass refers to the lower pitches in the audio range.

➤ **Wave**   For setting the level of playback for sound files such as WAV files.

➤ **MIDI**   For setting the level of playback for MIDI files.

➤ **Line input**   For setting the level of playback for items plugged into the Line in jack, such as a tape deck or audio CD player.

➤ **Microphone**   For the level for microphones.

➤ **PC speaker**   For the sound level for sounds that ordinarily would come out of your PC's built-in speaker.

Above each slider bar (except the bass and treble controls) are at least one and often two boxes. Clicking the boxes either makes a red dot or a green dot appear or disappear.

The green dots enable playback of that particular audio source. For example, if the green dot appears above the master setting, all audio sources can play. However, if you remove the green dot from above the MIDI setting, you won't hear MIDI sound.

Watch That Dot! Creative Mixer is fun to play with, but if you play around with it enough, eventually, you'll accidentally click off a playback button. If suddenly you don't hear, say, MIDI music, load Creative Mixer and make sure that the green dot above the MIDI playback slider bar is activated.

The red dots tell you whether you can record from an audio source. For example, a red dot above the slider bar for microphone levels allows you to record sounds with a microphone.

I suggest activating all green and red dots, which is the default. There is no particular advantage to deactivating any of these options. One final option is playback gain. This is the amount Sound Blaster amplifies the sound coming out of each channel. Ordinarily, there's no reason to change this setting.

But if you must change it, click the **Control-menu box** in the upper left corner of Creative Mixer and select **Output Gain**. The Output Gain dialog box appears.

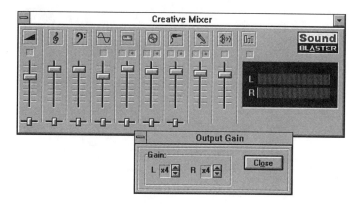

Changing output gain.

The default output gain, or amplification, is four times per channel. Change the gain for each channel by clicking the up or down arrows. But be careful: you will upset the balance of your playback by giving the different channels different gains. After you make changes to settings, click the **Control-menu box**.

After changing mixer settings, close Creative Mixer by double-clicking the **Control-menu box** in the upper left corner. You can set whether your changes are permanent or whether they are temporary, lasting only as long as you are in Windows. The next section describes how to do that.

Customizing Creative Mixer

Choices, choices, choices. Creative Mixer is highly customizable. You can set much of this customization in the Preferences dialog box. To access this dialog box, click the box in the upper left corner of Creative Mixer. From the menu that appears, select **Preferences**.

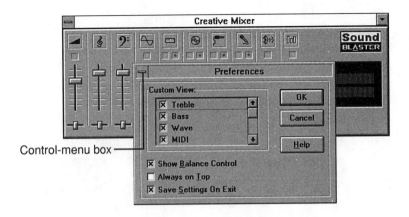

Control-menu box

Setting mixer preferences.

This dialog box enables you to select precisely which settings you can adjust in the main Creative Mixer window. To select or deselect an item, click the appropriate check box in the Custom View window. For example, if you don't want the bass and treble settings to appear, click the check boxes to the left of those listings so there is no X. Conversely, to make a setting appear in Creative Mixer, click the box until the X appears. The only reason you would hide elements is to save screen space.

At the bottom of the Preferences dialog box are some important options. They are:

➤ **Show Balance Control** Determines whether the balance slider bars appear below the level settings.

➤ **Always on Top** Makes Creative Mixer always appear on-screen above any other application. This is useful when you use another application such as a sound editor and want control over playback and recording levels.

➤ **Save Settings On Exit** Means that any changes you make in Creative Mixer are permanent (at least until you change them again) after you exit the program. If you don't check this box, the changes are in effect only until you exit Windows. The next time you load Windows, the previously saved settings are in effect.

When you finish setting preferences, click **OK**.

Getting Your Readings

Another way to customize Creative Mixer is to determine whether to view the display on the right side of the window and, if so, which display you view. You switch the display on or off by clicking the **Control-menu box** in the upper left corner of the Creative Mixer window and selecting **LED Display** from the **Control** menu.

There are three types of LED displays, each of which resembles the type of display you commonly see on stereo amplifiers. You toggle through them by placing your cursor over the LED display window. When the cursor turns into a hand, click the left mouse button to display the next type.

The three types of displays are:

➤ **Power spectrum**   Displays the different levels of output for different tones ranging from bass to treble.

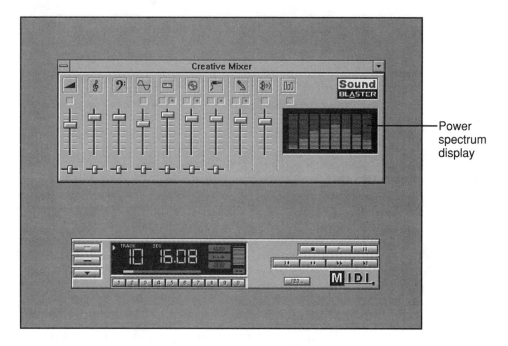

The power spectrum display.

➤ **VU meter**   Shows the sound levels from both the right and left speakers.

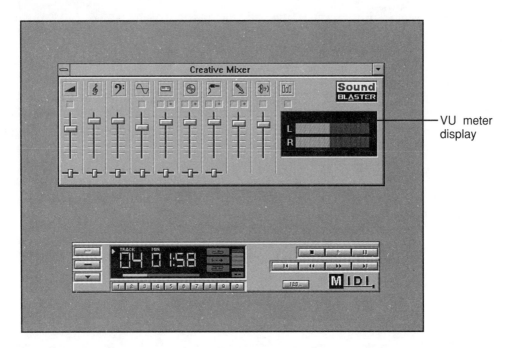

VU meter display

The VU meter display.

View the VU Meter

When playing around with Creative Mixer, it's easy to accidentally change the balance so a slightly higher level comes out of one speaker or the other. This diminishes the stereo effect. Using the VU meter setting is a good way to check the balance between speakers.

➤ **Scope**   Shows the combined volume of all the audio sources you selected for playback.

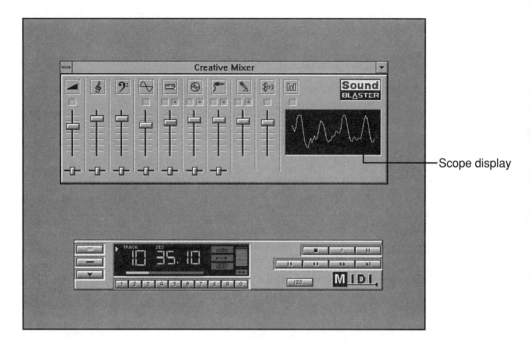

Scope display

The scope display.

Besides selecting the LED display, you also can determine whether the display shows readings at all. You do that by clicking the box above the display. When the green dot appears, readings appear in the display. When the green dot is not visible, no readings appear.

Finally, you can change settings for recording, although, again, in most cases, the defaults work perfectly well. To change these settings, click the **Control-menu box** in the upper left corner of the Creative Mixer window and select **Recording Settings**. The Recording Settings dialog box appears.

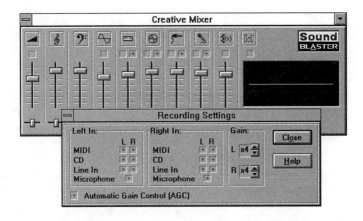

The Recording Settings dialog.

This dialog box provides the same options as the right side of the SB16SET window for DOS. To briefly reiterate, you set the channels for devices attached to Sound Blaster's MIDI, CD, Line In ports, and for the microphone. You also set the gain for recording on each channel.

One setting that I find useful is the Automatic Gain Control (AGC) setting at the bottom of the dialog box. This automatically sets the gain when recording to appropriate levels, which is a great convenience. To activate this setting, click the box until the red dot appears.

Using Mixer to Get It Right

In most cases, you won't have to bother with either SB16SET or Creative Mixer; the default playback and recording levels usually work just fine, thank you. However, "most cases" isn't the same as "always." So let me give you a few guidelines for setting recording and playback levels. (For more details about recording sounds, read Chapters 21 and 22).

First, here's a reminder: You must set volume separately for Windows and for DOS. Making settings in one doesn't have any effect on the other. Things are a bit simpler in Windows 95. As you learned in Chapter 11, you can use either the Creative Mixer in Windows 95 or the Volume Control dialog box. When you change settings with one of these mixers, it automatically changes the settings in the other. This isn't true in earlier versions of Windows. Again, though, simply making a change in Windows 95 doesn't effect levels in DOS.

Now, here are some general level setting guidelines:

➤ If you hear your speakers hiss, you may have one of two problems. The first problem may be bad speakers, and I can't help you with that. The second problem may be that your Master volume control is set too high. Go into SB16SET, Creative Mixer, or, in Windows 95, the Volume Control dialog box and experiment by turning down the Master volume.

➤ If you hear distortion, or crackling, in the sound you are listening to, you've set the playback levels too high. Use a mixer to turn down the volume for the specific item, such as MIDI music or WAV sounds, that you are playing back. Experiment until it sounds right.

➤ Similarly, you may need to turn down recording levels while you are playing back sounds or you can get strange, screechy sounds called *feedback*. This is particularly true if you have a microphone attached to Sound Blaster.

➤ If you change speakers, you may have to change all your playback levels. More specifically, this is true with powered speakers that have built-in amplifiers. Different amplifiers work at different levels—my newest set of speakers plays much louder than my previous set.

Finally, don't be afraid to experiment with playback and recording levels to find the levels that are optimal for you.

The Least You Need to Know

In this chapter, you learned how to set sound and recording levels for Sound Blaster. This is a simple but very important function. Specifically, you learned that:

➤ The SB16SET mixer works in DOS.

➤ The Creative Mixer utility is for Windows.

➤ You must make settings for DOS and Windows separately.

➤ Both mixers enable you to select the sound levels and balance for each type of sound source such as MIDI, waveform files, CD-ROM, and your microphone.

➤ Creative Mixer is highly customizable, including the ability to change the LED display.

The Sounds of Music

As I write this, I'm listening to Bach's Goldberg Variations through my Sound Blaster. Very nice, indeed. If you're ready to listen to sounds and music, your ship has come in.

In this chapter, you'll learn to use the Sound Blaster software for Windows and DOS that play MIDI and wave files and audio CDs. You can hear sounds and music by firing up your favorite game and playing your heart out, but if you want to listen to, say, the Goldberg Variations in the background while you work, read on.

The Sound Blaster Ensemble for Windows

The most thorough set of sound and music-playing tools is the interrelated set of Ensemble programs for Windows. These programs are:

➤ **EnsembleMIDI**   For playing MIDI files.

➤ **EnsembleWave**   For playing WAV files.

➤ **EnsembleCD**   For playing audio CDs.

➤ **EnsembleRemote**   An all-in-one controller for the other three programs.

Any of these programs can be on-screen at any time.

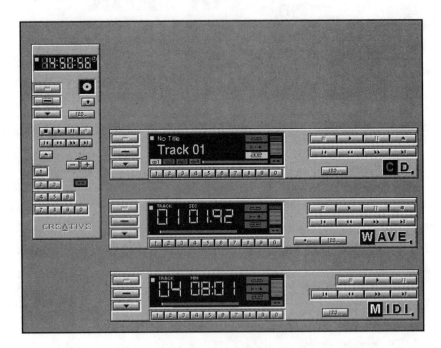

The entire Ensemble.

One nice thing about the Ensemble members is that they look and work about the same. This makes them easy to learn. The similar aspects of each player include:

➤ Identical buttons for closing the player, minimizing it for viewing the Options menu.

➤ VCR-like controls for starting, stopping, and pausing the play of sounds or music.

➤ The ability to create lists of songs or sound effects to play. These lists are called *playlists*.

Getting on the Playlist

Before describing the members of the Ensemble, let's talk about *playlists*. These are lists of songs or sounds you create for each of the three main Ensemble players. Playlists enable you to assemble all the sounds and songs you want to hear so you can hear them quickly without fumbling around in dialog boxes.

To create a playlist for any Ensemble member:

1. Click the button to the right of the main graphical display that has **123 ...** on it. For all three Ensemble players, this displays the playlist dialog box. The dialog boxes for EnsembleMIDI and EnsembleCD look like the following screen (it's slightly different for EnsembleCD).

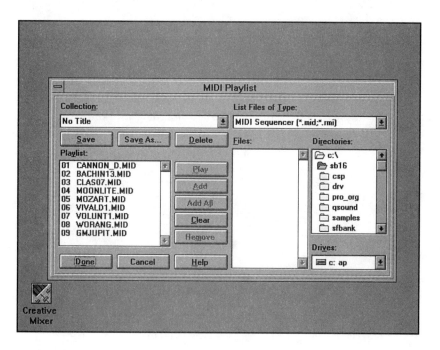

Making a playlist.

2. Select the types of files you are looking for in the **List Files of Type** drop-down list.

3. Select the directory in which the sound or music files are located in the **Directory** window. The sound or music files appear in the **Files** window.

4. To listen to a file before adding it to the playlist, highlight it in the **Files** window and click the **Play** button.

5. To add a file to the playlist, click the **Add** button. To add all the files in the **Files** window to your playlist, click **Add All**.

6. Change the order of an item in the playlist by highlighting it and then dragging it to a different place in the list while holding down your right mouse button.

7. To remove all files from the playlist, click **Clear**. To remove a single file, highlight it in the **Playlist** window and click **Remove**.

One at a Time, Please For most systems, you can't create an EnsembleCD playlist composed of songs from multiple CDs. The only ways you can do this are if you have either a multi-disk CD-player attached to your Sound Blaster (through the Line In jack) or if you have a CD-ROM player that can play multiple disks.

8. To save an existing playlist with your changes, click **Save**. To save an existing playlist that you have altered, click **Save As** and type a new playlist name in the dialog box that appears. To delete a playlist, select it from the **Collection** drop-down list and click **Delete**.

9. Click **Done** when you finish creating or altering your list.

The Playlist dialog box for EnsembleCD is a bit different. Obviously, because it plays audio CDs, there is no need to select a drive and directory. Instead of selecting those items, select a track in the **Track List** window and add it to the **Playlist** window.

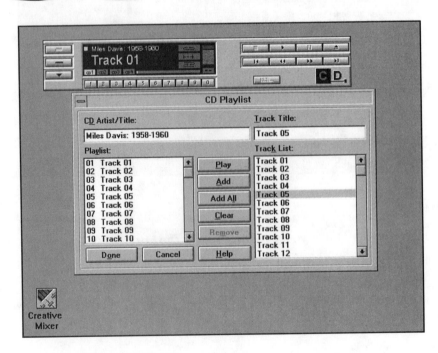

The EnsembleCD Playlist dialog box.

Playing a playlist is simple with any Ensemble member. Click the playlist button on the Ensemble member in the Collection drop-down list in the Playlist dialog box; then select the list you want. Click the numbered buttons at the bottom of the player. The numbers relate to a song's or sound's position in the playlist; clicking on number one, for example, plays the first song or sound in the list.

Using EnsembleMIDI

Now, let's get specific, starting with EnsembleMIDI. To load EnsembleMIDI, click the **EnsembleMIDI** icon in the Sound Blaster program group.

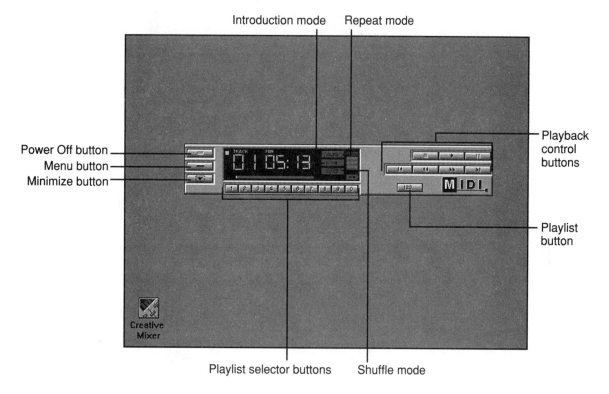

Playin' tunes with EnsembleMIDI.

The next two sections describe EnsembleMIDI. Read them even if you want to use one of the other Ensemble members. That's because the Ensemble members are more alike than different. I'll explain many of the basics as they pertain to EnsembleMIDI and I won't repeat them for EnsembleWave and EnsembleCD.

Running (Fast) EnsembleMIDI

Using EnsembleMIDI (and the other Ensemble members) is a lot like using your normal stereo equipment. For the most part, you simply click buttons on-screen. You can play either playlists or individual MIDI songs. You select a specific playlist from the Playlist dialog box as described previously. But you also can play a specific song from that dialog box, first by selecting the drive and directory on which the song is located.

You do this in the Drives and Directories part of the Playlist dialog box. The MIDI files appear in the Files window. Select the individual file you want and click **Play**.

While you do this, you can't use the buttons on the main part of EnsembleMIDI, which is one good incentive for creating playlists. After you select your playlist from the Collection drop-down list, click **Done** to return to the main EnsembleMIDI interface.

Let's examine that interface now.

Starting from the left, notice three buttons stacked vertically. From the top, they are:

➤ The Power Off button   Click it to close EnsembleMIDI.

➤ The Menu button   Displays the Options menu.

➤ The Minimize button   Turns EnsembleMIDI into an icon on your Windows desktop. This is useful for listening to music without cluttering up your screen.

To the right is the graphical display area. You can change the contents of the main display area by clicking it. The three graphical display views are:

➤ The standard graphical display shows an image of a floppy disk drive. If the disk is in the drive, EnsembleMIDI is playing music. If the disk isn't in the drive, EnsembleMIDI isn't playing music.

➤ The name of the file that is playing and the name of the playlist, if any.

➤ The current number of the song in the playlist (if any) and the running time of the song. These last two views provide more useful information than the standard graphical display.

Mixing Your MIDI

You can load the Creative Mixer whenever you play music with Ensemble MIDI. This enables you to precisely set the playback levels and balance of your MIDI songs. Read Chapter 15 to learn how to use Creative Mixer.

Personally, I find the standard graphical display mode a bit silly. The other two modes provide more useful information such as the title of the piece or the track number. They also display a time slider that indicates the length of the song or sound effect and how much longer it has to run.

Below the graphical display are numbered buttons. These work like the buttons on your car radio. Each number relates to a song on your playlist. For example, click button three and EnsembleMIDI plays the third song on your playlist.

On the right side of the display are three symbols. These can be a bit obtuse to new users. From the top, the symbols are:

➤ **Repeat mode** When you click this icon and it's active (it appears brighter than before), EnsembleMIDI restarts the playlist after playing the last song.

➤ **Introduction mode** When activated, EnsembleMIDI plays only the first few moments of the selection.

➤ **Shuffle mode** When activated, EnsembleMIDI plays the playlist (if you've selected one) in random order instead of the order you designated.

To the right of these three symbols are two more switches for controlling MIDI playback. The first is the volume indicator. This vertical bar indicates the volume level and enables you to change it. To increase volume, point your mouse cursor above the blue bar and click. To decrease volume, click the mouse cursor anywhere in the indicator bar.

If you click the tiny symbol beneath the volume indicator, you can select numbers greater than nine from the numbered selection buttons. For example, if you activate this button and then click 4 and then 5, you would play the forty-fifth item on the playlist. Obviously, this enables you to create long playlists.

At the bottom of the EnsembleMIDI window and toward the right is the playlist button (it has 123... on it). Above that are the two rows of buttons for controlling play-back. From left to right, the buttons in the top row are:

➤ Stop

➤ Play

➤ Pause

From left to right, the buttons in the second row are:

➤ **Skip reverse** Plays the previous track from the beginning.

➤ **Rewind** Rewinds the track.

183

➤ **Fast forward** Skips you ahead in the current song.

➤ **Skip forward** Plays the next playlist track from the beginning.

Eating off the MIDI Menu

Clicking the menu button (the middle button in the vertical stack of buttons on the far left) displays a menu. Of particular note in this menu are:

➤ **Mixer Settings** This loads the Creative Mixer for setting audio levels. Read Chapter 15 to learn how to use that program.

➤ **MIDI Mapper** This provides direct access to the Control Panel MIDI Mapper described in Chapter 14.

When you finish using EnsembleMIDI, close it by clicking the top button in the vertical stack of buttons on the left side.

Using EnsembleWave

As the name implies, EnsembleWave is for playing—and recording—WAV files. You load EnsembleWave by selecting its icon in the Sound Blaster program group.

As with EnsembleMIDI, you can play individual WAV files or create playlists of WAV files. The procedure is the same as I described previously.

Using EnsembleWave is similar to operating EnsembleMIDI, with a few exceptions. One difference is a button to the left of the playlist button. Clicking this button displays the Choose Wave Format dialog box in which you select the recording mode for WAV files. Use this dialog box to select whether you record in stereo or mono and the sampling rate and size; then click **OK** to close the dialog box.

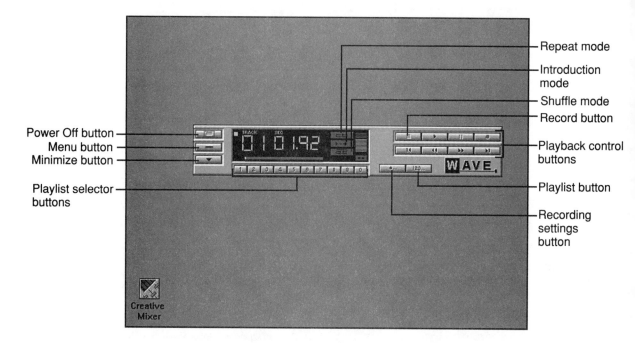

EnsembleWave for playing sounds.

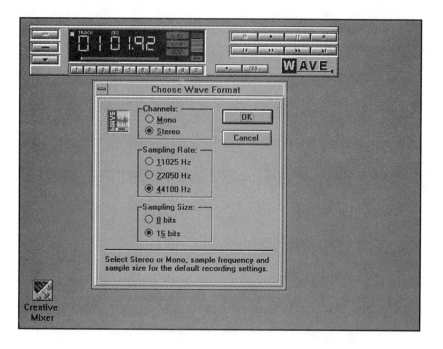

Selecting WAV recording mode.

Also, the playback control buttons are slightly different in EnsembleWave. It has two rows of these buttons. In the top row are:

➤ Stop

➤ Play

➤ Pause

➤ Record

To record a sound, first use the Choose Wave Format dialog box to choose how you want to record (as described previously). Then click the **Record** button. A dialog box then asks you to name the WAV file you are recording; the recording begins after you type a name and click **OK**. To stop recording, click the **Stop** button.

Use the Right Tool

For recording, I suggest using other programs such as Soundo'LE or WaveStudio, both of which come with most Sound Blaster cards. These programs provide more control over the recording process. Learn about Soundo'LE in Chapter 19 and WaveStudio in Chapter 22.

The bottom row of buttons for EnsembleWave are:

➤ **Skip reverse**   Plays the previous track from the beginning.

➤ **Rewind**   Rewinds the track.

➤ **Fast forward**   Plays the next track.

➤ **Skip forward**   Plays the next playlist track from the beginning.

A few final differences from EnsembleMIDI are in the menu, which you access by clicking the middle button on the left-hand side.

Specifically, selecting **Wave Editor** automatically loads the WaveEditor program and the current file in the playlist. This enables you to play and edit the WAV file.

Also in the menu, you can synchronize the start of a WAV recording to the start of a particular audio CD track or a specific MIDI file. This enables you to record as WAV files MIDI files and audio CD tracks. To do that, select either **CD Sync** or **MIDI Sync** from the menu. When you activate those options, a check appears next to them. Note: to make this option work, either EnsembleMIDI or EnsembleCD must be loaded.

Using EnsembleCD

Pheww... after explaining playlists, EnsembleMIDI, and EnsembleWave, there isn't much to describe about EnsembleCD. To load EnsembleCD, first put an audio CD disc in your CD-ROM drive. Then, double-click the **EnsembleCD** icon in the Sound Blaster program group in Windows.

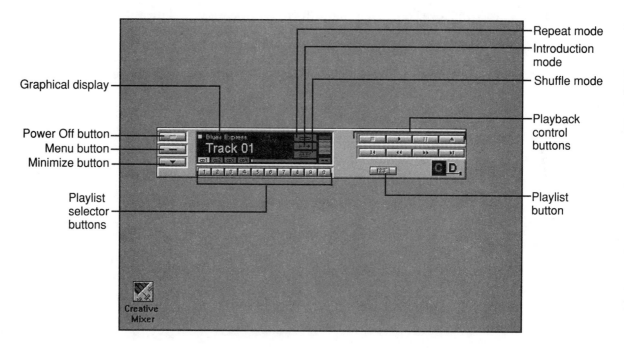

EnsembleCD.

There are four CD icons across the bottom of the graphical display modes. This enables you to control as many as four CD-ROM drives at a time. This would happen, for example, if you had a multitask CD changer attached to your Sound Blaster's Line In jack or if your CD-ROM drive can handle multiple discs.

Also, the playback controls are slightly different. Specifically, the controls in the top row are:

➤ Stop

➤ Play

➤ Pause

➤ Eject (Not all CD-ROM drives support this control.)

187

EnsembleCD is a wonderful tool for playing relaxing music in the background. I just slip an audio CD in my CD-ROM drive, fire up EnsembleCD, and then minimize it while I listen to my favorite tunes.

Using EnsembleRemote

Control freaks will love Ensemble Remote. It enables you to control the three other Ensemble members from a single source.

EnsembleRemote resembles a universal remote control. Frankly, I find those universal controls a bit confusing at first and, to be honest, I had the same response at first to EnsembleRemote. But the more I used it, the handier it became.

Load EnsembleRemote by clicking its icon in the Sound Blaster program group.

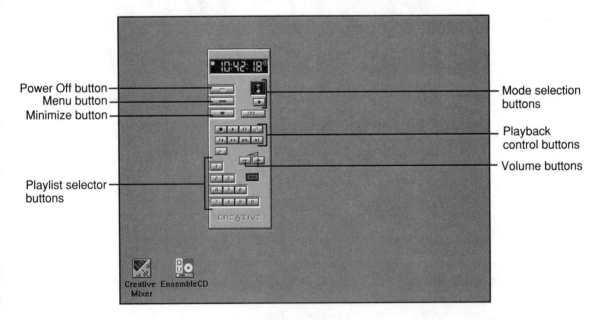

EnsembleRemote for controlling all Ensemble members.

Although EnsembleRemote has a different look, it works pretty much the same as the other Ensemble members. If you look closely, you'll see some familiar elements:

➤ The three familiar buttons: Power, Menu, and Minimize.

➤ The graphical display. In this case, the three displays are the current time, the name of your playlist, and the name of the currently playing track.

➤ The track selector buttons.

➤ The playback controls, which include all the playback controls for all the Ensemble members. For example, EnsembleRemote includes the Eject button from EnsembleCD and the Record button from EnsembleWave. When you use another Ensemble member, those buttons are not available for use.

➤ The playlist button for accessing the Playlist dialog box for the Ensemble member currently in use.

There are, however, some additions to EnsembleRemote. First, below and to the right of the graphical display is a button for selecting the specific Ensemble member you want to control. If you click the up arrow, EnsembleRemote shows a graphical dialog box with symbols for each player.

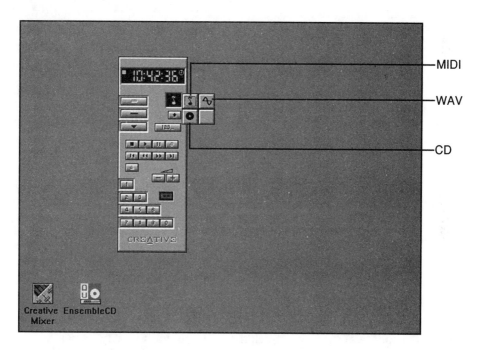

Selecting an Ensemble member.

The other new control is the master volume switch, which is below the playback controls. Click the plus sign to increase volume and the minus sign to decrease volume.

Also, there are a couple of new options in the menu. If you want all loaded players to be connected so they appear on-screen one on top of the other, activate the **Stack Players** menu option. A check appears when it is activated.

To load all players, select **Load All** and to close all players, select **Close All**. Finally, to change the color of players, select **Color Scheme** from the menu. Seven color schemes appear on-screen; click the color scheme you want, and the players and EnsembleRemote appear in that color.

Using the DOS PLAY and RECORD Utilities

If you have a "Windows shmindows" attitude, you can play and record sounds and music from the DOS prompt. Sound Blaster installation placed two programs, PLAY and RECORD, in your \SB16 directory. If you switch to that directory (first type C:\ and press **Enter**; then type **CD \SB16** and press **Enter**) and type **PLAY** and then press **Enter**, the utility displays a list of instructions. Because they're a bit obtuse, I'll summarize them here.

The simplest way to play music or sound is to type the word **PLAY** followed by a space, and then the path and file name of the file you want to play. Then press **Enter**. For example, I've copied a bunch of MIDI songs (such as those that come on the accompanying CD-ROM) to my \SB16\SAMPLES subdirectory. Let's say one of those songs is called JAZZ.MID. To play it, I would type **PLAY SAMPLES\JAZZ.MID.**

You can add songs by typing the above line, pressing the **Spacebar** and adding another path and file name. Note, though, that you can only play one type of file at a time. You can't, for example, type a command to play a MIDI song and a WAV file one after the other.

You also can play an audio CD track if the disc is in your CD-ROM player. To do that type the **PLAY CD** command, followed by a track number. For example:

PLAY CD /T:3

plays the audio CD starting at track three. If you don't specify a track, you must press **P** to start playing the CD. When PLAY is playing the file, you can press keys for specific actions.

```
Play Utility.   Version 1.03
Copyright (c) Creative Technology Ltd., 1993-94. All rights reserved.

During playing, you can use

   [Esc]    -Stop and Exit         [P]      -Play previous file

   [Space]  -Pause                 [N]      -Play next file

   [C]      -Continue              [↑ or ↓] -Change Tempo

   [> or <] -Select files and      [<- or ->] -Transpose
            hit Enter key to play
                                   [M]      -Change mapper

Format:    Extended MIDI
▶  PLAYING 001:001   SAMPLES\BACHXI.MID
```

Play options.

Specifically, you press:

➤ **ESC** to stop playing.

➤ **Spacebar** to pause and **C** to continue after a pause.

➤ The greater-than or less-than keys to select a different file to play.

➤ **P** to play the previous file, **L** to play the previous audio CD track, and **N** to play the next file you listed in the command line.

➤ **F** to fast-forward when playing an audio CD.

➤ The up and down arrow keys to increase or decrease the tempo.

➤ The left or right arrow keys to transpose the playing order.

➤ **M** to cycle through different modes of MIDI playback.

You also can record using the RECORD utility. To record, make sure you plug in the microphone. Then, at the DOS prompt, type the word **RECORD**, a space, and the name of the file you are recording. You also must add syntax that indicates the source of input and, optionally, the sampling rate. For example,

RECORD MYVOICE.WAV /A:MIC /S:11025

creates a file called MYVOICE.WAV from microphone input at a sampling rate of 11025Hz.

You must put your input source after the characters/**A:**. The other choices for input are CD (for your CD-ROM player), LINE (for anything connected to the Line in jack), and FM for MIDI. You put the sampling rate after the characters /**S:**. The other choices for sampling rates are 22,050Hz and 44,100Hz.

The Least You Need to Know

Sound Blaster comes with utilities for listening to and recording sounds and music.

➤ The Ensemble products for Windows include players for WAV and MIDI files and audio CD tracks playing in your CD-ROM drive.

➤ You can create playlists of the songs or sounds you want to hear.

➤ EnsembleRemote is a universal remote control for all three players.

➤ You also can use the PLAY and RECORD utilities in DOS to play sounds and music and to record them.

Chapter 17

Fine-Tuning Your Sound Blaster

In This Chapter

➤ Going to the (sound) bank

➤ Getting the concert hall effect

➤ QSound is your friend

Some people just love to tinker. If that's you, this is the chapter to read. No more of the basics from the previous chapters about how to listen to sounds and music. Nope, now we're getting into real techno dweeb territory. In this chapter, you'll learn how to control some of Sound Blaster's advanced features.

With many versions of AWE32 and Sound Blaster 16, you can uniquely alter the way Sound Blaster makes sounds. Specifically, its QSound capability makes sound seem three-dimensional; you can hear sound come from virtually any direction.

Also, the AWE32 lets you control effects such as reverb and simulate the acoustics in different "rooms," as if you are listening to a live performance. You also can change the instruments you hear during playback.

Why take advantage of these capabilities? Well, for one thing, they're fun to goof around with—if you have the time and inclination. Also, serious music aficionados are very picky about the nature of their sound, and these capabilities will satisfy even the pickiest of musicians.

In this chapter, we discuss those capabilities and how to use them. Remember, though, this information isn't necessary for everyday use of your Sound Blaster. Rather, these are more advanced topics.

Using AWE32 Control Panel

Unlike many other sound cards, the AWE32 does much more than simply play back sounds and music. You also can control the quality of MIDI sound and how it plays back, at least if your Sound Blaster is an AWE32.

You do this in Windows by double-clicking the **AWE32 Control Panel** icon in the Sound Blaster program group. The AWE32 Control dialog box appears.

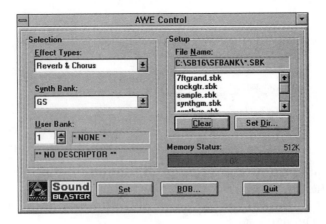

The AWE32 Control dialog box.

In this dialog box, you can choose to use QSound when playing MIDI songs or select a method of playback called reverb and chorus. This also is the dialog box in which you change "sound banks," or the specific collections of instruments used for playing back MIDI songs.

QSound? Yes, but...

QSound and reverb and chorus use the Advanced Signal Processing Chip (ASP) on the AWE32. Many versions of the Sound Blaster 16s also have the ASP chip, but only offer QSound. That's because, without the wave-table synthesis offered on the AWE32, which adds realistic MIDI playback based on actual sound samples, reverb and chorus are not of much benefit.

The next several sections discuss the specifics of setting the effects AWE32 uses for playing musical sounds.

Getting Familiar with Reverb and Chorus

Classical music aficionados will tell you that every concert hall sounds different. A musical ensemble playing in one hall sounds different when playing in another. That's because sound bounces off walls and other objects differently in different halls and rooms. One room may sound particularly crisp while another room may have a softer sound.

Set Sound Blaster to sound like different types of rooms with the Effect Types drop-down list in the AWE32 Control dialog box. In that drop-down list, there are two options: QSound and Reverb & Chorus.

I will discuss QSound in a later section of this chapter; the Reverb & Chorus option usually is the better choice. If you select the Reverb & Chorus option, two drop-down lists appear in the right side of the dialog box. They let you select specific reverb and chorus options. These options are subtle, but as you experiment, you'll notice the difference. If you have time on your hands, it's interesting and fun to see which room you like best.

The options from the Reverb drop-down list are called:

➤ Room 1 through 3

➤ Hall 1 and 2

➤ Plate

➤ Plate delay

➤ Panning delay

Reverb-b-b-b

To be a bit more specific, reverb adds a level of spaciousness to the playback of music. This is similar to the effect you get in real life when you hear sound in a large concert hall compared to, say, a practice room. By contrast, chorus adds warmth, depth, and resonance to the music.

The chorus options are called:

➤ Chorus 1 through 4

➤ Feedback delay

➤ Flanger

➤ Short Delay

➤ Short Delay FB

It's not as important to know the differences between the various settings as it is to know that these settings each create a slightly different feel. Since the effect depends on your speakers and the acoustics of your room, experiment until you find the specific effects that are most pleasing to you. So load a piece of MIDI music and have some fun.

Pickin' Your Standard

The next option in the Control dialog box is Synth Bank. In this drop-down list, you select a specific MIDI standard for playback or music creation. The three options are: General MIDI, GS (which stands for General Sound), and MT 32. Each of these options refers to a different standard for creating and playing back MIDI music. What's the diff?

Sometimes, MIDI creators write to one standard or the other, depending on their preferences and the hardware they use. However, in most cases they stay with the default selection, General MIDI. This is the most widely accepted standard and works well in virtually all cases.

You would switch to another standard if:

➤ You are playing a musical piece that was developed with one of the other standards.

➤ You want to create a musical piece based on one of the other MIDI standards.

The first case is reasonably uncommon. For the second case, I suggest creating your music to the General MIDI standard unless you absolutely must do it differently.

Listen!

There is no equivalent to the AWE32 Control dialog box for DOS. Usually DOS programs that play back MIDI, such as games, include a setup program in which you change MIDI settings.

By the way, I'll discuss some of the basics of creating MIDI music in Chapter 23.

Takin' It to the User Bank

In MIDI music, there are 128 general musical instrument sounds and 64 drum sounds. When you create a MIDI piece, you determine which of those sounds plays for a specific part of the music. For example, you can determine that one instrument in your composition is an oboe and another is the timpani drum.

With AWE32, however, you can create your own banks of sound (called, not surprisingly, *sound banks*, or *sound font banks*). So, for example, if you were in a goofy mood, you could replace the oboe with, say, a whistle or a car revving. You create these sound banks with programs such as the Vienna SF Studio program, which comes with your Sound Blaster.

You also can download sound banks created by others from online services. These sound banks are saved in files with the .SBK file name extension. The best source of public-domain sound banks is the Sound Blaster forum on CompuServe (type GO BLASTER). Also, the disc that accompanies this book has a number of sound banks.

In the AWE32 Control dialog box, you can assign a sound bank to a user bank, and then tell Sound Blaster to use the new bank. A *user bank* is a setting with a specific sound bank attached. To do that:

1. Select a user bank number (you can have as many as 128 different user banks) by clicking the up and down arrows. User banks are numbered, and you can attach a specific sound bank to a user bank.

2. In the File Name dialog box, the file names of various sound banks appear. AWE32 comes with a sampling of four banks.

3. Double-click the sound bank to which you want to attach to a specific user bank. Note the sound bank name and description appear next to the user bank number.

4. To detach a sound bank from a user bank, click the **Clear** button.

You don't have to load a sound bank; the default sound bank is always in effect until you load another one. The default sound bank isn't listed in the dialog box.

The four sound banks included with Sound Blaster are:

➤ **SAMPLE.SBK** Provides special sound effects for some MIDI sounds.

➤ **SYNTHGM.SBK** A sound bank designed specifically for General MIDI.

➤ **SYNTHGS.SBK** A sound bank designed specifically for General Sound.

➤ **SYNTHMT.SBK** A sound bank designed specifically for MT 32.

After you select the sound bank, click the **Set** button to put your selection into effect.

Introducing BOB

This section provides a quick explanation of one more advanced option in the AWE Control dialog box: the Break-Out Box, or BOB for short.

MIDI files consist of a series of instructions. Those instructions include which instrument to play, and its volume and other sound characteristics. In fact, there can be sixteen series of instructions in effect at any given time; each of those sets of instructions is called a *channel*.

Switching Channels

Channel is an often-used word when it comes to PC sound and can mean different things at different times. In this case, a channel is a series of MIDI instructions. However, the term also can refer to the sounds that come out of your right or left speakers.

BOB is a tool for fine-tuning each channel in a MIDI song during playback. Everyday, Sound Blaster users need never worry about this level of detail, but if you're a musician or technically inclined, you may want to use BOB to fine-tune playback of each channel.

Display BOB by clicking the **BOB** button in the AWE32 Control dialog box.

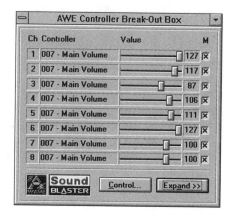

Controlling MIDI playback with BOB.

Initially, you see a contracted version of BOB that shows controls only for the first eight channels. If you click the **Expand** button, you'll see all sixteen channels.

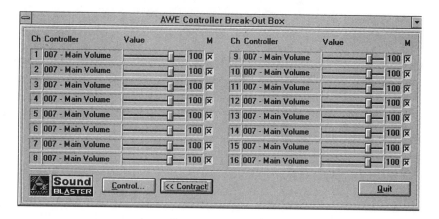

The full BOB dialog box.

To confuse matters a bit more, Creative Labs also calls each channel a *slot*. Each slot in BOB has the following settings:

➤ **Channel** The channel number.

➤ **Controller** The element of that channel you are controlling. The default element is Main Volume, but there are other elements you can control for each channel. I'll explain how to switch among these elements shortly. There is a slider bar for setting the precise value you want for that element.

199

➤ **Value**   The level you select with the slider bar.

➤ **Master control**   The check box. With an X in the check box, you can use BOB to control that particular channel element. Without the X, you won't be able to control the element.

As I mentioned, the default controller is Main Volume, which sets the volume for that channel, but you also can set other things to control with BOB. Those "things" are elements of MIDI that only a serious MIDI musician would care about, such as setting the level of variations of sound modulation for that channel (hey—I told you it was technical!).

If you're technically inclined, to use other settings:

➤ Click the **Control-menu box** in the upper left corner of the BOB window.

➤ From the menu, select **Slot Setup**. From the Slot Setup dialog box, select a different item to control.

➤ After you select a different type of controller, click the **Apply** button.

I want to repeat: this is complex stuff and unless you are a technically adept MIDI musician, don't mess with BOB.

You can save specific settings by clicking once on the **Control-menu box** in the upper left corner of the BOB window and selecting **Save As**. Give your settings a name of as much as eight characters and the .BOB file name extension. You can open previously saved settings by clicking on the **Control-menu box**, selecting **Open** from the menu, and then selecting the previously saved settings.

Now... with QSound

To be frank, at this writing QSound is more of an excellent idea than a reality. But that may change, and when it does, you'll be a very happy camper. That's why I devote a portion of this chapter to it.

QSound uses the ASP chip that is included on many models of Sound Blaster 16 and AWE32. It's a technology that enables you to hear sounds outside the physical boundaries of your speakers.

Here's an example of what this technology *could* do. Say you're playing DOOM. One of the curses of DOOM is that evil hellspawn can sneak up from the side and kill you. If— and this is a huge if—DOOM was programmed for QSound, you could hear the hellspawn sneaking up from the side, even if your speakers are located in front of you. This means you could spin, blow away the hellspawn, and be on your way.

It sounds wonderful (in a grisly sort of way), but the reality is that, at this writing, there are virtually no games or other applications written for QSound. So, when you play DOOM, you still must watch your backside.

That may change because Creative Labs is aggressively trying to convince developers to include QSound capabilities in their programs. They have a fair amount of leverage; Sound Blaster is, after all, by far the best-selling line of sound cards.

So, let's talk a bit about QSound, how to set it up and even how to play with it a little bit.

First, a Word About MIDI

The example I provided pertains to WAV files. To enable QSound for MIDI playback with the AWE32, open the AWE32 Control dialog box. Click the arrow of the **Effect Types** drop-down list, and select **QSound**.

Having told you how to do this, here's a strong suggestion: don't bother. If you select QSound, you won't get the full, richer sound you get by selecting Reverb & Chorus. What you hear will sound comparatively flat.

Sound Blaster does, however, come with a couple of demonstrations of the benefits of QSound with WAV files. The following sections describe how to get ready to use QSound and how to play with it a little bit.

Getting Ready for QSound

Speaker placement is critically important whenever you listen to sounds or music, but with QSound, it's particularly important. So let's take a moment and make sure that your speakers are:

➤ Evenly separated. That is, one speaker should be on each side of you and each should be equidistant from you. I suggest placing your speakers between eighteen inches and four feet apart. Experiment to find the distance that works best for you.

➤ At the same height.

➤ Slanted directly toward you.

To help you experiment with speaker placement, Sound Blaster comes with a DOS program called QSAlign. This program helps you align your speakers so that they provide the optimal sound when using QSound.

201

Before you use this program, remember you must load special DOS drivers. The initial Sound Blaster installation program asked if you wanted to load these drivers. If these drivers aren't loaded, QSAlign won't work. If you answered **No** during installation, rerun installation and answer **Yes**. When you finish re-installing, reboot your computer by pressing **Ctrl+Alt+Delete**.

Next, switch to the **\SB16\QSOUND** subdirectory. Do that by first typing **C:** and pressing **Enter**. Then type CD **\SB16** and press **Enter**. At the prompt, type **QSALIGN** and press **Enter**. You will see a screen showing a top-down view of your monitors and speakers.

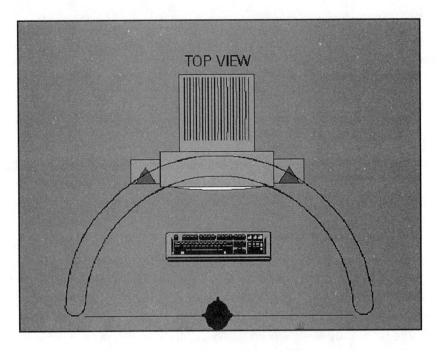

The QSAlign program.

Press the right and left arrow keys to hear QSound out of your right and left speakers. Move your speakers until QSound sounds right to you—this is a personal thing. To exit the QSAlign program, press **ESC**.

Using the QSound Dialog Box

You can adjust QSound from within Windows. To do that, in the Sound Blaster program group, double-click the **QSound** icon. You will see the QSound Control dialog box.

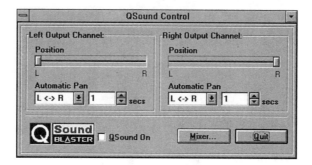

Controlling QSound.

In the QSound Control dialog box, you set specific QSound effects for each of your two speakers (called, in this case, *channels*).

➤ To separate the sound as much as possible, drag the right channel all the way to the right and the left all the way to the left.

➤ You also can set a *panning* effect for each channel. This effect gives the impression that the sound is moving from left to right or from right to left. Select the panning effect for each channel from the **Automatic Pan** drop-down list. If you don't want a panning effect, select **None** from the list.

➤ Select how frequently you want the panning effect to occur in each channel by clicking on the up or down arrows to the right of the **Automatic Pan** drop-down list.

➤ Make sure you activate the **QSound On** check box; it will have an **X** in it. If it doesn't, click the box and the X appears.

When you finish, click the **Quit** button.

Playing with QSound

As I mentioned, QSound is a fantastic technology but few software vendors have made their wares QSound-ready. Still, Sound Blaster comes with a couple of opportunities to experience QSound. One is in Windows and the other is in DOS.

For Windows, Creative Labs included a little game called Mosaic. This is a simple and self-explanatory game in which you rearrange the squares containing numbers or pictures so they are in the correct sequence. To play this game, click the **Mosaic** icon in the Sound Blaster program group. When you click a square, the resulting sound effect is played back with QSound.

There are several ways to hear sound effects in Mosaic:

➤ Click a square if there's an empty square next to it.

➤ Click a square that doesn't have an empty space next to it.

➤ Click an empty space.

➤ Reach 100 moves.

➤ You win.

➤ You start a new game.

An even better demonstration of QSound is in DOS. In DOS, switch to the **\SB16\QSOUND** directory. Then type **QSDEMO** and press **Enter**. As with the QSAlign program discussed previously, you must load the special DOS drivers to run QSDemo. If you didn't install these drivers, you must rerun the Sound Blaster installation program and reboot your computer.

When QSDemo starts, you'll see an on-screen text description of how QSound works. Then you'll see the following screen.

Shoot 'em up with QSound.

In this demo, the cowboy moves around the screen and fires his gun. You can hear the gunshot coming at you from various directions. True, it isn't the most dynamic demonstration in the world, but it does a good job of showing you what QSound is capable of.

The Least You Need to Know

This chapter covered some advanced topics.

➤ AWE32 users use the AWE32 Control dialog box to emulate the sounds heard in different types of rooms.

➤ You can use the AWE32 Control dialog box to change sound banks, which assigns different sounds to different MIDI instruments.

➤ You also can access the Break-Out Box (BOB) from the AWE32 Control dialog box. You use BOB to make some complex technical changes to how MIDI plays back.

➤ QSound, which is available in Sound Blaster 16 and AWE32 boards with Advanced Signal Processing, can make sound seem to come from outside the range of your speakers.

➤ You must precisely align your speakers with QSAlign to make QSound work well.

➤ There are relatively few programs that take advantage of QSound—so far. Sound Blaster does, however, come with two ways to demonstrate QSound.

Of Voice and Text

If you're aboard the Starship *Enterprise* and you want information, what do you do? You ask the computer—with your voice. The computer consults its knowledge base and it responds—in its voice.

Pretty futuristic stuff, huh? Nope. Some elements of that "fantasy" came with your Sound Blaster—at least if your Sound Blaster came with the Advanced Signal Processing (ASP) chip.

These futuristic programs go by the name of *TextAssist* and *VoiceAssist*. TextAssist turns the words you write with your PC applications into spoken words. VoiceAssist turns words you speak into commands that control your computing environment.

These are really cool programs, and this chapter tells you how to use them.

First Things First

If you want to use TextAssist and VoiceAssist with your Windows applications, you must be prepared. That's not difficult, but make sure before you proceed. Specifically, make sure:

➤ Your Sound Blaster includes the ASP chip. (Check the outside of the Sound Blaster box or your Sound Blaster documentation to find this information.)

➤ During Sound Blaster installation you installed TextAssist and VoiceAssist. Read Chapter 7 for information about installing Sound Blaster 16 and Chapter 8 for information about installing Sound Blaster AWE32.

➤ You connected your speakers to Sound Blaster.

➤ You connected your microphone to Sound Blaster for using VoiceAssist. Read Chapter 9 for information about connecting your microphone (and speakers).

➤ Know how to use Creative Mixer (described in Chapter 15) to set the correct input level for your microphone for VoiceAssist. This might take some trial and error.

Just thought I'd check. Now, on to the fun stuff.

Using TextAssist

TextAssist reads the words in your documents. It does this by using the ASP chip on your Sound Blaster to synthesize voices. TextAssist is fun, but it also can be useful. Specifically, it's useful in the following instances:

➤ People with vision impairments can hear words instead of reading them.

➤ It's an excellent way to proofread documents. It often is simpler and more accurate to hear what you wrote and correct it than to read it. This is particularly true with spreadsheets and other applications involving numbers.

➤ You can use the included Soundo'LE application (discussed in Chapter 19) to add voice descriptions and narrations that you include with e-mail or other applications.

So let's cut right to the chase. The next section tells you how to use TextAssist to read from your applications.

Hearing Your Text Quickly

We'll refine our usage of TextAssist later, but first let's get some instant gratification. With TextAssist, it's easy to get up and running quickly. To start, open an application such as a word processor. Then type something or open a document.

In the TextAssist program group created during Sound Blaster installation, double-click the **TextReader** icon. This adds four buttons to the title bar of your application, at the far left side.

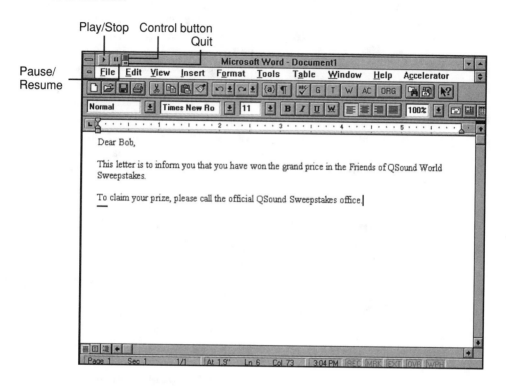

TextAssist in Word for Windows.

From left to right, the buttons are:

➤ The Play/Stop button.

➤ The Pause/Resume button

➤ The TextAssist Control button for displaying a dialog box in which you adjust the playback.

➤ The Quit button.

These latter two buttons are stacked, one on top of the other.

To have TextAssist read to you, highlight some text. Then click the **Play/Stop** button.

What If It Doesn't Work?

If you start TextAssist and get an on-screen message saying the proper driver (CSP.SYS) isn't installed, don't fear. The Sound Blaster installation program asked whether it should install drivers so you could automatically perform certain functions in DOS. If you selected **No** when the installation program asked if you wanted to install these drivers, you must rerun the installation program and answer **Yes**.

To stop the reading before it finishes, click the **Play/Stop** button. Note that while TextAssist is reading to you, the mark on the Play/Stop button is a square. To pause the reading, click the **Pause/Resume** button.

Speak Like a Nobel Prize Winner

If you've ever heard the Nobel Prize winning physicist Stephen Hawking "speak," you've already heard something like TextAssist. Hawking, who suffers from a debilitating disease sometimes called Lou Gehrig's Disease, has poor control over his vocal chords. As a result, he uses computerized speech synthesis such as TextAssist. He writes with his computer, which then converts his words to speech.

To adjust various aspects of the reading, click the **Control** button, which is in the top right side of the TextAssist group of buttons. When you click this button, TextAssist displays the TextAssist Reader Controls dialog box.

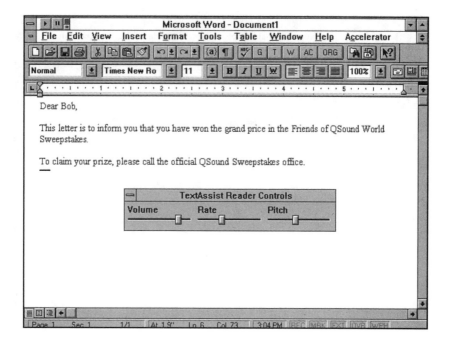

Controlling TextAssist.

The dialog box includes slider bars, which you adjust by dragging them with your mouse. The slider bars are for adjusting:

➤ Volume.

➤ Rate, which is how fast TextAssist reads back text.

➤ Pitch, which is how high or low the TextAssist "voice" sounds.

When you finish making your settings, double-click the **Close** button to remove the TextAssist Reader Controls dialog box from your screen. To close TextAssist, click the **Close** button, which is the bottom right button in the group.

Besides adding the four buttons to the title bar of your application, TextAssist also adds the Reader option to your application's Control menu. You access the Control menu by clicking once on the **Control-menu box** in the upper left corner of the application window. When you click the **Reader** command, you see a submenu with various options that enable you to play and control TextAssist.

More Than One Way... If for some reason the TextAssist buttons don't appear in your title bar, you still can control TextAssist from the Reader menu.

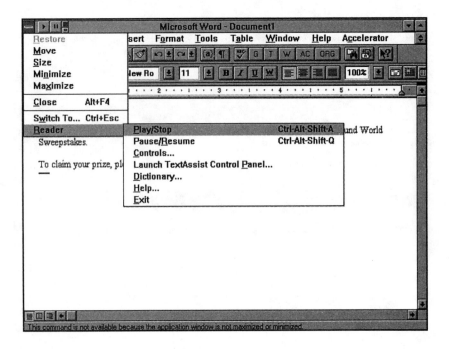

The TextAssist menu.

The first three options in the menu replicate the first three buttons in the title bar. The last command in the menu, Exit, replicates the fourth TextAssist button. Two other commands call up the TextAssist Control Panel and the Dictionary, which are the topics of the following sections.

Finding Your Voice in the TextAssist Control Panel

The TextAssist Control Panel is where you establish the characteristics of each of TextAssist's nine included voices. You also can create a new voice with the characteristics you choose.

After you load TextReader, display the TextAssist Control Panel by clicking on the **Control-menu box** and selecting **Reader**. Then select **Controls**. You also can display the TextAssist Control Panel by double-clicking on the **TA Control Panel** icon in the TextAssist program group.

TextAssist Control Panel.

The Control Panel has an extensive set of voice characteristics you can set for each voice. The first three characteristics—volume, rate, and pitch—are in the default view of the TextAssist Control Panel. To access even more voice characteristics, click the **Advanced** button. The dialog box expands to show more voice characteristics.

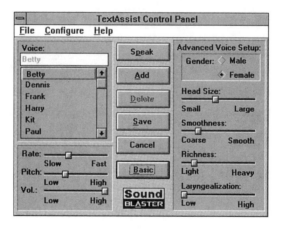

The advanced dialog box for precise settings.

To hear a voice, highlight it and then click the **Speak** button. While listening to the voice, you can change voice characteristics; you change most characteristics with slider bars.

The added options in the Advanced dialog box are for creating the voice you want to hear. They are:

➤ **Gender** Select between male and female.

➤ **Head size** Incredibly, the size of your head affects the tone of your voice. Larger heads produce richer tones.

➤ **Smoothness**

➤ **Richness**

➤ **Laryngealization** Refers to the level of "gravel" in the voice.

When you set a voice precisely as you want, click the **Save** button.

You also can create your own voices if you don't like the supplied voices. To do that:

1. Click the **Add** button.

2. Type a name for the voice in the text box that appears.

3. Set the characteristics for the voice.

4. Save the new voice. TextAssist adds it to the list.

Different Application, Different Voice

TextAssist is an agreeable application; besides changing the quality of the voices, you also can have a specific voice speaking in different applications.

To set different voices for different applications, from the TextAssist Control Panel select **Configure**, **Associations**. TextAssist displays the Application Associations dialog box.

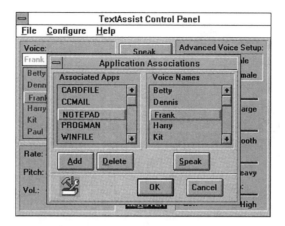

Associating voices to applications.

Next, click an application in the Associated Apps window and then a voice in the Voice Names window. To listen to a voice before selecting it, click the **Speak** button. To delete an item from the Associated Apps window, click **Delete**.

To add a new application, click **Add**. The right window turns into the Running Apps window, which shows all applications that currently are running. To add a program to the Associated Apps window, highlight it in the Running Apps window and click **Add**.

To associate a voice to the new application, highlight the program in the Associated Apps program and click **Change**. Then follow the procedures I just described for associating a voice to an application.

Making It Sound Right

You also can make sure that TextAssist pronounces your words the way you want them pronounced. This is useful if you use, say, a specialized set of technical words. To do this, you add words to a dictionary.

My Words Are Special

Using the dictionary for ensuring proper pronunciation is useful if you frequently use specialized words, such as scientific words or words that are specific to your industry or organization.

215

To add a pronunciation to the dictionary:

1. Click the **Dictionary** icon in the TextAssist program group. You will see the TextAssist Dictionary dialog box.

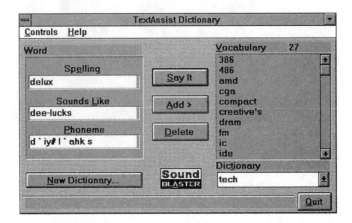

Adding words to the dictionary.

2. Select a specific dictionary you want to use from the **Dictionary** drop-down list. Or, create a new dictionary by clicking **New Dictionary**.

3. Type the word in the **Spelling** text box. As you do so, the technical pronunciation is automatically placed in the Phoneme text box.

4. Click **Say It** to see how the word sounds. If it doesn't sound right, spell it phoneti-cally in the Sounds Like text box. You may, for example, put dashes between syllables. Or you could spell the word to make the pronunciation more obvious.

For example, to put the emphasis on the first syllable of the word "deluxe," type **dee-lucks** in the Sounds Like text box. It takes a bit of practice, but you'll soon get the hang of it.

You determine which dictionary is in effect from the TextAssist Control Panel. Select **Configure, Dictionary**. You will then see a dialog box listing the dictionaries. Highlight the dictionary you want and click **OK**.

Using VoiceAssist

Here's the deal: Instead of typing or mousing out all those pesky commands, such as File Save, you can use words to tell your computer what to do. For some, this is an easier, more natural way to do things. Best of all, your computer won't talk back. That's what VoiceAssist is all about; it's *speech recognition software*. It converts spoken commands to computer commands.

To load VoiceAssist, click its icon in the Sound Blaster program group. Notice there are two parts to the main VoiceAssist Window.

Speech Recognition Software   This software recognizes your voice. You speak into a microphone and your computer does your bidding. VoiceAssist, which comes with versions of Sound Blaster that have the ASP chip, is a good example of this type of software.

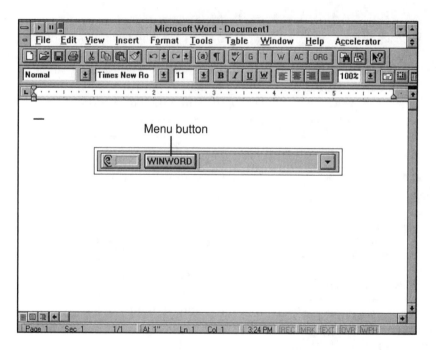

VoiceAssist carries out your commands.

➤ On the left is a button with an image of an ear. If the ear has an X over it, VoiceAssist isn't activated. If the ear has no X over it, the program is activated and is listening for your commands.

You switch between active and inactive modes by clicking on this button. When you speak into the microphone while VoiceAssist is active, this button also displays a voice meter showing the loudness level of your voice.

➤ The Menu button shows the currently active application. Also, clicking on it leads to a menu.

It is important to know that, when it's active, VoiceAssist knows which application you are using. That's because each application can have its own commands.

For example, as I write this, the word **WINWORD** appears in the menu button. This indicates that VoiceAssist is ready to accept and respond to voice commands for Microsoft Word for Windows.

Communicating and Controlling

Programs like VoiceAssist are known as *command and control* software because they only handle commands that control Windows and your applications. More advanced speech recognition products, however, let you dictate into your applications. At this writing, dictation software requires that you pause between words, which takes some getting used to. Vendors promise that continuous speech dictation software is just a few years away.

Problems with Mike Remember that many microphones, including the one that comes with Sound Blaster, are "on" as soon as you connect them to your sound card. So if they are close, say, to your keyboard, you may hear yourself typing through your speakers. You can minimize this problem by using Creative Mixer to lower the microphone input levels. Read Chapter 15 to learn how to use Creative Mixer.

VoiceAssist works best when you train it to recognize your voice. Also, you sometimes must teach it which commands to carry out. The next two sections describe how to do that.

VoiceAssist Quick Start

When you start using VoiceAssist, you must set yourself up as a user. This is important because VoiceAssist becomes more accurate the more you work with it and train it. Without your own "account," this increased accuracy can't happen.

To become a user:

1. Click the **Menu** button and select **User** from the menu. VoiceAssist displays the User & Application Files dialog box.

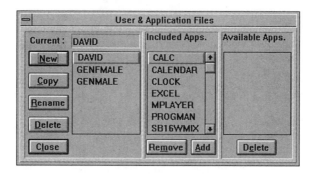

Becoming a VoiceAssist user.

2. If you are a female, click the **GENFMALE** selection; if you are a male, click the **GENMALE** selection. These are generic user files for males and females.

3. Click the **Copy** button and type your name in the ensuing text box. Click **OK** and then **Close**. This creates and loads a user file for you based on the generic user file.

In theory, you should now be able to use VoiceAssist. Try this: speaking directly into the microphone, say "calculator." If everything goes well, the Windows Calculator accessory program should appear on-screen. But, as we all know, things don't always go well. That means you must train VoiceAssist to work with your voice.

VoiceAssist Basic Training

Training is optional, but it makes VoiceAssist more accurate. It actually is two separate tasks: one task is getting VoiceAssist to recognize your voice and the other is creating and editing commands that you can launch with your voice. You accomplish both tasks from the training dialog box, which you can display by clicking on VoiceAssist's **Menu** button, and then selecting **Training**.

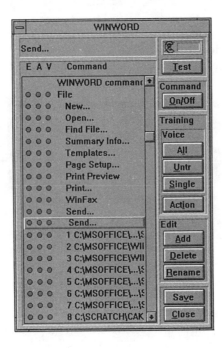

The training dialog box.

The large list in this dialog box contains all available commands. Some commands are generic and others work only with the currently open application. For example, the dialog box might include generic commands and commands for Word for Windows.

To the left of each command are three dots. The left dot, when it is green, indicates the command is named and listed. The second dot indicates the command has a specific task attached to it. The third dot indicates whether you trained VoiceAssist to launch the command.

To the right is a plethora of buttons, some of which may not have immediately obvious meanings. The top button, Test, lets you test to see if VoiceAssist recognizes your voice when you say the command.

To test a command, highlight it and click the **Test** button. Then speak the command into the microphone. If the command name appears at the top of the command window, the command is trained properly for your voice.

The On/Off button enables or disables a command. When disabled, the command won't execute when you say it into a microphone. To enable or disable a command, highlight the **On/Off** command and then click the button. Note that the leftmost dot indicator for the highlighted command toggles on and off as you click this button.

The next four buttons are for training. Let's start with the Single button. This trains VoiceAssist to work only with the command you highlighted. When you highlight a command and click this button, the Voice Training dialog box appears.

Training VoiceAssist.

The word or phrase you are training appears at the top of the Voice Training dialog box. You can determine how many times you train VoiceAssist to recognize this particular word or phrase by clicking on the up and down arrows.

Training... and Retraining

The more you train a word, the more likely it is to work correctly. However, in my experience, virtually all words and phrases work correctly with only one repetition.

When you are ready to train, click the **OK** button and say the word directly into the microphone. If you selected multiple trainings, you must repeat the word. After you repeat the word, the dialog box disappears and you should be able to successfully use that word to issue commands.

To train all the commands in the left window, click the **All** button. To untrain a command so you can retrain it, click the **Untr** button.

Creating Commands

To add a new command for a specific program, click the **Add** button and then type the name of the command in the Command Name dialog box. This adds the command to the list, but you're still not ready to use it. (Note that you can't add "generic" commands that work for all programs.)

First, of course, you must train it to your voice, as described in the previous section. You also must record the actual command, or sequence of events. For example, you could create a command that, at the verbal command "Save," saves a file.

To affix a sequence of events to the command, highlight the command name in the left window. Then click the **Action** button. The Recording Options dialog box appears.

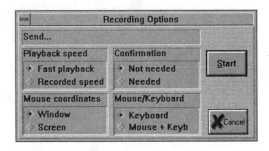

Setting recording options.

The options in the Recording Options dialog box determine how VoiceAssist records your actions. The options are:

➤ **Playback speed**   Refers to whether the command plays at the speed at which you recorded it or at the maximum possible speed.

➤ **Confirmation**   Refers to whether you receive on-screen confirmation of commands.

➤ **Mouse coordinates**   Refers to the position of your mouse. **Window** records mouse movements only within your application. **Screen** records them anywhere on your screen.

➤ **Mouse/Keyboard**   Refers to whether keyboard actions or both mouse and keyboard actions are recorded.

After you make your selections, click **Start**. This causes a blinking VoiceAssist icon to appear. All actions you take at this point are recorded. When you finish, press the **Pause** key on your keyboard. A dialog box asks if you want to save the actions or cancel the recording. Select the record action.

So, if you were creating a command called "Save," you would press **Alt+F** and then **S**, which are the keystrokes for saving files in Windows. When you return to the commands dialog box, click **Save** to confirm your new command. Then click **Close** to close the dialog box and resume using Voice Assist.

The Final Options

There are only a couple more options to set. If you click the VoiceAssist **Menu** button and select **Options**, you'll see the Options dialog box.

Setting options.

The Options dialog box only has two options:

➤ **Always on top** has VoiceAssist appear above other items on your screen.

➤ **Start active** tells VoiceAssist to automatically be in active mode awaiting your commands whenever you launch it.

Now, if there was some way that TextAssist could speak to VoiceAssist, we wouldn't need to work at all, would we?

The Least You Need to Know

Sound Blaster gives you two significant ways to hear voices.

➤ TextAssist turns the text you type in your applications into spoken words.

➤ TextAssist is useful for the vision-impaired and for proofreading documents.

➤ VoiceAssist turns spoken commands into actions that replace keyboard and mouse actions.

➤ VoiceAssist works in most Windows applications.

➤ You must train VoiceAssist to recognize your voice.

Sound Blaster on the Job

Sure, Sound Blaster is for having fun and playing games. But, alas, life isn't *all* fun and games.

Sound cards also are becoming increasingly important in the workplace. In this chapter, you'll learn about how to use Sound Blaster at work and also how to get up and running with more work-oriented tools that come with Sound Blaster.

At the Office with Sound Blaster

When it comes to Sound Blaster at work, I jumped the gun a bit in Chapter 18. That chapter was about using TextAssist to read text aloud. This is useful for proofreading documents, particularly those such as spreadsheets that have a lot of numbers.

Chapter 18 also discussed VoiceAssist, which turns your spoken commands into computer actions. This is useful in the workplace when your hands must be free for other chores. However, the number—and the importance—of other sound-related applications may surprise you. The next few sections describe some of those applications. Note, though, that you can only incorporate sound into your Windows applications; Sound Blaster doesn't provide tools for doing this in DOS.

Now Presenting...

Presentations are perhaps the single most important type of business application involving sound. Business presentation programs are one of the fastest-growing types of software.

Increasingly, these presentations include all multimedia elements, including video, animation, and still images, as well as sound and music. For example, you can include photos of products, corporate officers, and customers. Or you can include animated corporate logos or videos of the Big Boss sharing her wit and wisdom. You can also show instructional videos, such as how to accomplish a specific task.

It's important to realize these multimedia elements often are accompanied by music or sounds. Presentations often have background music, which are MIDI files. Or a photo of, say, your company's leading scientist accompanied by a *voice-over* of him describing the development process for a new product. This voice-over would be a WAV file.

Animations and videos also usually include sound such as voice-overs or background music. The bottom line is that if you are creating business presentations, you need a sound card.

Typical examples of presentations are:

➤ **Sales presentations**   Quickly fading into the past are the days of flip-chart-based presentations. Today, sales personnel tote laptop computers that they hook up to video projectors that display their computerized presentations. Part of these presentations are background music and sounds related to your product. The best part is that sales personnel often can leave behind copies of their presentations so potential customers can look at them at their leisure.

➤ **Training sessions**   These teach customers how to use a product. Or they teach employees how to sell a product or how to avoid workplace perils. These could include narrated videos.

➤ **Investor and corporate relations**   Looking for new investors? Explaining corporate strategies to current investors? These days, high stakes ventures almost always involve a multimedia presentation including charts showing sales and profits. These multimedia presentations may include audioclips of corporate officers or other investors.

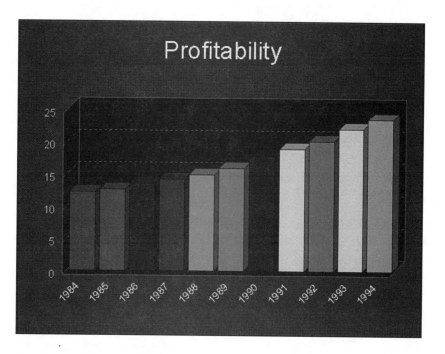

A presentation explaining your company's profits.

➤ **Organizational motivation**   Say your company is rolling out a new product or taking a new direction. Multimedia presentations are an excellent way to help employees understand—and become enthusiastic about—the new direction.

This Memo Speaks to Me

Your departmental budget is due today. Finally, you get the last piece you need to put the entire budget document together before you pass it on to your superiors: the spreadsheet developed by Filbert, a key manager and ace number cruncher. However, the spreadsheet is big and complex, and there are some parts that you don't understand. Even worse, Filbert took off for Bali as soon as he finished the spreadsheet.

The happy ending to this story is that Filbert annotated his spreadsheet with WAV sound files he recorded. Specifically, he added WAV files to explain the most difficult-to-understand parts of the spreadsheet. The result: your superiors congratulate you for the fine work done by you and your team. And Filbert has a job to come home to.

Voice annotations can be clearer and easier to follow than written comments. They also have a more immediate feel. That's why annotations are becoming increasingly common in the workplace. Besides adding them to spreadsheets, voice annotations can serve as:

➤ **Adjuncts to electronic mail.** For example, the text part of the e-mail message can say: "Mr. Flyspeck, we have received a lot of irate calls from customers about our new widgets. I've attached some recordings of customer calls so you can hear what they're saying."

➤ **Introductions to memos and reports.** This personalizes these often-impersonal tomes and, as a result, increases their impact.

"Edutainment" Can Be Fun

There is a glut of "edutainment" CD-ROM titles on the market. Many are aimed at home use, but many are useful in the office, too. I'm thinking, for example, of multimedia atlases and guides that are useful for business travelers. They can help you learn the customs of foreign lands in which you must do business or simply help you find your way around a distant city. Often these discs have sound such as music that is indigenous to a specific part of the world.

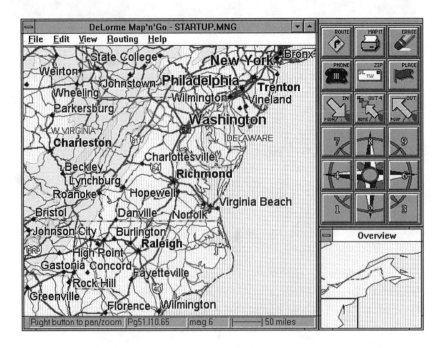

Learning about new places.

Also, an increasing number of reference works such as multimedia encyclopedias often are useful for business research.

Tools of the Trade

Having told you about some of the uses of sound cards in the workplace, now let's briefly discuss some of the tools you need—besides Sound Blaster and some speakers, of course.

Presentation Software Use this software to wow customers, employees, or investors. Well-known examples of presentation software include Microsoft PowerPoint and Harvard Graphics.

The most common type of software package used in the workplace that makes use of sound cards is *presentation software*. Presentation software specializes in—you guessed it—creating presentations. Even the most elementary of these programs integrates sound into presentations.

There are two broad categories of presentation software:

➤ **Business presentation software** This popular type of software creates traditional presentations based on slides you show in sequential order. These programs are a natural outgrowth of the old-fashioned slide shows—in fact, many people still use them to create slides.

However, more and more, people use these programs to create sophisticated on-screen presentations that include multimedia such as sound. Some of the better-known products in this category are Microsoft PowerPoint, Lotus Freelance Graphics, and Harvard Graphics.

➤ **Multimedia authoring tools** These create more sophisticated, interactive presentations. While average PC users can use relatively simple products such as Harvard Graphics to create professional presentations that include sound, authoring tools provide more sophistication still. And they are more difficult to use.

HSC InterActive, included with many Sound Blaster cards, is a sophisticated multimedia authoring program. However, it's different in one important way: while sophisticated, it is relatively easy to use. I will introduce HSC InterActive later in this chapter.

You also need software for creating and embedding sound annotations in your documents. There are many programs for recording sounds. You can, for example, record your voice using EnsembleWAVE, explained in Chapter 16. But for annotations, the software also needs the capability to *embed* sounds in your Windows applications. This takes a separate set of software capabilities that programs such as EnsembleWAVE don't have.

Specifically, the program must embed the sound in your Windows documents using Object Linking and Embedding. This also is known as OLE and is pronounced like what the crowd yells at a bullfight. It is a method of blending files created with one program into the files you create with another.

Happily, Sound Blaster comes with a program for embedding sounds in your documents: Soundo'LE. That's what the next section is about.

Embedding with Creative Soundo'LE

Say you want to impress your boss, Ms. Ratchet, with all the work you put into an important memo. You know she has a Sound Blaster card, so why not go hog-wild and embed a vocal introduction into the memo. It's easy to do with Soundo'LE, which comes with your Sound Blaster.

First, of course, you must properly connect your microphone to your Sound Blaster. That's easy enough—I described how to do that in Chapter 9.

The next step varies a bit from application to application. In all cases, you start from within the main application such as the word processor you're using to create a memo. There is a menu selection somewhere in your word processor for inserting an embedded object.

For example, in Microsoft Office products (such as Word for Windows and Excel) and Novell PerfectOffice products (such as WordPerfect for Windows and Quattro Pro), you would open the **Insert** menu and choose the **Object** command. For other applications, you may need to search through the menus a bit to find the correct option. At any rate, when you select this option, a dialog box appears listing all the different types of objects you can embed in your document.

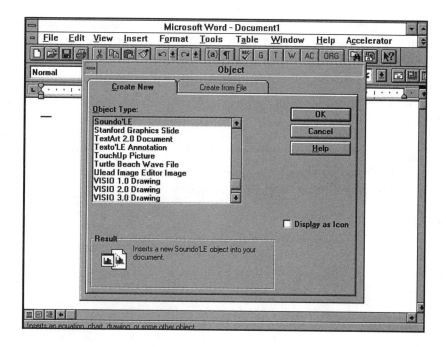

Inserting objects in Word for Windows.

Scroll through the Object Type list until you find the listing for Soundo'LE. Highlight it by clicking on it, and then click **OK**. The Soundo'LE window then appears.

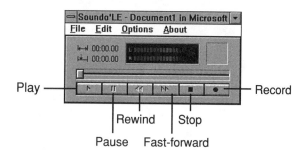

Soundo'LE for embedding sounds.

Soundo'LE lets you record sound in WAV format or use already-recorded sounds. It then embeds the sounds into your document. Let's start with sounds you record, like that description of the memo you are using to brownnose, uh, impress your boss.

First, tell Soundo'LE what type of sound you want to record. Do that by selecting the **Options** menu and choosing **Recording Settings**. Soundo'LE displays the Recording Settings dialog box.

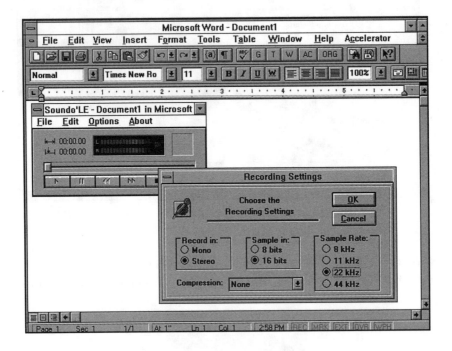

Making sound settings.

In the Recording Settings dialog box, you select whether you are recording in mono or stereo and in 8-bit or 16-bit mode. You also select the sampling rate. For a reminder about what these things mean, read Chapter 2. But to briefly reiterate, stereo sounds better than mono, 16-bit sounds better than 8-bit, and the higher the sampling rate, the higher the sound quality.

Also in this dialog box, you can compress the sound file so it takes less space on your disk. This is useful because WAV files, which you create with Soundo'LE, require a lot of storage space. If you create a longer recording, I suggest you use one of the compression options. Note, though, if you use the Creative ADPCM method of compression, the recipient of your recording must also have a Sound Blaster 16 or AWE32 sound card that supports this method.

After selecting your recording settings, click **OK**.

Recording It Right

Unless you are particularly demanding, I suggest recording voices in 8-bit stereo with a 22KHz sampling rate. This provides a good balance between sound quality and the need to conserve disk space for storing your WAV file.

The control buttons in Soundo'LE, from left to right, are: Play, Pause, Rewind, Fast-forward, Stop, and Record. Try a sample recording by clicking on the **Record** button and speaking directly into the microphone. Say something like, "Ms. Ratchet, after working day and night for the last three months, I'm proud to present you with this memo... ."

When you finish, click the **Stop** button. Change the recording characteristics if necessary. Also, you can change the volume and balance of the recording by selecting **Options, Mixer Settings**. This displays the Creative Mixer, which Chapter 15 discusses.

When the recording is the way you want it, select **File, Exit**. Soundo'LE closes and you return to your application. You should see a little icon in your application; this is the embedded sound.

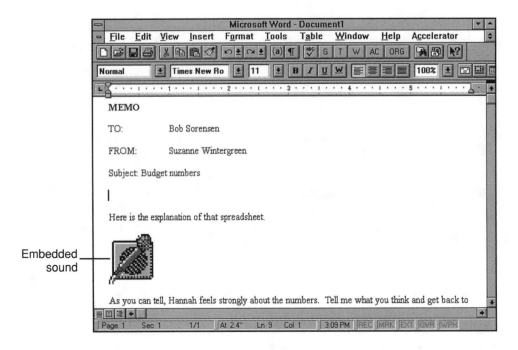

Embedded sound

The sound icon in a document.

To listen to the recording, double-click the icon for it in your document. The recording plays even if Soundo'LE isn't loaded. Note, though, that Soundo'LE or another program capable of playing WAV files must be present on the listener's computer in order to hear the sound.

Do It the Easy Way

Here's a neat shortcut for embedding the sound. After you finish recording, there is an image of a microphone on the right side of the Soundo'LE window. Click that image and hold down your left mouse button. Then drag your mouse to the place in your document where you want the sound icon to appear and release the mouse button.

To use an already-recorded sound, select **File, Open** and select the sound file in the dialog box. Click the **Play** button to make sure it is precisely the sound you want. Then follow the procedures I just mentioned to embed it in your document.

Ms. Ratchet is sure to be impressed.

Getting Started with HSC InterActive SE

For basic multimedia presentations, use presentation software such as Microsoft PowerPoint or my favorite—a little-known product called Astound from Gold Disk. These Windows programs are reasonably adept at handling multimedia, including sound.

However, if you want more sophisticated multimedia presentations, you must use a product like HSC InterActive. This is a Windows program that professional multimedia authors use to create multimedia titles, including many commercial titles.

A special, simplified version called HSC InterActive SE comes with many Sound Blaster cards such as the AWE32. My purpose here isn't to help you become an expert in this feature-rich program, but rather to set the stage for your explorations with it.

Before using it, you must install HSC InterActive SE; the Sound Blaster installation program doesn't do that for you. To install HSC InterActive:

1. Place the HSC InterActive disk in your floppy drive.

2. In Program Manager, select **File, Run**. In the text box, type **A:\SETUP.EXE** (substitute another drive letter if you're using a floppy drive other than A:) and press **Enter**.

3. Follow the on-screen directions for installing HSC InterActive SE.

When you finish installation, start the program by double-clicking on its program-item icon in the HSC program group that the installation program created in Windows.

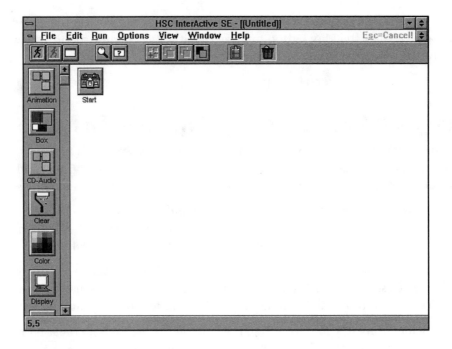

The HSC InterActive opening screen.

How HSC InterActive Works

HSC InterActive is comparatively simple because, unlike other multimedia authoring software, it doesn't require programming skills. Rather, you build presentations by dragging icons representing specific actions into a work area. You place these icons into a flowchart-like structure that determines the order of the presentation. You can change the order simply by dragging icons to a different location.

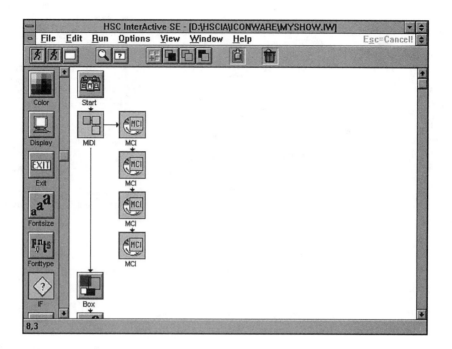

Creating an HSC InterActive presentation.

You start by selecting **File, New**. The icons you drag to the work area are along the left side of the screen. You drag an icon from the left side of the screen to the work area and drop it below or next to an existing icon.

You must be careful to place icons in the correct order. For example, if you want to add text to a presentation, you would drag the **Write** icon to the work area. But if you want to control the size, font, and other characteristics of the text, you must drag the **Size** and **Fonts** icons to the work area and place them sequentially before the Write icon.

To set specific characteristics for the action represented by an icon, you double-click it. A dialog box appears called a content editor.

In the content editor dialog boxes, you fine-tune how the icon acts on-screen. For example, you would type the words you want to appear on-screen in the content editor for the Write icon. You also set the text's on-screen location.

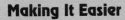

Making It Easier

To play sounds in HSC InterActive, you must use so-called MCI commands in the content editor dialog boxes. These are commands used within Windows to control playback of sounds, music, and other multimedia objects such as video.

This is complicated to learn, but HSC InterActive SE makes it easy—relatively. If you drag, say, a MIDI icon to the work area, HSC actually displays several icons, each of which performs a specific MCI function. Read the manual that comes with HSC InterActive SE to learn about these functions. Often with HSC InterActive, you need only know where to type in the name of a MIDI or WAV file to get it to play.

Even though this is easy compared to other multimedia authoring systems, you still need a fundamental understanding of how your PC and Windows operate to create presentations in HSC InterActive.

But give it a try—you won't break anything and I think you'll get the hang of it more quickly than you might expect. I found this program to be fun because, once I got over the initial learning curve, I could easily create some interesting and fun applications.

The Least You Need to Know

Sound Blaster isn't just for fun and games; it has many uses in the workplace.

➤ Presentations including sounds and music are effective tools for selling, training, and motivating.

➤ The HSC InterActive program that comes with many versions of Sound Blaster is a sophisticated way to create multimedia presentations.

➤ You also can embed sounds in business documents to annotate or explain them.

➤ The Soundo'LE program that comes with Sound Blaster enables you to embed sounds.

Giving Sound Blaster More Skills

Some people just can't get enough. You know the type—they crave power, fast cars…and the most complete sound card they can buy. If that's you, Sound Blaster is the right card to have. In Part 4, you'll learn about the advanced capabilities of Sound Blaster and how to make Sound Blaster even more powerful.

I assume that you own a version of Sound Blaster that is expandable. Certain cards such as the value editions of Sound Blaster 16 and AWE32 and the new Sound Blaster 32 have limited expansion capabilities. Expandability, of course, is something to keep in mind when you buy a sound card. Also keep in mind that if you just use your Sound Blaster for listening to sounds and music, you won't need most of these upgrades. Rather, these upgrades are for musicians and, as I mentioned, performance freaks.

If that's you, read on. If that's not you, close this book and go have some fun with your Sound Blaster.

Adding the ASP Chip

One of the things that gives Sound Blaster its unique capabilities is the Advanced Signal Processing (ASP) chip, but if you were on a budget when you bought your Sound Blaster, your card may not have this chip. That's because the "budget" versions of Sound Blaster don't include this little marvel.

To ASP... or Not to ASP...

The easiest way to find out whether your card has the ASP chip is to read the box in which your Sound Blaster came. Creative Labs is quite proud of the ASP chip and, if your card has it, your box will say so.

What can the ASP chip do for you? It enables you to make use of the following:

➤ The VoiceAssist program, which converts spoken words into commands that control your applications and Windows environment. Read Chapter 18 to learn about VoiceAssist.

➤ The TextAssist program, which turns text and numbers in your applications into spoken words you hear through your speakers. Read Chapter 18 to learn more about this program.

➤ Qsound, which is software that enables sound to seem like it's coming from outside the range of your speakers.

In addition, the ASP chip improves the performance of:

➤ **Soundo'LE**   This enables you to record sounds and embed those sounds in your documents. You can, for example, insert a spoken introduction into a memo. Read Chapter 19 for more information about Soundo'LE.

➤ **File compression**   This refers to the process of storing files on less disk space than they otherwise would require. (It's kind of like the computer equivalent of sitting on a suitcase so you can get more stuff into it.) Soundo'LE, described in Chapter 19, can compress sounds as it saves them. The ASP chip helps speed the process of compressing sounds and then uncompressing them when you use them. This process works without the ASP chip, but it's much faster with the chip.

If you bought the value edition of either the Sound Blaster 16 or the AWE32, you may want to upgrade to the ASP chip (the new Sound Blaster 32 doesn't provide the capability to upgrade). Chances are, you can buy the ASP upgrade from the retailer from whom you initially bought your card. If you can't find the upgrade, though, call Creative Labs at 800-998-1000.

Upgrading to the ASP chip is simple—follow the instructions that come with the chip. You must:

➤ Turn off and unplug your computer and take off the top as described in Chapter 6.

➤ Take the Sound Blaster out of the computer.

➤ Plug the ASP chip into the socket for the ASP. The instructions describe the precise location of the socket on the card.

➤ Insert the software disk that came with the upgrade pack into your floppy drive and run the installation program. Follow the on-screen instructions.

Be Chip-wise
Whenever plugging any chip into any socket, beware. Insert the chip very carefully so that you don't bend any of the prongs (also called pins) that plug into the socket. All pins must be firmly seated inside the socket. If you bend a pin during the installation process, it becomes much more difficult to use the chip.

When you finish, you will have the benefits of the ASP chip.

Adding Memory

If you are a serious MIDI musician (or if you want to be), you can add memory to your standard AWE32 card. This enables you to load additional sound font banks. Chapter 23 describes the uses of sound font banks and how to load them.

You already learned that wave-table synthesis cards such as the AWE32 play MIDI sounds by using digital sound samples. For example, a grand piano sound is a digital sample of that particular instrument. That's why wave-table synthesis cards sound more realistic than FM synthesis cards, which synthetically recreate the instrument's sounds.

Memory Limitations
You can't add memory to the AWE32 value edition, Sound Blaster 32, or to any 16-bit Sound Blasters.

A sound bank, as described in Chapter 23, is a custom set of digital samples for MIDI instruments that replaces the normal MIDI instruments. Serious musicians are very picky about the quality of the MIDI instruments. Put differently, they may want a slightly different sound quality for, say, the grand piano sound than they would normally get with AWE32. The CD-ROM that comes with this book includes a number of professionally created sound font banks that you can experiment with if you have a standard edition of the AWE32.

For musicians, one of the beauties of the AWE32 is that you can load multiple sound font banks at the same time. But when's the last time you came across something beneficial that was absolutely free? Loading sound font banks requires memory; the more sound banks you load, the more memory you need on your AWE32.

The standard version of AWE32 comes with 512K of on-board RAM, but if you're serious about adding sound banks, you'll need more. Much more. In most cases, 512K of RAM is only enough to load a single sound font bank, and some sound font banks require even more.

Was That a Tuba?

On a lighter note, you can use sound font banks for giggles even if you aren't a serious musician. There are sound font banks available with novelty sounds so that, say, the grand piano you hear is replaced by a pop or a whistle or a hilarious bodily function sound. Hey—different strokes... .

The purpose of this section is to tell you how to upgrade the memory of your standard AWE32 or Sound Blaster 32 card so you can load those sound banks.

Just like your PC, memory for your Sound Blaster comes on SIMMs, which stands for Single Inline Memory Modules. A single SIMM is typically an inch or so wide and several inches long. You plug SIMMs into Sound Blaster and you're done, which is much easier than inserting eight or ten individual chips for each megabyte of memory like you had to do in the old days.

SIMMs Standard Inline Memory Modules, or SIMMs, are the little wafers of memory you add to your computer to in-crease its RAM. You also use SIMMs to increase the RAM on your Sound Blaster card.

SIMMs typically contain either 1M, 4M, 8M, or 16M of RAM. Computer stores often carry SIMMs, but if you want to save money (and SIMMs aren't cheap), you can order them mail order. The mail order firm I use is H. Co (800-726-2477).

Your AWE32 comes with two empty SIMM sockets. Here are some rules of thumb about adding memory to your AWE32:

➤ You must add SIMMs to both sockets. To add 8M of RAM, for example, you must add two 4M SIMMs.

➤ The SIMMs you add must be identical, so you can't add a 4M SIMM and a 2M SIMM to create an additional 6M of RAM. Don't ask me why—that's just the way it is.

➤ You must buy precisely the correct type of SIMMs or they may not fit in the sockets or they may not work. Specifically (write this down!), you must order 30-pin, 1 X 9 (called one by nine) SIMMs. This refers to the construction of the SIMMs.

Leftover SIMMs

If for some strange reason you have SIMMs left over from your PC, don't assume they will work in your Sound Blaster—unless your PC is an older model. That's because, for the last couple of years, most SIMMs used for system memory on PCs are 72-pin SIMMs. Before that, though, 30-pin SIMMs were commonly used in PCs. These older SIMMs may well work with your Sound Blaster.

To install your new SIMMs, you must first, of course, turn off and unplug your PC, take the top off, and take out the AWE32 card. Reread Chapter 6 for a refresher on how to do this. The sockets for your SIMMs are in the upper left corner of the card.

Easy Does It

If you've never inserted new SIMMs into your PC to increase your computer's random-access memory, this is a good way to learn. That's because the principles of inserting SIMMs into a Sound Blaster are the same, but it is much simpler to do. When inserting SIMMs into your PC's motherboard, you typically must contort yourself to fit the SIMMs in between the other components. With your Sound Blaster, the SIMM sockets are, almost literally, in your lap and are easier to get at.

Hold the card so that all the circuits and electronic doodads face you and that the gold-plated connectors are facing down. Notice in the upper left corner there are two long horizontal slots. That's where the SIMMs go.

Now, if you haven't already, take a good look at a SIMM. Notice that there are little chips on it and that there are holes at each end. Now look at the SIMM sockets on the AWE32. Notice that there are little latches into which the holes on the SIMM fit. You don't need a degree in engineering to figure out what to do next.

Slide each SIMM into the slot so that the chips face you. Do it in such a way that the holes snap into the latches. (It's easier to do than to describe.) When you finish this, press gently down on the SIMMs to make sure they are firmly in place and firmly latched. The SIMM shouldn't flop around if it's firmly seated.

You are almost finished. Put the sound card back in your PC and reconnect items such as your speakers. If you want, run the DIAGNOSE program from the DOS prompt (as described in Chapter 8). Among other things, this program tests on-board memory to make sure it's properly connected. If it isn't, take the board out and reseat the SIMMs.

All This and Wave Blaster II

Say you already own a Sound Blaster 16 and you want wave-table synthesis playback. Whatcha gonna do? Well, you could fork over the dough, buy an AWE32, and toss the old sound card. Or for about half that much, you can buy a Wave Blaster II card.

Wave Blaster II is what's known in the computer biz as a daughtercard. No, that doesn't mean it has big cute eyes and looks at you with loving appreciation as you read to it before bedtime.

Nope, a daughtercard is an add-on adapter that snaps onto another card. If you snap Wave Blaster into a Sound Blaster 16 card, you will have instant wave-table playback. If you snap it into an AWE32, your wave-table playback capabilities increase.

You also can connect a Wave Blaster to a number of other 16-bit sound cards not manufactured by Creative Labs. The only requirement is that the card have a so-called Wave Blaster connector. This is a 26-pin connector near the top of your sound card and toward the right side. Installation is a simple matter of snapping Wave Blaster into the Wave Blaster connector. Bingo bango—that's all there is to it. You're done. Finished. Have fun.

While it's simple, there are a couple more things you should know. First, there are two flavors of Wave Blaster II.

The standard edition is aimed at musicians and includes a copy of Cakewalk Apprentice, the MIDI sequencer I will describe in Chapter 23. However, there's also a version called Wave Blaster II GamePak. This version comes with a CD-ROM containing a number of games, but it doesn't come with Cakewalk Apprentice.

When a Wave Isn't Enough

Simply adding a Wave Blaster II to an FM synthesis card won't create a sound card that will satisfy serious MIDI musicians. That's because you still can't do things such as add memory so you can add sound font banks. Rather, adding a Wave Blaster to an FM synthesis card is aimed primarily at increasing your MIDI music playback pleasure.

It's important to understand why somebody would add a Wave Blaster II to an AWE32. At first, it doesn't make any sense. After all, Wave Blaster adds wave-table MIDI playback and the AWE32 already has that capability. But Wave Blaster II increases the quality of AWE32's MIDI capabilities. In musical techie terms, Wave Blaster II provides 64-note polyphony and 32 voice multitambral capabilities to AWE32.

Put differently, Wave Blaster II doubles these particular capabilities on your AWE32 card. For more information about these capabilities, read Chapter 23, which provides background about creating MIDI music.

The Least You Need to Know

You can increase the capabilities of many models of Sound Blaster. In this chapter, you learned that you can:

➤ Add an ASP chip to Sound Blasters that don't come with one. This improves your ability to record sound and to compress sound files to take less disk space.

➤ Serious musicians may want to add RAM to their AWE32 card. This enables them to load more sound font banks of customized instruments.

➤ The Wave Blaster card clips on to existing Sound Blaster 16 and AWE32 cards. It adds wave-table MIDI playback to Sound Blaster 16 and increases the MIDI music capabilities of the AWE32.

Part 4
Making Sound Blaster Sing and Dance

OK—I'm kidding about making Sound Blaster dance. But, boy, can this thing sing if you know how to use it.

In this part, you'll learn how to make your Sound Blaster more powerful so it sounds even better than when you bought it. You'll also learn about some of Sound Blaster's advanced skills of making sound effects and music.

And, proving once again that the best things in life are free, you'll also learn what's on the absolutely free CD-ROM that comes with this book. I'll give you this hint: there's a lot of fun on that disc.

parp parp
parp

Chapter 21

Recording Your Own Sounds

In This Chapter

➤ Getting the right settings

➤ Learning about mics

➤ Compressing sounds tightly

I just love to hear the sound of monsters dying in DOOM. And a good edutainment CD-ROM title that includes music and sounds really makes me happy. That's about all most people use their Sound Blaster for, but Sound Blaster also is an excellent tool for recording and creating music.

Chapter 22 describes how to create and edit WAV sound files using Creative WaveStudio. Chapter 23 is where you'll learn the basics about creating MIDI music. In this chapter, though, we cover the basics of sound recording. This background will prove quite helpful as we move into the specifics of creating sounds and music.

Doin' the Analog to Digital Dance

Let's start at the beginning—literally. Way back in Chapter 2, I discussed analog sounds and digital sounds. To briefly review:

➤ **Analog sounds** are those that occur continuously. For example, hitting a drum with a stick creates sound waves that travel through the air and enter your ear. The qualities of the sound, such as its pitch and loudness, depend on the qualities of the sound wave. Recording analog sounds is an old technology, usually involving magnetic tape that stores the analog signals.

➤ **Digital sounds** are those that a computer creates and stores. Computers don't understand physical waves. Rather, they understand computer language. Recording digital sounds is a newer technology. These digital sounds most frequently are stored in WAV files.

Recording the WAVs

A WAV file is, literally, a digital recording of a sound. But MIDI files aren't recorded music files. Rather, MIDI files are a series of instructions to Sound Blaster's synthesizer chip about which instrument to play and how to play it. This is a fine distinction but an important one, as we will discuss in Chapter 23.

Analog and digital sounds are two quite separate things. Computers can't intrinsically play analog sounds, and you could never hear digitized sounds. Unless you use a device like a sound card, what we would have here (to paraphrase an old movie) would be a failure to communicate.

Among its many talents, however, your Sound Blaster converts analog sounds from a microphone or a device such as an attached tape recorder to digital sounds. It also takes digital sounds and converts them to analog sounds that come out of your speakers.

Your Sound Blaster does this with a chip built into the board called a digital to analog converter, or DAC. Conversely, the capability to convert digital code to analog signals is managed by an analog to digital converter, called ADC. If you read Chapter 2, you already know this, but I wanted to remind you because I will go into more detail about this process in the rest of this chapter. I will go into more detail because if you're reading this part of the book, which covers more advanced topics, you are exploring the limits of your Sound Blaster's capabilities. The more you know about these processes, the more successful you will be.

Starting the Recording Process

We all know that some recordings sound better than others. If you create digital sound with your Sound Blaster, you undoubtedly will want to create the highest quality sounds possible. In this case, there are several critical elements that contribute to sound quality. The next few sections walk through those elements.

The purpose here isn't to turn you into a technical dweeb who thinks it's funny to wear a propeller beanie. Rather, the purpose is to help you make wise decisions when recording your sounds and creating your music.

Here's a Sample of Sound

When it comes to recording—whether it's analog or digital recording—it all begins with the microphone. Whether you are doing your best Tony Bennett imitation, speaking into it, or making funny sounds, the sound waves enter the mic and cause a little diaphragm to vibrate. The vibrating diaphragm causes tiny but important changes in voltage. Those changes in voltage reflect the nature of the sound waves.

If you make an analog recording, these fluctuations are sent to the recording head of a tape device, which translates them into magnetic patterns stored on the tape. The playback mechanism of the tape recorder reads those patterns and plays them back as they were recorded.

If you record directly into your Sound Blaster, the signal goes from the microphone to the sound card. There, the ADC takes *samples* of the incoming sound. The number of times per second that samples are taken and processed is the sampling rate, first mentioned in this book in Chapter 2.

So here's the first lesson in recording sounds with Sound Blaster: the higher the sampling rate, the better the playback sounds. Put differently, more samples make more realistic sound.

Even relatively poor sound quality takes samples many thousands of times per second. With Sound Blaster (and most other sound cards), the lowest sampling rate is 11,025 samples per second (also known as 11,025 hertz, or 11KHz (for *kilohertz*). You also can record using sampling rates of 22,050 and 44,100 samples per second.

To use a simple analogy, think of listening to a symphony while covering and uncovering your ears with your hands about twice a second. This represents a low sampling rate since you'll hear relatively little of the music.

If you increase the speed with which you cover and uncover your ears to four times a second, you will hear more of the music. This represents a higher sampling rate. (In real life, higher sampling rates don't cause headaches like you would get from quickly covering and uncovering your ears.)

Obviously, then, higher sampling rates sound better because you hear, quite literally, more sound. This, in turn, enables you to hear more nuances of the sound. More specifically, a higher sampling rate increases the range of frequencies that you hear. You'll hear more highs, more lows, and richer sounds in between.

However, the downside is this: a higher sampling rate requires that more data be stored in the WAV file, which requires much more disk storage space. As you'll learn later in this chapter, though, there are solutions and compromises to this problem.

A Lot About Bits

Here's another critical component to sound quality: *bits*. The ADC uses digitized bits of information that describe such factors as loudness. The more bits of information used to determine this information, the more accurate the digital recording and playback.

Early Sound Blasters were 8-bit cards because they handled 8 bits of information at a time. In fact, you can still buy 8-bit cards if you are on a tight budget or aren't demanding about sound quality.

Sound Blaster 16 and AWE32 are 16-bit cards. In the logarithmic world of computers, the switch from 8-bit to 16-bit capabilities is an order-of-magnitude improvement in sound quality, not just a twice-as-much improvement. But, once again, 16-bit digital sound files require much more storage space than 8-bit digital sound files. Hey—nothing that's good in life is free.

Mono and Stereo

Here's yet another important component to sound quality: stereo or mono. A mono recording is simpler; it has one channel of data, and that channel comes out both speakers. Stereo, on the other hand, has two channels of information. Often those channels contain the same information but, as described in Chapter 22, sometimes the channels contain somewhat different information.

However, even if both channels contain the same information, having two channels provides fuller, richer sound. That's why stereo sounds better than mono. And, not to sound repetitive, stereo requires more disk storage space than mono.

Comparison Shopping

If you're following all this techie talk, give yourself a pat on the back (being careful not to break your arm in the process). That's because you're getting ready to record and this information will help you make good decisions about how to do so.

When making decisions about the levels at which to record, consider:

➤ 16-bit stereo recordings with a 44.1KHz sampling rate are, technically speaking, audio CD quality recordings. Obviously, this is the way to go if you have unlimited disk storage space. A recording with these maximum settings requires roughly thirty times more disk space than the same recording using the lowest possible levels.

Audio CD Sound? Not!

True, technically speaking, 16-bit stereo recordings with a 44.1KHz sampling rate are audio CD quality. But in the real world, recordings with those levels made with your Sound Blaster (or any PC sound card) won't sound as good as a CD. That's because professional recording studios use higher quality equipment that costs thousands (or hundreds of thousands) of dollars. The result of this expensive equipment is, inevitably, higher sound quality.

➤ The highest sound quality for recordings is probably overkill for many applications. For simple voice recordings, I suggest either 8-bit or 16-bit stereo recordings at a 22KHz sampling level.

➤ For recording simple sound effects with many low, rumbly tones, lower recording settings may be satisfactory. For example, you may be able to get away with 8-bit stereo or mono settings at 11KHz or 22KHz.

➤ If you record complex sounds with a variety of tones and textures, err on the high side of the settings.

Complicating factors is the use of tape recorders. You can use a tape recorder to record sounds, and then plug the recorder into your Sound Blaster's Line in jack to capture the tape recording in digital form.

This is a common way to capture sounds because it's not always practical to drag your PC around. However, each time you transfer a sound from one source to another, you lose a bit of sound quality. It's kind of like photocopying an original laser-printed document. If you copy the copy, eventually it doesn't look so good anymore. If you transfer a magnetic recording device to your computer via your Sound Blaster card, err on the side of higher recording levels.

Master Digital

Until recently, many original professional music recordings—called *masters*—were made on magnetic tape and then transferred to the recording medium you bought in record stores. In the old days, these masters eventually led to vinyl records, so creating masters on tape made sense. However, creating a tape master and converting it to a digital medium such as audio CDs caused some loss of sound quality. That's why, until it became increasingly common, record companies bragged when their music was "digitally mastered."

Why Mic Is Important

Enough! Let's stop this technical discussion for a moment and return to the mic. Since the whole recording process starts with your microphone, that device is critical to sound quality.

When selecting a microphone, remember that:

➤ The quality of the microphone's materials, such as the diaphragm I mentioned previously, is critically important. If getting the highest possible sound quality is important, then spend the money to buy a quality microphone.

The microphone that comes with many models of Sound Blaster is adequate for tasks such as recording voice-overs for multimedia presentations (as we discuss in Chapter 22). But it frankly isn't adequate for demanding, professional-level uses.

➤ You also must consider the directionality of the microphone. Some microphones such as the one that comes with Sound Blaster are *unidirectional*. That is, they accept sounds from a relatively narrow physical range. Put differently, you must speak directly into them or sound quality drops off.

Unidirectional mics are good for recording voices. That's because they pick up relatively little background noise (sometimes called *ambient* noise) such as the fan on your PC.

Other microphones are *omnidirectional*: they are good at collecting sounds from many directions. This makes them better for tasks in which you want to capture a lot of ambient sounds. For example, you would use an omnidirectional microphone if you were in the woods capturing the sounds of nature. However, this type of microphone isn't always particularly good for recording voices because it picks up much background sound.

Let's Compress

I've talked quite a bit about file size and how, as you add quality to the recording, the file size increases dramatically. Sound Blasters with the Advanced Signal Processing (ASP) chip offer an alternative: *file compression.*

File compression temporarily alters files so they take less disk space. Sound Blasters support file compression in two ways:

➤ The Soundo'LE program, discussed in Chapter 19, can record and automatically compress sound files.

➤ Sound Blaster automatically plays compressed files. When it finishes playing the files, it automatically recompresses them.

Recordings made at the highest quality level can require a humongous amount of disk space. I just recorded a WAV file, for example, that chewed up 1M for every twenty seconds of recording time. Compression decreases those disk requirements by as many as eight times.

This is getting repetitive, but we all know this sad reality of life: nothing is free. When you compress files, you lose some sound quality. As a result, if you are going to compress the file, increase the recording settings. It takes some experience, though, to find the right balance between storage requirements and sound quality.

Another thing to remember is that Sound Blaster doesn't play the sound file while it's compressed. Rather, it rapidly uncompresses the file, plays it, and recompresses it. This means that you need enough disk storage space available to handle the file when it is uncompressed.

One Compresses, the Other Doesn't While Soundo'LE can record and compress files, WaveStudio, which is the subject of the next chapter, can't compress as it records. However, WaveStudio automatically compresses and uncompresses sound files created by Soundo'LE. That means you can use Wave-Studio to edit compressed files.

For example, a three-minute high-quality recording can require about 10M of storage space when it is uncompressed. Compression can cut that to a quarter of that requirement, or about 2.5M. However, you need the full 10M of free disk space to actually play the file.

The compression levels vary according to the method of compression you use. Some methods compress as tightly as 8:1. The tighter the compression, the more sound quality you lose.

If compression causes a loss of sound quality and you need the disk space to uncompress the file anyway, why bother with compression? For one thing, most people only listen to one file at a time. If you store many of these 10M (or higher) monster sound files on your disk, you'll still save disk space by compressing them. In general, though, don't use compression unless you need to.

On the (Recording) Level

Setting the correct recording level is important. Set a level that's too soft and, not surprisingly, you can't hear. Set a level that's too high and you get what's known as *clipping*, which is a form of distorted sound.

The Creative Mixer, discussed in Chapter 15, is the tool that comes with Sound Blaster for setting recording and playback levels.

Creative Mixer sets recording and playback levels.

To review, Creative Mixer has nine vertical slider bars for setting recording and playback levels. You drag the slider bars up and down with your mouse to increase and decrease the levels. Below most of the slider bars are other slider bars to control the balance between your speakers for playback or recording.

If you are transferring sounds from a device such as a tape recorder or CD player that you attach to Sound Blaster's Line in jack, use Creative Mixer's line input control. This is the seventh controller from the left.

If you are recording with a microphone, use the microphone input controller. This is the eighth controller from the left in the Creative Mixer window.

While recording, I suggest using the VU meter display in Creative Mixer. As described in Chapter 15, this shows the levels for both the right and left channels during both recording and playback.

Get It Right!

Setting the correct recording level is something of an art. The bottom line, though, is that you want the highest possible recording level without it being so high that you get periodic sound distortion. The only way to perfect this art is to experiment a bit before you record.

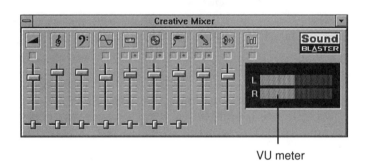

VU meter

Creative Mixer's VU meter display.

If you consistently "bury" the VU meter display all the way in the right side of the display, your recording level is too high and you'll get a lot of distortion. Rather, the recording level should be as high as possible without bumping into the right side of the display. To set the correct level, take some sample recordings and experiment.

Recording Other Sounds

Sometimes, you must record items from other sound sources. For example, you may need to record MIDI and audio CD tracks as WAV files and other times you must create a sound file from a tape recording.

When would you record a MIDI song or an audio CD track to a WAV file? Not often. Most applications that use sound and music support both WAV files and MIDI files.

However, say you want to use a music clip from a royalty-free clip-media collection and combine it with a voice-over. Then, you would need the music in WAV format and record the voice directly over the music using a program like Creative WaveStudio.

The process for gathering sounds from other sources is relatively straightforward. If you are grabbing sound from a tape recorder, connect the recorder to Sound Blaster's Line in device.

Honor Thy Copyright

I've said it before and I'll say it again: do not use copyrighted material. The contents of audio CDs that you buy in a record store are almost always protected by copyright laws. Unless you enjoy becoming entangled in the legal system and potentially suffering severe penalties, you won't enjoy being caught using copyrighted material.

If you are recording from a CD in your CD-ROM player or from a MIDI file, you need not make any special connections. Simply load both your recording software, such as WaveStudio or Soundo'LE, and the player for audio CD (such as EnsembleCD) or MIDI (such as EnsembleMIDI).

In the application you are using for recording, make all your recording settings like the sampling rate. Also, use your mixer, such as Creative Mixer, to set the playback and recording levels and balance for both pieces of software.

Finally, start recording and then begin playing the piece with either the tape recorder or the MIDI or CD player. The recording application records the music. When you finish, press the **Stop** button in the recording application. Then stop the player or tape recorder.

There may be a lag of a second or two at the beginning of the recorded file. However, that is easy to eliminate using a sound editor like WaveStudio, which is the topic of the next chapter. (Chapter 22 goes into more detail about the recording and sound editing process.)

The Least You Need to Know

If you care about the sound quality of items you record, you need to know the basics in this chapter.

➤ Higher sampling rates result in fuller, richer sound.

➤ Similarly, the higher the number of bits, the better the sound. A 16-bit recording sounds much better than an 8-bit recording.

➤ There is a trade-off between sound quality and disk storage space. Recordings with better quality have steeper storage requirements.

➤ If you record with Soundo'LE, your Sound Blaster can compress sound files to take less space and uncompress them when you want to play them.

More Complex Sounds

In This Chapter

➤ Cutting out unnecessary sounds

➤ Professional sound recording

➤ Sound effects galore

There are sounds… and there are sounds. Sure you can record any old sound, but if you are picky, any old sound isn't good enough. As you learned in the last chapter, there are many elements that contribute to sound quality. These elements include sampling rates, the number of bits used in the recording, and whether you record in mono or stereo. But there's more still to sound quality than those elements. When you record digitally, you also have great latitude to alter and edit those sounds, fine-tuning and polishing them so they are exactly like you want.

Many versions of Sound Blaster come with Creative WaveStudio. This is a full-featured program for editing WAV files that you record or obtain from other sources, like the CD-ROM that comes with this book.

In this chapter, you'll learn how to use Creative WaveStudio. It's fun and very helpful if you are using sounds for things such as business presentations.

Catching the Wave(Studio)

Say you need to record a sound and you want to record it precisely. That means you want to "trim" unnecessary parts from the beginning and end of the recording. Or perhaps you want to merge it with other sounds or change the playback characteristics of the sound such as the volume of a specific section. That's what Creative WaveStudio is all about. It provides a thorough tool chest for those who are recording and fine-tuning sounds.

Here's an example of when you'd use Creative WaveStudio. You are creating a business presentation about your company and an exciting new line of products. As part of the presentation, you record the boss, Ms. Ratchet, describing the company and its product line.

Ms. Ratchet's thoughts are brilliant, but her delivery is something less than stellar. Specifically, Ms. R. adds a lot of *um's* and *ah's* and her voice fades out every now and then. Before you put the recording into a multimedia presentation (such as one you'd create with HSC InterActive, which is described in Chapter 19), it needs some work.

Creative WaveStudio is like a recording studio on your PC. When you finish with Ms. Ratchet's voice recording, she'll not only say brilliant things but she'll sound brilliant saying them. And we all know what that means for your career... .

Firing Up Creative WaveStudio

Let's start with the easy stuff: starting Creative WaveStudio. To do that, double-click the **WaveStudio** icon in the Sound Blaster program group.

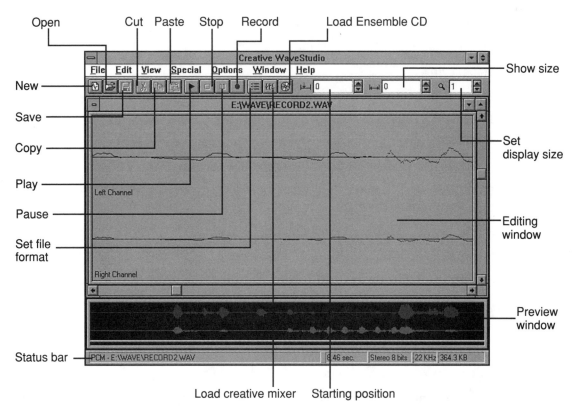

Creative WaveStudio.

Now for a quick guided tour. Just below the menus is the toolbar. You click toolbar buttons to accomplish common tasks. From left to right, the toolbar buttons are:

➤ Create a new sound file.

➤ Open an existing WAV file.

➤ Save the current WAV file.

➤ Cut a part of a WAV file to the Windows Clipboard. This eliminates that section from the current file.

➤ Copy a part of a WAV file to the Windows Clipboard. This keeps that section in the current file.

➤ Paste the portion of the WAV file you cut or copied into the current file.

➤ Play the currently loaded WAV file.

➤ Stop playing.

➤ Pause or continue playback.

➤ Record a WAV file.

➤ Set the recording format.

➤ Load Creative Mixer, which you learned about in Chapter 15.

➤ Load CreativeCD, which plays audio CDs in your CD-ROM player. This enables you to re-record audio CD tracks as WAV files.

➤ Set the beginning point of the sound in the WAV file.

➤ Show the size of the WAV file or selected section.

➤ Set the size of the display of the WAV file.

Below the toolbar is the editing window. This is a window that displays, in graphical format, the WAV file. It's also the place in which you edit WAV files.

Below the edit window is the preview window. This shows the entire WAV file. Use the preview window to select a portion of the file to edit.

At the bottom of WaveStudio is the status bar. This shows the name of the file and its length, file format, and size.

Takin' WaveStudio Out for a Spin

Let's keep it simple a while longer by loading an existing sound file and listening to it. To load a file, click the **File Open** button in the toolbar.

In the Open Sound File dialog box, select the drive on which the sound files are located in the Drives drop-down list. Select the directory of the files in the Directory window. If you don't know the location of some WAV files, select your Windows directory, which is probably **C:\WINDOWS**.

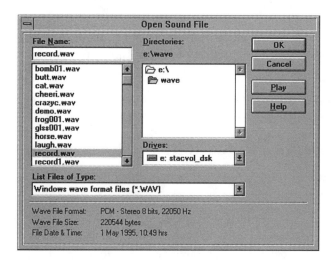

Opening a sound file.

The Open Sound File dialog box is like most Open dialog boxes in most Windows applications, but with a couple of differences.

First, at the bottom of this dialog box is information about the format and size of the file and when it was created. Also, you can hear the file before you load it by clicking the **Play** button.

Highlight a WAV file in the File Name window; play it first if you want. Then click **OK** to load it into WaveStudio.

The contents of the file show up as a series of oscilloscope-like waves in the edit and preview windows. Play the file by clicking on the **Play** button in the toolbar. Notice that a progress bar beneath the preview window shows progress through the sound file as it plays.

They're Not the Same

At first, the editing and preview windows may seem similar, but the preview window shows the entire file at once, while the editing window shows only a small portion. Also, you can't perform all sound editing functions in the preview window. You can, however, drag to highlight a portion of a sound in the preview window and cut or copy that portion. Notice that when you highlight a portion of a file in the preview window, it also becomes highlighted in the edit window.

263

Think of the file displayed in WaveStudio as you would a word processing file. Just as letters and words are the editable form of your thoughts, the display in WaveStudio is the editable form of a sound. You can cut, copy, and paste portions of the sound like you do with words in a word processing document.

Also, like you change fonts and font sizes in a word processor, you can change the characteristics of the sound file. You'll learn how in the next section.

Playing Around in WaveStudio

Now, let's play with the sound you selected. After all, we learn better when we're having fun. I do, anyway.

However, just like a mother, I have a caution before you go out and play. We will be changing the sound. If you want to keep the original sound, either back it up or don't save any of the changes you make. Saving changes to a WAV file is like changing and saving a word processing file; once you do it, there's no going back.

With a WAV file loaded, let's explore the Special menu. Many of the options in this menu enable you to apply special effects to the entire sound or a selected portion of the sound.

In the preview window, highlight a portion of the sound. Do that by clicking your mouse on the beginning point of the section you want to hear. Hold down the left mouse button and drag to the end of the section you want to edit or hear. Release the mouse button; notice that you've highlighted the section of the file.

Click the **Play** button on the toolbar to hear the portion of the clip you highlighted.

Now You Hear It...

Particularly if it's short, highlight enough of the sound clip so you can hear it clearly. If you only highlight one-fourth of a two-second clip, the sound comes and goes very quickly.

Now, let's play—and learn how to use WaveStudio. Among the options in the Special menu are:

➤ **Reverse**   This plays the selected section backward. Depending on the sound clip, you may not notice. For example, unless you're a cat, a meow sounds pretty much the same forward and backward. But if you're editing Ms. Ratchet's speech, you'll certainly notice.

➤ **Add Echo**   Adds the echo effect to either the entire sound clip or the part you highlighted. When you select this option, you will see the Add Echo dialog box.

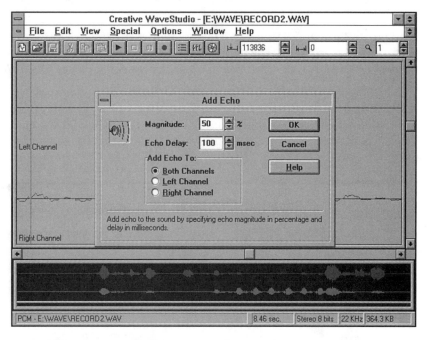

Adding echo effects.

In this dialog box, you adjust the magnitude, which is the loudness of the effect, and the delay before you hear the echo. If the WAV file is stereo, you also can choose the channel for playing back the effect.

➤ **Invert Waveform**   Essentially plays the WAV file back "inside out." This is different from the reverse option; it's more like a mirror image of the sound. If the WAV file is in stereo, selecting this option displays a dialog box in which you select the channel to apply this effect to.

➤ **Rap**   One of my favorites. It repeats the highlighted section of the WAV file, a common effect in rap music. But be careful in choosing when to use this effect. If you apply it to Ms. Ratchet's audio clip, she could become extremely angry.

➤ **Insert Silence**   Adds a period of silence into the sound clip. The silence doesn't replace or mute any recorded sounds.

➤ **Force to Silence**   Mutes the part of the file you highlighted. If you are using a stereo clip, a dialog appears in which you tell which channels should be silent.

➤ **Fade In** and **Fade Out**   As the names imply, you can fade the sound you selected in and out. If you select either option, you will see a dialog box in which you select the magnitude of the effect.

➤ **Pan Left to Right** and **Pan Right to Left**   Causes the stereo sounds to appear to move from one speaker to the other. These effects, which you probably have heard in musical recordings, are sure to make your listeners say things like, "Wow, man!" and "far out."

➤ **Phase Shift**   Another effect with "Wow, man" potential. It delays the playback of a channel in a stereo WAV file. If you select this option, you will see the Phase Shift dialog box in which you select the delay and the channel to which you want to apply it.

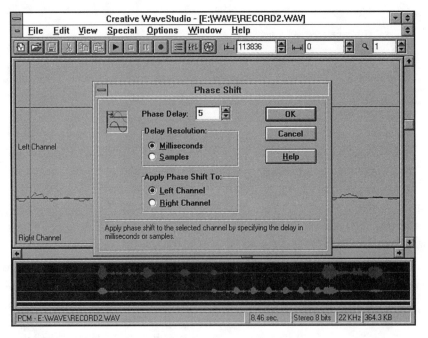

Applying a phase shift.

After making each change, click the **Play** button on the toolbar to hear what your change sounds like. Even if you don't have a serious purpose such as perfecting a recording by Ms. Ratchet, this is a lot of fun. But remember—if you add a special effect and save the file, you can't undo the effect.

Enough fun! Now it's time to get back to work and learn about some of the more practical aspects of WaveStudio. There are a few options in the Special menu I skipped over. I didn't mention them because they aren't fun to play with and I wanted to start out with the fun stuff.

But here are some more menu options:

➤ **Swap Channels**   Simply switches channels in stereo WAV files. What was in the right channel switches to the left and vice versa.

➤ **Convert format**   Enables you to change the recording settings. You can, for example, increase the sampling rate and sampling size or switch from mono to stereo. Read Chapter 2 for a reminder about what those terms mean. You would do this either to increase sound quality or to decrease quality to save space.

➤ **Amplify Volume**   Increases the volume of the portion of the file you select. This is useful, as you'll learn, so you can better hear specific parts of a recording.

Cutting, Copying, and Pasting Sound

As you get serious about sound editing, cutting and pasting is an essential operation. It's also relatively simple; conceptually, it's similar to cutting and pasting in your word processor. Here's how:

➤ Highlight the section you want to cut or copy in either the editing or preview windows. Play the highlighted section to make sure it's precisely the sound you want.

➤ In the **Edit** menu, select, as appropriate, **Cut**, which deletes the sound and places it in the Windows Clipboard, or **Copy**, which copies the highlighted sound to the Clipboard. Or use the **Cut** and **Copy** icons in the toolbar.

➤ Click precisely the spot in the sound file where you want to place the cut or copied sound.

➤ Select **Edit**, **Paste** to paste the information into the sound file. This adds the sound to the file without eliminating any other sound. Or use the **Paste** button in the toolbar.

➤ Select **Edit**, **Paste Mix** to add the sound saved to the Clipboard to the existing sound. If you do this, you'll hear both sounds.

Try it a few times. You can create some interesting effects with pasting. Open up a second sound file without closing the first and copy and paste between the two files.

Recording Ms. Ratchet with WaveStudio

Let's go back to the recording of Ms. Ratchet (a.k.a. The Big Boss) you are using in your multimedia presentation. In that clip, Ms. Ratchet talks about the company and the new product line. You plan to put this clip at the beginning of the presentation and it must be right. After all, this presentation is going to stockholders and big customers. If Ms. R. sounds like a dork, things won't go well for you.

So, let's quickly review how to record The Big Boss using WaveStudio. To do that, sit her down in front of a PC that has Creative WaveStudio and a Sound Blaster card. Needless to say, you need to connect a microphone to Sound Blaster and load WaveStudio. Next, open the **File** menu and choose **New**. This displays empty edit and preview windows. Then click the **Record** button in the toolbar. You will see the New Recording dialog box.

Helpful Hints on Recording

Here are some quick recording tips. It might seem obvious, but make sure the room in which you are recording is quiet and there will be no interruptions. If possible, block the fan noise coming from the PC by putting a cover on the PC or any other material between the microphone and computer. Make sure that, if Ms. Ratchet is reading from a script, that she doesn't rustle the papers or, even worse, bang them against the microphone during recording. Finally, don't let her get too close to the microphone or it will sound like she's spitting and sputtering into it.

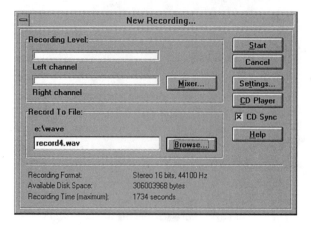

Starting a recording.

In this dialog box, click the **Settings** button to set the recording characteristics. You will see the Record settings dialog box.

Making your settings for a new recording.

Using a Recorder

Remember, you also can use a tape recorder to record Ms. Ratchet. When you finish, connect the tape recorder to Sound Blaster's Line in jack. Start playing the recorder, and then click WaveStudio's **Record** button. WaveStudio captures the recording.

Determine whether the recording is in mono or stereo and the sampling rate and sampling size. If necessary, read Chapters 2 and 22 to review what these items mean. Click **OK** when you've made your choices.

Next, select the directory and the file name for the WAV file in the Record To File part dialog box. I also suggest clicking on the **Mixer** button so that Creative Mixer is on-screen so you can quickly change recording levels.

Compression? Try Another Program If you need to compress the recording to save disk space, you are using the wrong program: WaveStudio can't compress as it records. To do that, record using the Soundo'LE program discussed in Chapter 19.

Finally, rush around yelling things such as "Quiet on the set." After that's out of your system, click the **Start** button and ask Ms. Ratchet to read the first paragraph of her statement. Notice that, during recording, a status window appears on-screen. When the recording is complete, click the **Stop** button in the status dialog box.

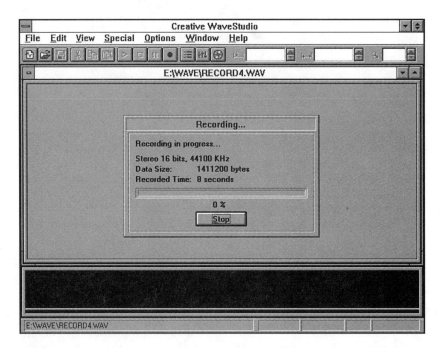

The recording status dialog.

Using Audio CDs

I don't mean to make short shrift of it, but you can use WaveStudio to record music from an audio CD. To do that, put the disc in your CD-ROM player and click the **Record** button. In the Record dialog box, activate the **CD Sync** check box and click **CD player** to load EnsembleMIDI. Click **Start** and WaveStudio automatically starts EnsembleMIDI and records the contents. Remember, though, that most material on audio CDs is copyrighted and, even for a simple presentation, you can run afoul of the law if you use copyrighted material.

Play back the test recording and see if you like it. If you don't, use Creative Mixer to make any adjustments you need to the volume, bass, treble, or other settings. Or change the recording settings by clicking on the Settings dialog box. When you finish testing, it's time to record all of Ms. Ratchet's immortal words.

Getting It Right with WaveStudio

Simply recording Ms. Ratchet isn't enough. As she read, she threw in a bunch of unnecessary *um's* and *uh's* and her voice kept getting louder and softer. If you really want that promotion, bonus, or whatever else trips your trigger, make sure that Ms. Ratchet sounds her best. So, let's get to work with her file—and resist the temptation (for now, anyway) to use the Rap special effect to make her sound really cool.

First, let's attack those pesky *uh*s and *um*s. As you play back the recording, click the **Stop** button to stop at the first *uh*. In either the edit window or the preview window, click the start of the ***uh*** and drag your mouse until the end of the ***uh***.

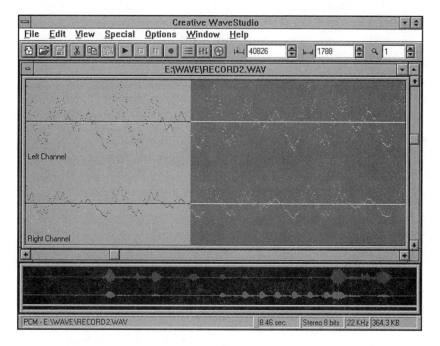

Highlighting a part of the sound file.

Click the **Play** button to hear what you highlighted. If you didn't get the entire errant sound—or if you got too much—try highlighting it again until you get it right.

When you get it just right, open the **Edit** menu, select **Cut**, and kiss that *uh* goodbye. Repeat the process until you eradicate all the errant sounds.

Oops! You realized that Ms. Ratchet forgot to begin with, "Hello, my name is Ms. Ratchet." Find that busy executive and get her to record that sentence. Then, open both the original WAV recording and the newly recorded addition (in WaveStudio you can keep multiple files open at the same time).

Highlight the entire introduction, and then select **Copy** from the **Edit** menu and close its editing window. Click the editing window with the main part of Ms. Ratchet's speech and click at the very beginning of the file. Finally, select **Edit, Paste**. This pastes the second sound clip into the main file.

You aren't finished yet. The way you pasted the second sound clip into the first makes the whole thing sound hurried. Ms. Ratchet sure will appreciate it if you place a thoughtful pause between the newly pasted "Hello, my name is Ms. Ratchet" and the rest of the file.

This time, highlight a part of the file immediately after the newly inserted introduction. Then, open the **Special** menu and choose **Insert Silence** to insert a pause. Now, Ms. Ratchet sounds thoughtful, serious, and not hurried.

Next, move to the section in the file where Ms. Ratchet's voice dropped. Highlight that section, open the **Special** menu and choose **Amplify Volume**. In the Amplify Volume dialog box, you determine how much to increase the volume of the highlighted part of the file. Also, if it's a stereo clip, you can determine the channels to amplify.

Now you're done. You deleted the *um*s and *uh*s, inserted an introduction and increased the volume where Ms. Ratchet's voice dropped. Now, she sounds professional and polished where before she sounded, uh, less than her usual perfect self. Who said you can't make a silk purse out of a sow's ear?

The Least You Need to Know

Creative WaveStudio is a powerful way to create and edit WAV sound clips. It is fun to play with, but it also has many serious uses.

➤ WaveStudio lets you create professional-level sound effects that help you create professional-sounding presentations.

➤ You can apply special effects such as the echo effect and panning the sound from left to right or right to left.

➤ You can use WaveStudio to cut out unnecessary elements of the sound clip.

➤ You also can use WaveStudio to increase the volume of specific sections of a sound file. This is useful, for example, in a voice recording in which the speaker's voice volume drops.

➤ Similarly, you can use WaveStudio to copy and paste the contents of another sound file.

Creating That Old MIDI Music

If I've mentioned the term MIDI once in this book, I've mentioned it a hundred times. MIDI is, by far, the most common form of digital music that you can play with your computer. Until now, however, we've mostly been concerned with playing back MIDI. In this chapter, however, we turn the tables a bit—we discuss creating and editing MIDI music.

Here's what you can't accomplish here. You *won't* learn how to be a MIDI musician in this chapter. That requires you to be a musician and, of course, this book is about Sound Blaster.

My purpose is to introduce you to MIDI and to Cakewalk Apprentice, which accompanies the AWE32 Standard Edition and the Wave Blaster II daughtercard. You also will learn more about sound font banks, which enable musicians to fine-tune the "instruments" played by Sound Blaster. Perhaps, this chapter will embolden you to learn more about creating MIDI music. Just like a proud parent, that would leave me with a warm glow.

The MIDI Backgrounder

Let's start at the beginning. MIDI stands for *Musical Instrument Digital Interface*. It's simple for beginners to think of MIDI as simply files with the .MID file name extension that play through a Sound Blaster card. MIDI is far more than just that, though.

MIDI dates back to the early '80s, which, not coincidentally, also was when personal computers became popular. MIDI is a standard that describes a variety of characteristics from how MIDI devices connect to each other to the contents of MIDI files.

The word *interface* is key to MIDI. Among other things, MIDI is a standardized method of connecting electronic musical equipment. The MIDI specification includes standards for the cables that connect MIDI devices and the interface ports to which you connect those cables. However, you don't even need a PC to create MIDI music. Rather, you need only MIDI devices. Such devices typically include "instruments" such as synthesizers. Your Sound Blaster includes a built-in synthesizer chip.

Are Digital Instruments Real?

I put "instruments" in quotes because traditionalists may not consider MIDI devices to be instruments. Before the advent of digital music, the term *instrument* referred to a device that made sound by creating vibrations or waves. It turned sounds into music by managing those vibrations or waves to create different tones. MIDI instruments, however, are digital. They create music synthetically (which is why they are sometimes called synthesizers) using something more similar to the code used in a computer program. The playback of MIDI music, of course, comes out of speakers and, in that way, it recreates the vibrations or waves of "old-fashioned" analog instruments.

Another type of MIDI device is a *MIDI interface*, which is the device that connects other MIDI devices. Your Sound Blaster includes a MIDI interface, but you also can buy free-standing MIDI interfaces with a variety of capabilities not found on your Sound Blaster card, such as the capability to handle multiple instruments.

For a musician, these standards are important. They mean that you can create chains of MIDI devices using standard, off-the-shelf cables and equipment.

So you have a series of interconnected MIDI devices, each of which can produce a different sound. Somewhere in there, however, you need a mixer or sequencer program to merge and save the sounds, keep all the tracks straight, and give you the opportunity to edit each track. Cakewalk Apprentice, which comes with some versions of Sound Blaster, is a slightly scaled back version of one of the most powerful sequencers available.

Here's one more important thing to remember about MIDI. Whether we are talking about a MID file or even an interconnected chain of instruments, a MIDI file doesn't contain music. Rather, MIDI files contain instructions about how to play the device that creates the music. This is a seemingly small distinction, but it's important for budding MIDI musicians to remember.

The instructions tell the MIDI device, such as the synthesizer built into your Sound Blaster, which "instrument" to play. They also tell the synthesizer precisely which characteristics it should use for the instrument it plays, such as pitch or volume.

In practical terms, it means that you can change instruments—also known in MIDI-speak as *voices*—literally in midstream. The MIDI standard supports 128 general instrument sounds and 64 percussion sounds.

If you are creating music and you don't like the way one instrument sounds, you can try another. It's easy to do while the song is playing either on the synthesizer itself or with a sequencer. As far as MIDI is concerned, changing instruments is just a change in instructions, similar to changing pitch or volume.

For AWE32, these instruments are part of a sound font bank. These are collections of sounds for all 128 instruments and 64 percussion sounds.

Sound font banks, some of which are on the CD-ROM that accompanies this book, provide different sound characteristics for each different type of sound. If you're a picky MIDI musician, you can obtain precisely the sound font bank you want so that, say, a piano sounds precisely right to your ear.

> **Sound Font Bank** A specialized collection of MIDI voices that you can add while creating or playing back MIDI compositions. Serious MIDI musicians love sound font banks because they help provide precisely the right sound.

General(ly) MIDI

MIDI provides standard ways of transmitting signals between your computer and a synthesizer. This is handy because it enables MIDI musicians to mix and match equipment without worrying about plugs, ports and connectors.

MIDI also provides for such details as requiring sixteen channels of sound to be available in any given MIDI piece. Each channel can have a different voice and each voice can have a wide variety of precisely set characteristics. Sequencers such as Cakewalk Apprentice provide this precision control and mix together the sounds of each channel.

Other MIDI details include the format of MIDI files. This means you can play the same MIDI file with any sound card and synthesizer. All this is handy and saves a lot of hassle. After all, it would be a royal pain if somebody handed you a MIDI file created on a Brand X sound card and you couldn't play it with your Sound Blaster. The MIDI standard ensures that won't happen.

However, this level of standardization wasn't enough. That's because, without further standardization, the music you create on one system would still sound different from one system to another. Put differently, if you create a MIDI piano concerto on one keyboard or sound card, you want to make sure that it doesn't come out as a flügelhorn concerto on another system.

Hence, the General MIDI standard was born. At the most superficial level, General MIDI requires that a system be able to play at least twenty-four instruments (also called voices) at a time. This is so-called twenty-four note polyphony.

General MIDI is justly famous among MIDI musicians for the *instrument patch map*. This takes 128 instruments and sound effects and gives each a number. It starts with number one (acoustic grand piano) and ends with number 128 (gunshot special effect). It does the same for the 64 percussion sounds.

That means that if you create a composition that adheres to the General MIDI standard and you specify instrument number one for a specific track, that instrument will always be an acoustic grand piano. With the addition of this consistency, musicians were ready to cook. MIDI now provided a stable, predictable platform for creating music. The General MIDI standard made it even more stable and predictable.

Polyphony
The capability to play multiple instruments, or voices, at the same time. The AWE32 gets its name, in part, from the fact that it has 32-voice polyphony.

General MIDI This is a MIDI standard that is best known for its instrument patch map. This assigns a number to 128 types of instruments and 46 types of drum sounds. That way, the same instrument plays on every system every time.

Marching to Different Tubas

Just because the General MIDI standard states, say, that number 59 is a tuba, it doesn't mean that every tuba sounds the same. That depends on the qualities of the synthesizer that creates the sound of the tuba. The differences between instruments have become particularly pronounced with wave-table synthesis, which plays actual samples of an instrument. A bad sample can make the instrument sound strange. One of the reasons that serious musicians like the sound font banks is that they augment the specific instrument characteristics created by your Sound Blaster.

Sure, there are other standards. One standard isn't necessarily better or worse than another, but General MIDI is the most widely accepted—it's the one most PC-based musicians use when creating music. So, how do you make sure that your Sound Blaster is set to play General MIDI (also known as GM)? As described in Chapter 17, that occurs in the AWE32 Control Panel. To display this dialog box, double-click the **AWE32 Control Panel** icon in the Sound Blaster program group.

MIDI types —————

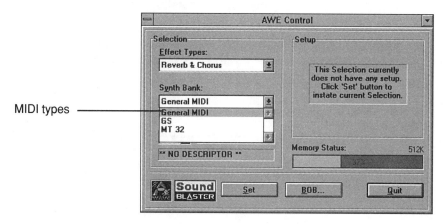

Use the AWE32 Control Panel to set your MIDI type.

In the **Synth Bank** drop-down list, make sure you select **General MIDI**.

As an aside, you also can have two other choices: GS (which stands for General Sound) and MT 32. These are other standards with other instrument maps. Depending on how deeply you get into MIDI music creation, there may be times when you'll need to use those standards. However, as I already mentioned, General MIDI is usually the way to go.

Making Sound Font Bank Deposits

Musicians love sound font banks—just love them to pieces. In fact, there are a handful of great sound font banks on the CD-ROM that comes with this book. They come from E-Mu Systems, a long-time MIDI music vendor.

First, copy the sound font banks from the disc into your **\SB16\SFBANK** subdirectory. Next, let's return to the AWE32 Control Panel and load the sound font bank.

1. Double-click the **AWE32 Control Panel** icon in the Sound Blaster program group.

2. Make sure that your Synth Bank setting is set to **General MIDI**.

3. Click your mouse on the bottom part of the dialog box just to the right of the number in the User Bank section. On the right side of the dialog box, in the File Name window, a listing of all the sound font banks should appear. If it doesn't, click the **Set Dir** button and, in the ensuing dialog box, select the directory in which you store your sound font banks.

4. Click the **Set** button.

5. Select a user bank by clicking on the up and down arrows. If you are loading only one sound font bank, select **user bank one**.

6. In the File Name window, double-click the sound font bank you want to attach to that particular user bank. The name of the file and a description appear in the User Bank section of the dialog.

7. Click the **Quit** button to close the AWE32 Control Panel.

Notice how, when you select a sound font bank, the amount of available memory shown in the Memory Status section of the Control Panel goes down. In fact, some of the sound font banks require more memory than comes on a standard AWE32 card. When that happens, you will see a dialog box informing you of that fact.

Read Chapter 20 to learn how to add memory to your AWE32. With more memory, you can load more sound font banks.

Taking It to the (Correct) Sound Banks

You just learned how to load sound font banks. But what if you want to switch sound banks or have as a default a particular one? Many sequencers provide the method to switch from one loaded sound font bank to another. As you'll learn soon, that's a bit of an obtuse operation in Cakewalk Apprentice.

Here's a special trick if you want one particular sound font bank to be your default. It involves a file called **SBWIN.INI**. The Sound Blaster installation program placed that file in your \WINDOWS directory when you installed Sound Blaster. It contains instructions that tell AWE32 how to operate when you are in Windows.

You can edit that file with any text editor, such as the Notepad program that comes with Windows. From Windows Program Manager, double-click the icon for the **Accessories** program group. Then double-click the **Notepad** icon. After Notepad starts, open its **File** menu and click **Open**. In the Open dialog box, type C:**WINDOWS\SBWIN.INI**. This loads the file.

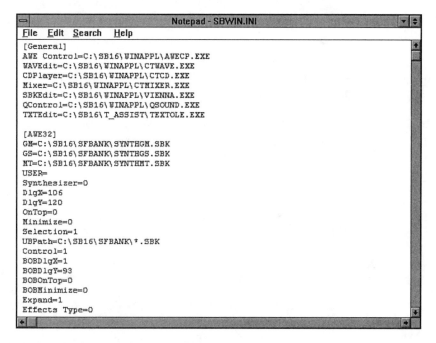

Sound Blaster Windows configuration file.

Notice there is a section of the file that begins with [**AWE32**]. In this section, there are, among others, the following four lines:

GM=C:\SB16\SFBANK\SYNTHGM.SBK
GS=C:\SB16\SFBANK\SYNTHGS.SBK
MT=C:\SB16\SFBANK\SYNTHMT.SBK
USER=

These lines refer to the default sound font banks for each MIDI standard (General MIDI, General Sound, and MT 32). The fourth line, which shouldn't have a listing in it until you put one there, is for setting a default sound bank.

If you find a sound font bank that you really, really love, after **USER=** type the drive, path, and name of the bank. This isn't a mandatory thing—only bother with this if you have a strong preference for a specific sound bank.

Life Is a Cakewalk Apprentice

Cakewalk Professional is a MIDI sequencer that's popular among professional MIDI musicians because of its power and its flexibility. It enables musicians to fine-tune their MIDI compositions.

Cakewalk Apprentice, which comes with the AWE32 card, is a slightly scaled back version, but it still is very powerful. The price beginners pay for this power is that Cakewalk initially can be complex to use.

In this section, we take a quick stroll through Cakewalk Apprentice. Remember, though, this is a deep, rich program and the only way to really get to know it is to spend time with it. Also, you should read the more detailed documentation that comes with your AWE32.

Just for Grins

If you simply want to play with a sequencer to see how you can modify the instruments in each track and how they play back, take a look at Midisoft Studio. This is a sequencer from a well-known company named MIDISoft and it comes on the CD-ROM attached to this book. Midisoft Studio, while a bit less powerful than Cakewalk, is simpler to use. Read more about Midisoft Studio in Chapter 24.

Unlike most of the programs that come with Sound Blaster, you must install Cakewalk Apprentice separately. To do that, place the Cakewalk Apprentice disk in your floppy drive and, from Windows Program Manager open the **File** menu and click **Run**.

In the Run dialog box, type **A:\SETUP.EXE** (assuming your floppy drive is the A: drive) and click **OK**. Follow the on-screen instructions to complete installation of Cakewalk Apprentice. After installation, run the program by double-clicking on its icon in the Cakewalk Apprentice program group.

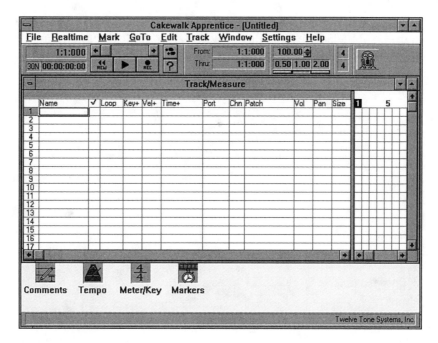

Cakewalk Apprentice.

When Cakewalk Apprentice first starts, the following screen elements appear:

➤ A message box may appear saying you haven't selected MIDI output devices and that, until you do, you won't be able to hear anything. To rectify this situation, select **Settings**, **MIDI Devices**. In the Output window of the MIDI Devices dialog box, select all the items listed and click **OK**.

➤ The control bar enables you to quickly control a musical piece. From the left, the control bar shows you the current position in a MIDI song and lets you start, rewind, or if you have a synthesizer connected, record a song. Continuing to move to the right, you can set the specific parts of a piece you want to hear, set the meter and key, and set a piece to stop quickly (the panic button).

➤ The Track/Measure window has two parts. The left side shows which instruments are playing in each track (also called a channel). On the right side is a measure-by-measure display showing whether the instrument for that track plays in that specific measure.

Let's start simply by loading a MIDI file and playing it. To load the file, open the **File** menu and click **Open**. In the Open dialog box, find the drive and directory in which you store MIDI files. Select the file and click **OK**. For example, I loaded a rendition of

Mozart's Jupiter Symphony. You can find this file on the CD-ROM that accompanies this book. It's in the \MIDISOFT\MIDI directory. You can run it from that directory, although I suggest copying it to your hard drive.

Playing Mozart's Jupiter Symphony in Cakewalk Apprentice.

Notice that in the left part of the Track/Measure window there is a listing of each channel and the instrument attached to that channel. For example, channel 1 of the Jupiter Symphony is Violin I and channel 14 is Timpani.

To play the piece, click the **Play** button in the control bar. That's the button with the forward-facing arrow. Notice that, as the song plays, a large cursor at the top of the right side of the window shows the current measure.

To start the song at a specific measure, click that measure in the right side of the window; then click the **Play** button. To stop the playback, click the panic button on the far right or the **Play** button again.

Noodling Around in Cakewalk

Okay—you loaded a MIDI file in Cakewalk Apprentice. Now, you can explore a bit. This is exploration with a purpose, though. The goal is to acquaint you with some of the major parts and capabilities of the program.

First, let's look at the different ways you can view music. In either the left or right side of the Track/Measure window, click a specific track with your *right* mouse button. Select a track that is in regular use in this piece, as indicated by dots in the right side of the dialog box. Remember that a dot indicates that a particular instrument plays in a particular measure.

After clicking with your right mouse button, you will see a dialog box with four options, each of which provides a different view of the track you selected. Those views are:

➤ **Piano roll**   This shows a window with a piano keyboard on the left. To the right is a measure-by-measure display with the specific notes for that channel and their durations. If no instrument is playing in a specific measure, there is no notation.

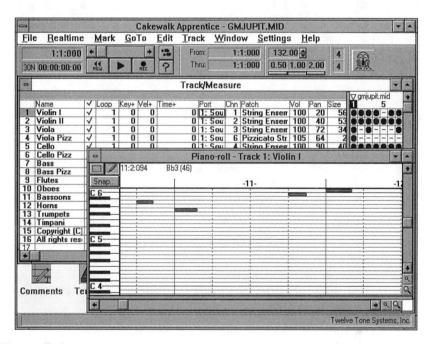

The Piano-roll view.

Here's a bit of fun that will help you become accustomed to Cakewalk. If you are playing a piece while viewing the piano roll, click the **Play/Stop** button in the command bar to stop the music. Notice how, if you point the cursor at the keyboard, it turns into a hand. Move the hand over a specific key and press your *left* mouse button. The instrument and the note you selected plays.

283

➤ **Event list**   A nitty-gritty information window that lists in text format every bit of information about every part of the composition. An "event" can be a specific note, but it also can be instructions such as which sound font bank to play.

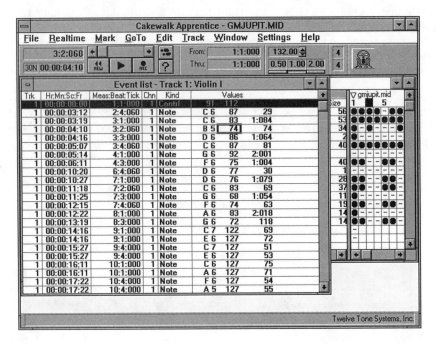

The Event list view.

➤ **Controllers**   Displays the controllers dialog box. This is even more technical than the Event list. It enables you to set, for the channel you selected, the controller used to make specific settings. One obvious type of controller is for the volume of that track, but there are many other types of controllers. This is a dialog box that a MIDI expert would use to tweak the composition. Read the Cakewalk Apprentice documentation for more details.

➤ **Staff**   Shows the music for that track in a traditional staff. Play an individual note by clicking it or watch the music flow by as you play the entire piece. Again, only the music for that particular channel is displayed in the staff view.

At the bottom of the Cakewalk window are icons on which you can double-click for some aids in creating music. Those aids are:

➤ **Comments**   Displays a window in which you can type random comments about the piece.

➤ **Tempo**   Here you set the tempo for measures you select.

➤ **Meter/Key** Sets both the meter and the key for the sections you select.

➤ **Markers** Enables you to mark specific times in a composition. This is useful for precisely synchronizing music to say, videos or audio.

Makin' Music

Even without a synthesizer attached to your AWE32, it's easy to create a song in Cakewalk Apprentice. To start, select **File**, **New**. You will see an empty Track/Measure dialog box.

Click the name box in the Track 1 row and type a name for the track. Next, double-click the **Channel** box. The Track parameters dialog box appears.

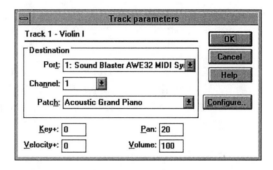

Setting track parameters.

Don't worry about the port. From the **Channel** drop-down list, select a channel. In this case, select channel 1. In the Patch dialog box, select a patch, or instrument. Any instrument will do. Select other parameters such as volume. For now, change volume to 100.

One final thing: make sure the letter "m" isn't visible in the mute column for that track. If it is, you won't be able to hear your work. Double-click the mute box so that a check mark appears.

If you have a synthesizer connected, click the **Record** button in the control bar. You will see and hear a count-down box. When the box disappears, it's time to boogie. Click the **Record** button to stop recording.

If you don't have a synthesizer connected, go into staff mode. Hold down the **Control** key and click the staff to add notes. To add different types of notes such as half notes instead of quarter notes, click the button at the top of the view for the specific note type. You can drag and drop notes anywhere in the staff. Enjoy—this is a blast, even if you aren't a serious musician.

Save the work by selecting **Save**. Note, though, that you are not saving in .MID format. Rather, Cakewalk initially saves the file in its own .WRK format that only Cakewalk can read.

To save your masterpiece as a MIDI file, click **File**, **Save As**. To save it as a MIDI file, select **MIDI File** in the Save File as Type drop-down list.

Switching Sound Banks

One final thing before we finish our quick walk through Cakewalk Apprentice. After all the discussion earlier in the chapter about using sound font banks, you may want to experience it for yourself in Cakewalk. That's especially true because you get some great sound font bank samples on the included CD-ROM.

First, load the sound font bank you want, as described earlier in the chapter. Remember the user bank number to which you attached the sound font bank. For simplicity, select user bank number 1.

Next, copy **TESTFILE.WRK** from the **\SNDFONTS** directory on the CD-ROM to your Cakewalk directory. By default, that directory is **C:\WCWLITE**. Then load **TESTFILE** in Cakewalk. Play it through once to get a feel for what it sounds like. It should play using instrument number 1, which is the acoustic grand piano.

Now, things get a tad complicated.

1. In the left-hand side of the Track/Measure window, click your right mouse button anywhere in the listing for channel 1 and select the Event list. The Event List window displays.

2. Move to the very top of the list and highlight the first line. In the Kind column, the word **Control** should be listed.

3. With that first row of the Event list highlighted, click any box in that row. Then press the **Insert** key. A new row, identical to the first, should appear.

4. Notice the numbers 0 and 1 in the Values column. If you chose user bank 1 for your sound font bank, you're finished. If you used another user bank, change the second number in the second row to the user bank number.

5. Play the test file once. It should still play the old instruments. When you play it the second time, it should play the new sound bank. Note that adding the new sound font bank changes the .WRK or .MID file to include those particular sound fonts.

The Least You Need to Know

In this chapter, you learned more about MIDI music and took some initial steps toward making it. You also learned about Cakewalk Apprentice, the MIDI sequencer that comes with some versions of Sound Blaster.

➤ MIDI is a series of standards that makes connection to MIDI devices predicatable and consistent.

➤ The MIDI standard also dictates the content of MIDI files.

➤ General MIDI dictates which MIDI voices play under which circumstances. It ensures that a certain type of piano in a MIDI piece sounds roughly the same no matter what device is playing it back.

➤ Sound font banks, some of which are included with this book, are specialized sets of MIDI instruments.

➤ Cakewalk Apprentice provides precise control over creating and editing MIDI music. In this chapter, you received just a brief walk-through of the program.

Chapter 24

What's on the CD-ROM?

In This Chapter

➤ Listen to MIDI and WAV files galore

➤ Play with more sequencers

➤ Install your very own sound font banks

Hey—enough talk about Sound Blaster. Now it's time to use it. It's easy to start: just start playing your favorite game and wail, shoot, and blast away.

You also can use your Sound Blaster with the software that comes with it. Even budget versions of Sound Blaster come with tons of software for listening and using sounds and music. You learned about those programs in other chapters of this book.

As a super-duper, special extra bonus, this book comes with a CD-ROM chock full of stuff to make your Sound Blaster even more fun. There are tons of WAV and MIDI files created by professionals and some additional programs to use and enhance those files. This chapter describes what's on the disc and how to use it.

Playing with MIDI

In Chapter 23, you learned the basics of MIDI music and became acquainted with Cakewalk Apprentice, which accompanies some versions of Sound Blaster. It's cool to listen to some professionally created MIDI tunes, so with the help of several software vendors, I included a bunch of them on the CD-ROM.

You can play the included MIDI tunes directly from the CD-ROM. Or copy them using File Manager (in Windows 3.11 and Windows for Workgroups) or Explorer (in Windows 95) to your hard disk. In either case, you play the songs using a MIDI player such as EnsembleMIDI (described in Chapter 16), which came with your Sound Blaster.

If you feel particularly adventurous, load the MIDI songs into a sequencer such as Cakewalk Apprentice, which comes with some versions of Sound Blaster. Or use the Midisoft Studio and Cakewalk Professional demos, which are on the CD-ROM. Then, you can play around with the various tracks and get a better idea about how MIDI music is created.

The MIDI music files on the disc are in several directories. Each directory is named after the vendor that contributed the files. In describing the location on the disc of these files, I'll refer to your CD-ROM drive as D:\. Remember, though, that yours might have a different drive letter.

Also remember (and I can't stress this strongly enough) that *all MIDI compositions are copyrighted by the contributors*. You may listen to them, play with them in a sequencer and use them for your private applications, but you can't use them in commercial applications without permission of the vendor.

So as to not play favorites, I'll describe the MIDI files as they occur in alphabetical order.

➤ **D:\MIDISOFT\MIDI**   These are five files contributed by Midisoft, four beautiful classical pieces and a top-notch rendition of the Maple Leaf Rag. This company has long been devoted to helping composers create MIDI music; they created the excellent Midisoft Studio sequencer also included on this disc.

➤ **D:\NOVELL**   These are thirty MIDI compositions developed (and copyrighted by) Novell Corporation. These MIDI files are a cross-section of different musical styles. While Novell is best-known as a vendor of networking and word processing programs, it also is the developer of WordPerfect Presentations, a multimedia-oriented presentation graphics program. Novell developed these delightful tracks for that program.

➤ **D:\VOYETRA\MIDI**   Like Midisoft, Voyetra is a long-time serious player in the MIDI music world contributing eleven MIDI professional MIDI compositions. Its products include sequencers in the Sequencer Plus and the MIDI Orchestrator Plus series. Voyetra also sells a series of MIDI sampler discs and various utilities for playing and modifying MIDI music.

Playing with Midisoft Studio

Some versions of Sound Blaster come with Cakewalk Apprentice from Twelve Tone Systems. This is a scaled-back version of a sequencer that has a large following among professional MIDI composers.

I included two other sequencers on the CD-ROM. The first is a demo version of Midisoft Studio. I'm including this sequencer for several reasons. First, not all versions of Sound Blaster come with Cakewalk Apprentice. If you don't have Cakewalk, you can use Midisoft Studio to learn how sequencers work. Also, Cakewalk Apprentice, while extremely powerful, can take a while to learn. Midisoft Studio is very self-evident to learn.

This demonstration version has all the capabilities of the full version of Midisoft Studio, but you won't be able to print or save MIDI compositions you create or alter. Rather, this demo is meant to show you what a good sequencer can do and to provide an alternative to Cakewalk Apprentice for those with a bit less time for scaling the learning curve.

Midisoft Studio runs right off the CD-ROM drive. To get ready to run it:

1. Insert the disc in your CD-ROM drive.

2. From File Manager open the **File** menu and choose **Run**. In Windows 95, click the **Start** button, and then select **Run**.

3. Type **D:\MIDISOFT\STUDIO SETUP.EXE** and click the **OK** button. This sets up Windows so you can run Midisoft Studio.

4. To start Midisoft Studio, double-click its icon in the Midisoft Studio for Windows program group.

To start working in Midisoft Studio, open the **File** menu and choose **Open**. Load a MIDI file from the dialog box and click the forward-facing arrow in the lower right part of the screen to start playing.

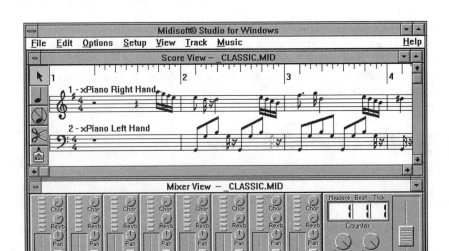

Playing MIDI in Midisoft Studio.

Notice that the music scrolls by as it plays. Also notice that each track has a series of controls and a VU meter to show that the particular track is active. I suggest clicking buttons and dragging slider bars to start experimenting. You'll quickly learn how to change how each track works.

For some, the best part of Midisoft Studio is that it comes with fifteen more MIDI songs. You can use them with the sequencer or simply play them with a MIDI player such as Ensemble MIDI. They are located in the **\MIDISOFT\STUDIO** directory on the CD-ROM drive.

Playing the Virtual Piano

I also included a demo version of Cakewalk Professional version 3.0. This gives you an idea of what the full-blown Cakewalk is all about. Like Midisoft Studio, this is a full working copy, except that you can't save or print the contents of MIDI files.

Chapter 23 describes how to get up and running in Cakewalk Apprentice. The Cakewalk Professional demo works about the same way.

Even more exciting is that the Cakewalk Professional demo also installs a little program called Virtual Piano. This lets you "play" music by clicking on the keys of an on-screen piano keyboard.

To install both the Cakewalk Professional demo and Virtual Piano:

1. Insert the CD-ROM in your drive.

2. From File Manager open the **File** menu and choose **Run**. In Windows 95, click the **Start** button, and then select **Run**.

3. Type **D:\12TONE\SETUP.EXE** and click **OK** to install both programs.

Note that the Cakewalk Apprentice demo comes with about twenty .WRK music files. These are music files saved in Cakewalk's proprietary format.

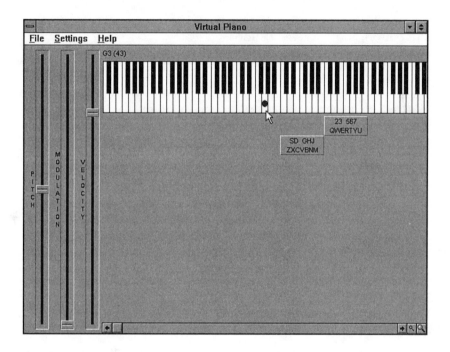

Playing with Virtual Piano.

As you tickle the virtual ivories in Virtual Piano, you can record those sounds in Cakewalk Apprentice or Professional. To do that, select **Settings**, **MIDI Devices**. Highlight **Virtual Piano** in the dialog box and click **OK**.

Next, follow the procedures in Cakewalk for creating a new composition. I told you about those procedures in Chapter 23. Finally, click the **Record** button in Cakewalk and, after the countdown, wail away on Virtual Piano. When you finish, click the **Record** button again to stop recording.

This is way cool stuff. Have fun!

You Can Hear I-cons

Just for giggles and grins, I included a copy of Icon Hear-it Too Lite from Moon Valley Software. This is a fun little program for Windows 3.1 and Windows for Workgroups that lets you attach interesting sounds to actions such as opening and closing specific programs. If you like the program, you can buy the full-blown version that has even more features.

To install Icon Hear-it Too Lite:

1. Insert the disc in your CD-ROM drive.

2. From File Manager open the **File** menu and choose **Run**. In Windows 95, click the **Start** button, and then select **Run**.

3. Type **D:\MOONVALL\IHEARIT\INSTALL.EXE**. Follow on-screen installation instructions.

To start the program, double-click its icon in Program Manager. Clicking on the various icons in the Icon Hear-it Too Lite window displays self-evident dialog boxes for setting up the program.

Catching the Sound Blaster Wave(file)

There's more to life than MIDI. The CD-ROM also includes zillions of WAV files for your listening pleasure. Okay—I'm exaggerating. There are only about 240, but they're darned good.

Here's where to find those WAV files:

➤ Most of the WAV files are in the **\MOONVALL\WAVE** subdirectory on your CD-ROM. Moon Valley, which also provided the Icon Hear-it Too Lite program described previously, contributed those files.

These top-notch WAV files were all recorded in 16-bit, 22KHz stereo, so they sound great. Beware, though. Some of the files are large and, if you copy them willy-nilly to your hard disk, your disk will fill up quickly. But you can play them directly from the CD-ROM drive and copy over only the files you want. To listen to the files, use a WAV player like EnsembleWAVE.

➤ There also are some fine WAV files in **\VOYETRA\WAVE**. Sure, these guys are best known for MIDI, but they're in the WAV business, too.

294

Your Very Own Sound Font Banks

For you serious musicians, the CD-ROM also offers seven sound font banks from E-Mu Systems. These are among the highest-quality sound font banks you can obtain. E-Mu Systems not only has been in the MIDI business for a long time, but they also make the wave-table synthesizer chip for the AWE32. Put differently, these guys know their stuff and their stuff sounds fantastic on AWE32 sound cards.

You learned about using sound font banks in Chapter 23. As a quick reminder, using File Manager or Explorer, look in the **\SNDFONTS** directory. The files with the .SBK file extension are the sound font banks.

Copy the sound font banks you want into your **\SB16\SFBANK** directory. Then, follow the instructions in Chapter 23 for using them.

The sound font banks (for which E-Mu uses the trademarked name SoundFont Bank) included with this disc are:

➤ 7Foot Grand Piano

➤ 9Foot Grand Piano

➤ B3 Organ

➤ Haunt Fonts

➤ Rock Instruments

➤ Woodwinds

➤ World Instruments

One caution is in order about the SoundFont banks. Some of them require more than the 512K of RAM that comes standard on AWE32 cards. Chapter 20 describes how to add more memory to your AWE32.

The Least You Need to Know

This chapter told you about the contents of the CD-ROM that comes with this book.

➤ There are hundreds of high-quality WAV files and MIDI files.

➤ There are demonstration versions of two sequencers: Cakewalk Professional and Midisoft Studio.

➤ There is a novelty program called Icon Hear-it Too Lite that enables you to attach sound effects to specific events in Windows such as opening and closing files or specific programs.

Speak Like a Geek:
The Complete Archive

amplitude   This is a measure of the intensity, or loudness, of a sound wave. The higher the amplitude, the louder the sound. It makes sense, then, that when you *amplify* sound, you increase its amplitude.

analog   Analog means that something occurs in the physical world that is constantly changing. When it occurs, you hear, see, feel, smell, or touch it, but it consists of constantly changing forces, like sound waves. I have a computer geek friend who refers to a handshake as an *analog interpersonal interface*. He's spent way too much time in front of his monitor, but I like him anyway.

analog control chip   This chip, which resides on your sound card, is as adept as any translator at the United Nations. In this case, the analog control chip converts analog sounds to digital—and vice versa.

CD-ROM interface   This is the intermediary between your CD-ROM drive and the rest of your computer. It routes information from your CD-ROM to the proper place in your computer. It can either be a separate add-on card or it can be part of your Sound Blaster card.

digital   This refers to a "language" that your computer understands. Instead of analog, in which natural forces like sound waves are constantly changing, digital items are instructions encoded with a long series of 1s and 0s. Taken as a whole, this string of 1s and 0s tells your computer what to do.

digital signal processor (DSP)   These are handy little chips that come on Sound Blaster cards. Because they assume some of the duties that creating sounds normally imposes on your computer, they prevent your computer from bogging down.

direct memory access (DMA) channel   No, this isn't a cable channel that helps you remember things better. It's the direct pathway to RAM used by a device such as your Sound Blaster. If more than one device uses the same DMA channel, malfunctions can occur.

driver   This is a little bit of software that's kind of like an arbitrator. It gets your hardware (such as Sound Blaster) and software (such as your multimedia titles) to work together. A number of drivers are necessary for Windows to work correctly with Sound Blaster.

frequency   Frequency is the number of times per second a sound wave vibrates. It is measured in *hertz* (abbreviated Hz), which simply refers to the number of times in a second that something occurs. Experts say the sounds humans normally can hear range from those that vibrate twenty times per second (20Hz) to those that vibrate 20,000 per second (20 kilohertz).

frequency modulation (FM) synthesis   This is a common method used by sound cards for creating MIDI music. Although effective and even beloved by some people, it creates synthetic-sounding instruments. That's why music created this way often is called *synthesizer music*.

General MIDI   This is a MIDI standard best known for its instrument patch map that describes precisely what instrument to play at what time during a MIDI song. This assigns a number to 128 types of instruments and 46 types of drum sounds. That way, the same instrument plays on every system every time.

Hertz   Named after Heinrich Hertz who made a study of such things, hertz refers to the number of times per second something occurs. Kilohertz refers to how many *thousands* of times per second something occurs.

I/O base address   The specific chunk of your computer's random-access memory used by a hardware device such as your Sound Blaster card. Just like a row of suburban tract houses, each device must have its own address.

interrupt request (IRQ)   This is a priority number assigned to a device such as your Sound Blaster that you connect with your computer. This priority number helps your computer's central processing unit sort out the flood of data being sent to it by your Sound Blaster and all other devices in your computer.

joystick   Computer joysticks are a favorite of hard-core game players. They are modeled after the joysticks in airplanes, which explains joysticks' popularity for use with games involving simulated flight. However, they're also popular for many other types of games, particularly action games.

magnetic media   This refers to the most common method of storing digital data. It involves creating specific magnetic patterns that represent data on a magnetic medium like a hard or floppy disk. The disk both creates these magnetic patterns and reads them back.

MIDI   MIDI, or Musical Instrument Digital Interface, is a method by which your computer and sound card create synthesized music. MIDI first became popular in the early '80s before PCs as we now know them became popular. In fact, some of the early MIDI synthesizers now are highly prized for the "retro" sounds they create.

mixer software   It sounds like software for planning one of those famous mixer parties in college. In this case, mixer software for Windows and DOS enables you to determine volume levels and other settings for different types of audio, such as MIDI files and sound effect files.

Multimedia PC (MPC)   This is supposedly a standard. It was developed by multimedia hardware and software vendors to tell you what software and hardware—including sound cards—you need to successfully run multimedia on your PC. It's not much help, though—the current "standard" is barely acceptable for many of today's multimedia titles. Read Chapter 10 for specifics about this standard.

optical media   Optical media such as CD-ROMs use light to discern patterns of tiny pits etched into the media. Those patterns determine the data.

polyphony   The capability to play multiple instruments, or voices, at the same time. The AWE32 gets its name, in part, from the fact that it has 32-voice polyphony.

presentation software   Use this software to wow customers, employees, or investors. Well-known examples of presentation software include Microsoft PowerPoint and Harvard Graphics.

samples   This is what Willie Loman carried in *Death of a Salesman*. It also refers to a sample of a real sound. When many samples are played at a rapid rate, the samples combine to re-create a sound.

sampling rate   This *could* refer to how fast I eat my way through the dessert section of a buffet. In this case, though, it refers to how many sound samples per second a sound card plays.

sequencer   Software you use to edit MIDI music. A good sequencer will let you assign a specific synthesized instrument to each track and also assign specific characteristics such as pitch and volume to each track.

SIMMs   Standard Inline Memory Modules are the little wafers of memory you add to your computer to increase its RAM. You also use SIMMs to increase the RAM on your Sound Blaster card.

Small Computer System Interface (SCSI)   This is the long-time standard for CD-ROM interfaces. However, SCSI isn't limited to CD-ROM drives. You also can use SCSI adapters for connecting other devices such as SCSI-compatible hard drives and tape backup devices to your computer.

sound font bank   A specialized collection of MIDI voices you can add while creating or playing back MIDI compositions. Serious MIDI musicians love sound font banks because they help provide precisely the right sound.

sound waves   Sound is created by waves, or vibrations, moving through the air. Our ears collect these waves and send them to the brain for processing. We don't "hear" until our brain processes the sound waves, which reminds me of the old riddle about whether a tree makes noise if it falls in the forest and nobody is around to hear it.

speech recognition software   This software recognizes your voice. You speak into a microphone and your computer does your bidding. VoiceAssist, which comes with versions of Sound Blaster that have the ASP chip, is a good example of this type of software.

system software   System software is, in many ways, the master arbitrator. Among its many chores, system software routes data and instructions to the proper component in a PC so that, to the user, everything occurs in the precise sequence that it should.

wave-table synthesis   This is a method of creating MIDI music that uses waveform sound samples of actual instruments rather than synthesized versions of those instruments. The result is MIDI music that is much more realistic than FM synthesis.

waveform (WAV) files   Birds chirping, bigwigs speaking, cars roaring—if you've heard sounds such as these on your computer, chances are they were stored as WAV files. WAV files are essentially digital recordings of sounds that occur in the real world.

Index

E

S